A Is for American

A Is for American

Letters and Other Characters in the Newly United States

Jill Lepore

Alfred A. Knopf · New York · 2002

Library of Congress Cataloging-in-Publication Data
Lepore, Jill, [date]
A is for American : letters and other characters in the newly United States /
Jill Lepore. — 1st ed.
p.   cm.
Includes bibliographical references.
ISBN 0-375-40449-X
1. English language—United States—History—18th century. 2. English language—United
States—History—19th century. 3. English language—Social aspects—United States.
4. National characteristics, American—History. 5. English language—18th century—
History. 6. English language—18th century—History. 7. Americanisms—History. I. Title.
PE2809 .L46 2002
306.44'973'09033—dc21   2001038057

Manufactured in the United States of America

First Edition

*In memory of
my favorite character,
Jane F. Levey, 1960–1999*

CHAR′ACTER, *n.* 1. A mark made by cutting or engraving, as on stone, metal . . . ; hence, a mark or figure made with a pen or style, on paper. . . . 4. The peculiar qualities, impressed by nature or habit on a person, which distinguish him from others. . . .

—NOAH WEBSTER,
An American Dictionary, 1828

Contents

A Is for American

Samuel F. B. Morse, Noah Webster, *1823.* (Courtesy of the Mead Art Museum, Amherst College.)

Prologue

A Likeness

COIN'CIDENCE, *n.* The falling or meeting of two or more lines, surfaces, or bodies in the same point.

—NOAH WEBSTER,
An American Dictionary, 1828

In 1823, Noah Webster sat for a portrait. He was sixty-five, stiff, vain, and about to leave home for a year of study in Europe. There he would pore over crumbling pages at the British Museum and the Biblio-thèque Nationale, trying to track down the elusive origins of words. Meanwhile, the portrait was to be kept by his wife, Rebecca, to remember him by during his long absence. And on his return it was to serve as fron-tispiece for his soon-to-be-published *American Dictionary of the English Language,* his magnum opus, his life's work. Ever since 1783, when a very young Webster published his first "American" spelling book, his pas-sion had been to develop—and, literally, to spell and define—what he

Samuel F. B. Morse, Self-Portrait,
1812–13. (Courtesy of the Addison Gallery
of American Art, Phillips Academy, Andover,
Massachusetts.)

called the American language. "*Language,* as well as government should be national," Webster insisted in 1789. "America should have her *own* distinct from all the world."[1]

In 1823, when Webster, now an aging man of letters, sat in his crimson-cushioned chair and stared at his portraitist with a kind of grim curiosity, his eyes fell on the familiar face of a man half his age. The artist, Samuel Finley Breese Morse, was the son of Webster's longtime friend and new neighbor Jedidiah Morse. Noah and Jedidiah had just missed each other at Yale in the 1770s (Webster graduated in 1778; Morse entered in 1779), but both men had recently resettled near their alma mater, just a few doors apart on Temple Street, not far from the New Haven Green. Now, in 1823, Morse's eldest son, Finley to his friends, was called upon to take Webster's likeness.

And so it came to pass that the inventor of the code painted the man who wrote the dictionary.

That day, in the humble parlor of Webster's New Haven home, Samuel Morse and Noah Webster stared at each other, sniffing as oil paint fumes filled the space between them. They paused, no doubt, to stretch, to take a cup of tea, to chat. What they said went unrecorded. Still, what brought Webster and Morse together bears looking into, not least because both men are central figures in the story this book has to tell, a story about how a few early Americans tried to use letters and other characters—alphabets, syllabaries, signs, and codes—to strengthen the new American nation, to string it together with chains of letters and cables of wire, even as other Americans strained to break those chains and labored to stretch those cables across ocean floors.

"A national language is a national tie," Noah Webster had insisted in 1786, "and what country wants it more than America?" What country, indeed? Already larger and more racially, ethnically, and linguistically diverse than any western European country, America in Webster's lifetime tackled the problem of unifying itself as a nation by stirring nationalist sentiment. The new United States cast off all things British and instead created its own holidays (the Fourth of July, Washington's birthday), produced its own literature (Cooper, Emerson, and more), invented its own founding moments (including the Pilgrims' landing at Plymouth Rock), and adopted new, decidedly un-English ancestors, the noble but savage American Indian. To Webster and his supporters, the passion for American distinctiveness naturally extended to language:

THE

AMERICAN

𝕾𝖕𝖊𝖑𝖑𝖎𝖓𝖌 𝕭𝖔𝖔𝖐:

CONTAINING AN EASY

STANDARD of PRONUNCIATION.

BEING THE

FIRST PART

OF A

GRAMMATICAL INSTITUTE

OF THE

ENGLISH LANGUAGE.

BY NOAH WEBSTER, JUN. ESQUIRE.
AUTHOR of " DISSERTATIONS on the ENGLISH LANGUAGE,"
"COLLECTION of ESSAYS and FUGITIVE WRITING," &c.

Thomas and *Andrews's* SECOND EDITION.
With additional LESSONS, corrected by the AUTHOR.

PRINTED AT BOSTON,
BY ISAIAH THOMAS AND EBENEZER T. ANDREWS.
At FAUST's STATUE, No. 45, NEWBURY STREET.
Sold, Wholesale and Retail, at their Bookstore ; by said THOMAS at his
Bookstore in *Worcester*, and by the Booksellers in Town and Country,
MDCCXC.

Noah Webster's American Spelling Book, *1790.* (Courtesy of the Library of Congress.)

America could never be fully independent from England, or fully united as a nation, without its own peculiar but common tongue. As one writer asked in 1815, "How tame will his language sound, who would describe Niagara in language fitted for the falls at London bridge, or attempt the majesty of the Mississippi in that which was made for the Thames?"[2]

In the 1780s and 1790s, fully convinced that the fledgling United States must break free from England in language as in politics, Webster encouraged Americans to spell differently from their English neighbors— and more like one another. Americanizing spelling, he believed, would help Americanize Americans. By making American spelling different from

English spelling, Webster hoped to cultivate a kind of orthographical independence; by eradicating spelling variations within the United States, he hoped to build Americans' fragile sense of national belonging. He largely succeeded. While Webster's more radical spelling proposals—writing *dawter* for *daughter,* for instance—subjected him to scathing attacks (one hostile critic dubbed him No-ur Webstur, and even his adoring brother-in-law once complained, "I ain't yet quite ripe for your *Orthography*"), his patriotic *American Spelling Book* sold wildly. Between 1783 and 1801 it was reprinted fifty times, for a total of one and a half million copies. By 1829 ten million copies had been printed, and by the time Webster died in 1843, nearly every schoolchild in the now-sprawling American Republic had learned to spell using one of the millions of cheap blue-backed copies of Webster's beloved speller.[3]

In 1800, flush with success, Webster turned to a new linguistic project: he boldly announced plans to compile a dictionary full of Americanisms, arguing that "new circumstances, new modes of life, new laws, new ideas of various kinds give rise to new words." Critics were appalled at Webster's audacity. An editorial in the New England *Palladium* snickered, "If he will persist, in spite of common sense, to furnish us with a dictionary we do not want, . . . let, then, the projected volume of *foul* and *unclean* things bear his own christian name and be called NOAH'S ARK." Meanwhile, the *Gazette of the United States* printed fictitious fan mail for Webster's "nue Merrykin Dikshunary" from the most mocked of America's polyglot masses. African slave "Cuffee" wrote: "Massa Webser plese put sum HOMMANY and sum GOOD POSSUM fat and sum two tree good BAN-JOE in your new what-you-call-um Book for your fello Cytzen." "Hans Bubbleblower" recommended, "As I find der ish no DONDER and BLIX-SUM in de English Dikshonere I hope you put both in yours." And the entrepreneurial "Martha O'Gabble" inquired whether Webster intended to "buy words by the hundred or by the dozen," while her husband certified that his foulmouthed Irish wife had "the best knack of coining new words of any I ever knew."[4]

But that had been in 1800. Nearly a quarter century later, when Webster sat to have his portrait painted, he had greatly recovered from the derision that had greeted much of his earlier work. In the intervening years his spelling book had become a publishing phenomenon, work on the dictionary had progressed, and largely through his own impassioned and prolific public defense of it, more and more Americans had come around to Webster's point of view, becoming convinced that there was indeed such a thing as an American language and that if anyone could define it, that man was Noah Webster. Webster at sixty-five was a failed schoolmaster, a passable flutist, a lousy lawyer, an intriguing essayist, an inexhaustible lobbyist, a shrill editor, a pompous lecturer, and a man once dubbed "critick and coxcomb general of the United States," but he was undoubtedly also a prominent American citizen and, to many Americans, an eminent and admirable man of letters.

To promote his work, Webster had great need for a good portrait; he was desperate to replace the crude and outdated woodcut that served as the frontispiece of his spelling book. At least one reviewer worried that the so-called porcupine portrait was so ugly that it might even "frighten children . . . from learning to read."[5] Before leaving for Europe and befitting his decades of labor in preparing the *American Dictionary,* including the learning of more than twenty languages, Webster wanted a mature, scholarly, and most decidedly nonporcupine portrait to accompany his lasting legacy to the American people, a work that, for many Americans, would make "Webster" a synonym for "dictionary." For that, he turned to his neighbor's son Finley.

The "porcupine portrait" of Noah Webster. (Courtesy of the Library of Congress.)

I n 1823 Samuel Finley Breese Morse was thirty-two and broke. He had always wanted to be a painter, even as a boy, and his loving parents had indulged him by sending him to England in 1811 to train with Benjamin West and Washington Allston. In London, Morse was a star; his eight-by-six-foot *Dying Hercules* won prizes and praise when it was exhibited there in 1813. Two years later he returned to the United States seeking fame and fortune. He was profoundly disappointed. A friend had warned Morse in 1816, "Portrait painting alone is profitable in this country, our rich men not having yet obtained that relish for the fine arts

Samuel F. B. Morse, Dying Hercules, *1812–13.* (Courtesy of the Yale University Art Gallery.)

which would lead them to admire a painting for its own sake, or to patronize Genius from the noble principles of love for excellence, & love for country."[6] Morse found these words painfully prophetic. In America no one would pay him to paint epic art, and when he exhibited his work, no one would pay to see it. By 1823, married with two children, Morse found himself living in his decrepit New York studio, farming his family out to the care of his father, Jedidiah, in New Haven. To help pay for their charge, he diligently traveled to New Haven to paint the portraits of the Elm City elite: Eli Whitney, inventor of the cotton gin; Jeremiah Day, president of Yale; and No-ur Webstur, spelling fanatic.

"You may read Pedant in his very phiz," William Dunlap once said of Webster.[7] And you may read a pedant in his portrait too. Morse was a fine portraitist, and however much he hated hackwork, his rough portrait captures Webster's character well: he painted him as a tight-lipped, supercilious, embittered patriarch, all true to contemporary descriptions and to everything knowable about Noah Webster, who was as a man rather Pecksniffian.

Webster's wife considered Morse's portrait a wonderful likeness and years later the lexicographer's great-granddaughter reported that it "was considered by most of the family as the best ever painted of him."[8] In 1823, Webster himself must have admired the likeness. When he returned from Europe, he chose to include an engraving based on it in the *American Dictionary,* first published in 1828, after which Morse's painting toppled the notorious porcupine portrait, becoming the most common image of the great lexicographer, even long after his death.

Pages from Morse's 1832 sketchbook, with his first plans for the telegraph and numerical code. (Courtesy of the Library of Congress.)

Yet despite Samuel Morse's obvious talent, favorable critical reviews, and occasional important commissions, he never found fortune as an artist. Within a decade of painting Webster, Morse had nearly abandoned his art altogether in favor of pursuing "new plans." In 1832, returning from a trip to Europe, he fell into dinner conversation with other ship's passengers on the question of electromagetism, a small interest of his since his college days. Inspired, he drew plans in his sketchbook for a refined electromagnetic telegraph and a coded system of dots and dashes by which it could be used to communicate at a distance. He hoped that this invention might bring him the wealth that, as a painter, he had found so elusive.

Initially Morse devised a numerical code of dots and dashes, a cipher to be used only by government operatives for secret communiqués. Why a secret code? Morse never said. But at the time he believed there was a clandestine, international conspiracy to overthrow the U.S. government, a plot led ultimately by the pope, by which European monarchs were exporting Catholics to the United States to undermine and eventually to destroy American democracy. In 1835 Morse's ferocious nativism led him to publish *Imminent Dangers to the Free Institutions of the United States through Foreign Immigration,* advocating the passage of a new naturalization law whereby "no foreigner who comes into the country after the law is passed shall ever be allowed the right of suffrage."[9]

Morse's first telegraph message, 1844. (Courtesy of the Library of Congress.)

Morse never gave up his hatred of immigrants, but by the late 1830s he had abandoned his secret numerical cipher as impractical and inefficient and had settled instead on an ingeniously simple dot-and-dash alphabet. In 1844 he achieved his long-awaited public triumph when he sent his now-famous message along a forty-mile test wire built between Washington and Baltimore. Sitting at a desk in the chambers of the U.S. Supreme Court, Morse tapped out on his telegraph, "W-H-A-T H-A-T-H G-O-D W-R-O-U-G-H-T?"[10]

What indeed? From the start Samuel Morse's invention was hailed as a glue that, like Noah Webster's spelling book, might help bind Americans to one another. As early as 1838 Morse himself had predicted that before long "the whole surface of this country would be channelled for those *nerves* which are to diffuse, with the speed of thought, a knowledge of all that is occurring throughout the land; making, in fact, one *neighborhood* of the whole country." The telegraph, the *American Telegraph Magazine* reported in the 1850s, "renders us emphatically 'ONE PEOPLE.' " By 1860 fifty thousand miles of telegraph wires would stretch across the country, connecting over fourteen hundred stations, staffed by ten thousand telegraph operators, sending millions of messages in Morse's simple, elegant code. On the eve of the laying of a cable under the Atlantic, many people on both sides of the ocean expected the international telegraph to go beyond tying Americans together to paving the way for "universal harmony" and global peace; in 1855, Morse himself predicted, "I trust that one of its effects will be to bind man to his fellow-man in such bonds of amity as to put an end to war."[11]

In 1823, when Samuel Morse and Noah Webster sat in the parlor of Webster's New Haven house, sniffing at oil paint fumes, neither man could have predicted that although in their lifetimes both would be hailed by Americans from Albany to Albuquerque as men whose innovations helped hold the growing nation together, Morse's legacy would eventually loom larger, especially on the global stage. From the perspective of the twenty-first century, Morse's alphabetic code of dots and dashes, even if it didn't "put an end to war," began the worldwide revolution in communications we ourselves participate in each time we log on to the Internet, while Webster's greatest global legacy is the kind of petty parochialism by which Americans write *honor* and the British write *honour.*

But surely our modern-day perspective misses the point. To see Morse as a man of technology and Webster as a man of letters, to call Morse's code a technological innovation and Webster's spelling a literary one is to draw artificial, ahistorical boundaries. And to consider Morse a visionary globalist and Webster a stubborn nationalist is to forget that both despised foreigners and their influence on American life (Webster once memorably grumbled that "the country would be as prosperous and much more happy if no European should set his foot on our shores"); both placed the nation above all; and both were swept up in nineteenth-century fantasies of universal harmony (Morse hoped his code would put an end to war; Webster expected American English to become the global language).[12]

One remedy for this blurry hindsight is to focus on Webster and Morse as they sat together in Webster's parlor in 1823. Picturing them in that room and thinking about how they came to be there and where they went next remind us that while Webster's critics worried he would let foreign words into his dictionary, Morse worked to keep foreigners out of American ballot boxes. Webster wanted to nationalize language, and Morse ended up internationalizing communication, but both embraced early America's passionate nativist prejudices and nationalist fervor.

This book commits many such acts of juxtaposition. *A Is for American* is a collection of character sketches, in which I've attempted to take the likenesses of seven men: Noah Webster (1758–1843), William Thornton (1759–1828), Sequoyah (c. 1760–1843), Thomas Hopkins Gallaudet (1785–1860), Abd al-Rahman Ibrahima (c. 1762–1829), Samuel F. B. Morse (1791–1872), and Alexander Graham Bell (1847–1922). By most conventional measures, these men had little in common. And, although they meet time and again on the pages of this book, most of them never caught a glimpse of one another while they walked the earth. What binds the characters in this book is something other than personal acquaintance. Here Webster is compared with Morse, and Morse with Bell, and Bell with Gallaudet, and on and on, because all of them explored the idea that letters and other characters—alphabets, syllabaries, signs, and codes—hold nations together, and not because they shared a cup of tea.

Webster, Thornton, Sequoyah, Gallaudet, Abd al-Rahman, Morse, and

Bell are a motley crew, but they are also, each of them, fascinating characters, men whose lives are rich with irony and passion and a certain kind of
flawed earnestness. Taken singly, it would be easy to get lost in these lives.
Taken together, they bear on the most pressing issues facing the newly
United States on the roller coaster ride from Revolution to Reconstruc-
tion: the need for an educated citizenry, the problem of faction in a large
republic, the fear of disunion, and the challenge of unifying a diverse people. And they also trace several major trajectories of nineteenth-century
American history: from arts and letters to technology and progress; from
nation to race; from union to disunion.

In the pages that follow, I consider these characters one at a time, to
share with you their small, sometimes thrilling stories, and all together, to
tell a tale, sometimes chilling, of the birth and growth of the American
nation. Noah Webster is a kind of beginning for the tale I have to tell, and
Samuel Morse is a kind of end. That they met, somewhere in the middle,
and stared at each other for a good long while, seemed a fine place to
begin.

A Cobwebs

CON'STITUTE, *v.t.* 1. To set: to fix; to enact; to establish. 2. To form or compose; to give formal existence to; to make a thing what it is. . . .

—NOAH WEBSTER,
An American Dictionary, 1828

1

An American Language

On July 23, 1788, the people of New York spilled out onto the streets of the city, streets that had been specially swept and watered the night before. In the summer sun, five thousand New Yorkers formed a procession a mile and a half long, while thousands more watched from sidewalks, windows, doorways, and rooftops. The Federal Procession was meant both to stir and to display the people's passions in support of the Constitution, drafted in Philadelphia in 1787, already ratified by ten out of the thirteen states, and now being debated at New York's ratifying convention in Poughkeepsie. Meanwhile, in Manhattan, marchers expressed their support for the Constitution with a splash of panache and a fair bit of wit. A contingent of confectioners carried a ten-foot-long "federal cake," one foot for each state that had ratified. Thirty-one skinners, breeches makers, and glovers wore "buckskin waistcoats, faced with blue silk, breeches, gloves, and stockings, with a buck's tail in their hats," and waved a standard bearing the motto "Americans, encourage your own manufactures." The butchers' stage carried a thousand-pound ox and a flag reading, "Skin me well, dress me neat, and send me

*Noah Webster in 1788, from a
miniature by William Verstille.*
(Courtesy of the Litchfield Historical Society,
Litchfield, Connecticut.)

aboard the federal fleet." Even the solitary equine veterinarian was
dressed in "an elegant half shirt, with a painted horse on his breast," over
which was written, "Federal Horse Doctor." From early morning until
nearly dusk, a parade of trumpeters, artillery pieces, mounted horses,
floats, and citizens from physicians to upholsterers inched its way down
Broadway, through Hanover Square, and, still more slowly, back again. At
the end of it all, Noah Webster, who marched with the rest, wearily
summed it up in his diary: "Very brilliant, but fatiguing."[1]

Webster trudged along the streets of New York that day as a member of
the New York Philological Society, "whose flag & uniform black dress," he
noted with pride, "made a very respectable figure." The society, founded in
March 1788, "for the purpose of ascertaining and improving the *American
Tongue*," had spent much of July preparing for the grand procession,
where, dressed in black, the philologists marched in a division with other
pen-pushers—lawyers, college students, merchants, and traders. Perhaps
they hoped to keep their distance from more muscular marchers whose
displays they could not hope to rival. But if the philologists could not bear
the weight of a federal cake or pull a half-ton ox, they did manage to carry
four symbolic props: a flag ("embellished with the Genius of America,
crowned with a wreath of 13 plumes, ten of them starred, representing the

ten States which have ratified the Constitution. Her right hand pointing to the Philological Society, and in her left, a standard, with a pendant, inscribed with the word, CONSTITUTION"); a copy of "Mr. Horne Tooke's treatise on language" (an influential linguistic tract); a scroll "containing the principles of a *Federal* language" (the text of which unfortunately has not survived); and an extraordinarily elaborate coat of arms. Designed in part by Webster himself, the coat of arms depicted three tongues; a chevron; an eye over a pyramid inscribed with Gothic, Hebrew, and Greek letters; a crest and key; and a shield ornamented with oak and flax, supported, on one side, by Hermes with a wand and, on the other, by Cadmus in a purple robe (holding, in his other hand, papyrus covered by Phoenician characters).[2]

In the aftermath of the bloody War for Independence, New York's philologists hoped that peacetime America would embrace language and literature and adopt, if not a federal cake, a federal, national language. Winning the war had gained the former colonies their political independence from Britain, ratifying the Constitution would unify the states under a national government, but what would hold ordinary Americans together? Inhabitants of the thirteen "united" states were both too much like the English and not enough like one another. Americans in the 1780s shared very little by way of heritage, custom, and manners, and what little they did share, they shared with England. What, then, made them American? Noah Webster and his supporters believed that Americans needed, first, a national government and, second, a national language.

That any group of people form a "nation" is a kind of fiction, an act of imagination. A common ethnicity, heritage, and culture make this act of imagination a bit less strenuous, and a common language can make it a great deal easier. As early as the seventh century Isidore of Seville observed: "Nations have arisen from tongues, not tongues from nations." Yet national boundaries and language boundaries are rarely one and the same. Spain is not a nation of only people who speak "Spanish," nor do all Spanish speakers live there. According to one recent estimate, "there are some four to five thousand languages in the world but only about 140 nation-states."[3] Much as their governments might claim, or wish otherwise, all the world's nations are multilingual to one degree or another. Why, then, do so many people believe, and some insist, otherwise?

A "nation" is a relatively recent Western invention. And the idea that languages define nations—that how we speak and write and even spell is a necessary marker of our national character—is an assumption or really an invention that many people now take for granted but that first became commonplace and assumed special prominence during Noah Webster's lifetime. By 1849, six years after Webster's death, the French minister Paul de Bourgoing could declare with confidence that "this principle of the division of nationalities by their languages thus appears to be in truth the ruling political idea of our times."[4]

During the early modern era, when modern nation-states were founded, the idea that languages define nations had a special resonance. In Europe, nations fully emerged as political bodies only when vernacular languages began to stabilize. Before the invention of the printing press in the fifteenth century, books that circulated in manuscript were usually written in Latin and read only by scholars and nobles; literacy among the common people, who spoke a variety of vernacular languages and dialects, remained very low. With printing came not only a proliferation of print and a sharp rise in literacy rates but also printing in vernacular tongues. Over time a single French dialect out of the many spoken in France came to be favored by printers, and that "French" became a national standard. That the people of France began increasingly to read and eventually to speak something that came to be called the French language made it easier for them to consider themselves as belonging to a single nation. They might continue to speak different dialects and even different languages, but the fiction of linguistic uniformity made the fiction of nationhood easier to swallow: the French are French because they speak French.[5]

The new United States could adopt no such seemingly simple solution. An American is an American because he speaks . . . English? In the aftermath of the American Revolution, Americans faced the same problem many postcolonial nations face today: speaking the language of the now-despised mother country. As one American put it in 1787, "In most cases, a national language answers the purpose of distinction: but we have the misfortune of speaking the same language with a nation, who, of all people in Europe, have given, and continue to give us fewest proofs of love." Noah Webster believed he had found the solution. "*Language,* as well as government should be national," he insisted. "America should have her *own* distinct from all the world. Such is the policy of other nations, and such must be *our* policy."[6]

On that sultry New York summer day in 1788, a phalanx of philologists dressed in black and carrying a flag, a scroll, a treatise, and an extraordinary coat of arms insisted that a national language was nearly as necessary to national unity as the Constitution itself, a main but missing ingredient in a half-baked nation. Were they right?

Our Pretended Union

Noah Webster was an ardent Federalist, an admirer of the Constitution and a vigorous proponent of its ratification. He admired the Constitution so much that he liked to take credit for it, even though he wrote not a line of it and was nowhere to be found among the fifty-five delegates to the convention in Philadelphia in 1787 who debated and revised a document initially drafted by James Madison. (Although Webster was at the time *in* Philadelphia, serving as schoolmaster and delivering lectures on language). What Webster liked to take credit for was not the text of the Constitution but the idea of it. In 1785 he had published a pamphlet in Hartford, titled *Sketches of American Policy,* that included an essay on a "Plan of Policy for improving the Advantages and perpetuating the Union of the American States," and later in life he claimed that this essay contained "the first public proposition" urging "the establishment of a National Constitution."[7]

At the time Webster wrote his *Sketches of American Policy,* very many Americans were eager for a new plan of union. Since 1777 the thirteen states had been united under a legal pact called the Articles of Confederation, but especially because Article II declared that "each state retains its sovereignty, freedom and independence," America under the Articles was basically a loose alliance of wholly independent states over which the Continental Congress had almost no authority. When the war ended in 1783, terms of peace had to be negotiated with all thirteen states, and after the peace, the states only fragmented further. With no executive or judicial body, and with a legislative body lacking any real power, the federal government was unable to intervene in the disputes between states that became all too common in the war's aftermath, not least because seven of the thirteen colonies printed their own money, nine had their own navies (likely to seize the ships of other states), most passed tariff laws against neighboring states, and many quarreled over boundaries. Eyeing this state of affairs, Alexander Hamilton complained that the Articles had created "little, jealous, clashing, tumultuous commonwealths, the wretched nurseries of unceasing discord," while George Washington called the Continental Congress "a half-starved, limping government, that appears to be always moving upon crutches, and tottering at every step."[8]

Noah Webster agreed. "Our pretended union is but a name," he declared in his *Sketches of American Policy,* "and our confederation, a cobweb." Before the Philadelphia convention met in 1787, most critics of the existing government had called for revisions to the Articles that would give more power to the Continental Congress, including the power to tax. Webster, however, believed increasing the powers of Congress required a wholesale reconstitution of the federal government and the establishment of a wholly national union. "Must the powers of Congress be increased?" he asked, and answered: "This question implies gross ignorance of the nature of government. The question ought to be, must the American states be united?" If yes, "there must be a supreme head, in which the power of all the states is united."[9]

Webster was neither the first nor the only pundit to advocate abandoning the Articles in favor of a federal constitution (his own distant relation Pelatiah Webster had earlier published *A Dissertation on the Political Union and Constitution of the Thirteen United States of North America*).[10] And, although Noah Webster urged modeling the national constitution on state constitutions (specifically, on the Connecticut constitution), his "Plan of Policy for Improving the Advantages and Perpetuating the Union of the American States" was more polemic than plan. Still, he did write with passion about national union. In his *Sketches,* Webster contended that "three principles . . . have generally operated in combining the members of society under some supreme power: a standing army, religion and fear of an external force." None of these "can be the bond of union among the American states." Americans would never allow a standing army, a weapon of despots. The Protestant religion might bring peace and harmony to the United States, but it would never compel union as do religions of "superstition" by keeping people in ignorance. And America, remote from Europe, need not fear invasion or conquest. "We must therefore search for new principles in modelling our political system," Webster concluded. "We must find new bonds of union to perpetuate the confederation."

In Webster's mind, those new bonds of union would derive in large part from a strong national government that would serve as the "supreme power" necessary to hold the states, and the people, together. Yet, he hinted, something more was needed. The Articles of Confederation were not all that weakened the Union, weaving it together with the slender threads of a cobweb. Poor education, which fueled local prejudices, especially between New Englanders and southerners, pulled the nation apart. And, just as ignorant Americans cherished the ways in which they were different from one another, they also stupidly aspired to be more like Europeans. "Nothing can be more ridiculous," Webster complained, "than a servile imitation of the manners, the language, and the vices of foreigners. . . . Nothing can betray a more despicable disposition in Americans, than to be the apes of Europeans." And nothing, but nothing, nauseated Webster more than those preposterously affected Americans who "must, in all their discourse, mingle a spice of *sans souci* and *je ne scai* [*sic*] *quoi*."

"America is an independent empire," Webster insisted, "and ought to assume a national character." A national constitution would strengthen political union, but Americans must also constitute themselves as a distinct and united people. "We ought not to consider ourselves as inhabitants of a single state only," he implored his readers, "but as *Americans,* as the common subjects of a great empire."[11] To develop a "national character," America must first cast off its cultural subservience to Europe and, second, eradicate local prejudices. Language, Webster believed, was the stone that could kill both those birds: if Americans could be shamed into silencing their pretentious *je ne sais quoi*s and coached out of their provincial twangs and drawls, the resulting national, homegrown American language would go a long way toward establishing a national character. It was a nice, neat plan, one that Webster had first contemplated in 1783, even before he'd come up with the idea for a national constitution.

Our Political Harmony

The Revolutionary War officially ended with the signing of the Peace of Paris in 1783. That same year young Noah Webster published his American spelling book. It was, he asserted, an act of passionate patriotism: "The author wishes to promote the honour and prosperity of the confederated republics of America." Webster's readers received the book in the spirit in which it was offered: Timothy Pickering, quartermaster general of the Continental army, wrote to his wife, "I think the work will do honor to his country."[12]

It's tempting to class Webster's spelling book with a number of other patriotic post-Revolutionary schemes promoting a distinctive national language. In 1787 the Marquis de Chastellux observed that Americans were considering abandoning English altogether and adopting Hebrew as the national language, both to distance themselves from Britain and to signal themselves as a chosen people. Meanwhile, an English observer reported that American revolutionaries had contemplated making French the national language as a means of "revenging themselves on England." Greek too was apparently considered. Yet as one commentator remarked in 1815, "ninety-nine, out of a hundred, and more probably nine hundred and ninety-nine, out of a thousand, *Americans,* never heard" of such plans.[13]

Webster's solution was both more practical and infinitely more popular: he proposed to teach Americans to spell and speak the same as one another, but differently from people in England, thereby creating an "American language," which over the years would become "as different from the future language of England, as the modern Dutch, Danish and Swedish are from the German, or from one another."[14]

Not only was Webster's solution more practical than adopting Hebrew, French, or Greek as the national language, but it also remedied another problem altogether. To Webster's way of thinking, the obstacle to the formation of a "national character" wasn't simply that Americans spoke English, the language of the people who "give us fewest proofs of love," but that they spoke it differently from one another. Variant pronunciation between northerners and southerners, Webster observed, "affords much diversion to their neighbours," while "the language of the middle States is tinctured with a variety of Irish, Scotch and German dialects which are justly censured as deviations from propriety and the standard of elegant pronunciation." A uniform, national standard for spelling, Webster believed, would create a uniform, national standard of pronunciation and "demolish those odious distinctions of provincial dialects, which are the objects of reciprocal ridicule in the United States." More than mere mockery was at stake. "Small differences in pronunciation at first excite ridicule—a habit of laughing at the singularities of strangers is followed by disrespect," and soon enough Virginians come to despise New Englanders, and vice versa. "Our political harmony is therefore concerned in a uniformity of language."[15]

Webster could attempt to standardize spelling because before the eighteenth century very few standards existed. Before the advent of printing, spelling was altogether personal and erratic; by Webster's lifetime it had become less so, but spelling still varied by region and even by individual (a writer might even spell the same word two different ways on the same page). This highly irregular state of affairs was a good part of what had led

The alphabet from Webster's American Spelling Book, *1789.* (Courtesy of the American Antiquarian Society.)

several European nations to establish language academies to dictate both spelling and usage. (It was in an attempt to standardize orthography, for instance, that the Académie Française, founded in 1635, codified French's diacritical marks over accented vowels.)[16]

Webster believed the establishment of an American academy to regulate the language was unlikely. Although he expected that "the reformation of the language we speak will some time or other be thought an object of legislative importance," in the meantime, a humble fourteen-shilling spelling book would have to do, and it might even achieve the same end.[17] If every American learned proper pronunciation by reading Webster's spelling book, all Americans would eventually speak and spell alike. And what, other than a national government, could be more important for national unity?

OF PRONUNCIATION. 25

INDEX OR KEY.

Long.			Oo proper.	
1	1		6	6
a	name,	late.	oo or oo move,	room.
e or ee here,	feet.			
i	time,	find.	Oo short.	
o	note,	fort.	7	7
u or ew tune,	new.		oo book,	stood.
y	dry,	defy.	u bush,	full.
	Short.		Short u.	
2	2	2	9	9
a	man,	hat.	i fir,	bird.
e	men,	let.	o come,	love.
i	pit,	pin.	e her.	
u	tun,	but,		
y	glory,	Egypt.	Long a.	
	Broad a or aw.		10	10	10
3	3	3	e there,	vein.
a	bald,	tall.		
o	cost,	fought.	Long e.	
aw	law.		11	11	11
	Flat a.		i fatigue,	pique.
4	4	4	oi } diphthong ; voice, joy,	
a	ask,	part.	oy }	
	Short aw.		ou } diphthong ; loud, now.	
5	5	5	ow }	
a	what,	was.		
o	not,	from.		

EXPLANATION of the above INDEX.

A figure stands as the invariable reprefentative of a certain found. The figure 1 reprefents the long found of the letters *a, e, i, o, u,* or *ew,* and *y*; number 2, the short found of the fame characters; number 3, marks the found of broad *a,* as in *hall*; number 4, reprefents the found of *a* in *father*; number 5, reprefents the short found of broad *a,* as in *not, what*; number 6, reprefents the found of *o* in *move,* commonly expreffed by *oo*; number 7, reprefents the short found of *oo* in *root, bush*; number 9, reprefents the found of *u* short, made by *e, i,* and *o,* as in *her, bird, come,* pronounced *hur, burd, cum*; number 10, reprefents the first found of *a* made by *e,* as in *their, vein,* pronounced *thare, vane*; number 11, reprefents the French found of *e,* which is the fame as *e* long. See table 34th.

C

A guide to pronunciation in Webster's American Spelling Book, 1789. (Courtesy of the American Antiquarian Society.)

Speaking the Same Language

"All America waits anxiously for the Plan of Government," Webster wrote in his diary from Philadelphia on September 18, 1787, as Benjamin Franklin presented the Constitution of the United States to the Pennsylvania Assembly. The day before, thirty-nine of the remaining forty-two delegates to the Constitutional Convention had signed the final draft (thirteen of the original fifty-five had already gone home), and Franklin, upon signing, had memorably declared, "Thus I consent, Sir, to this Constitution, because I expect no better, and because I am not sure it is not the best."[18]

Whether it was the best, or at least good enough, was for Americans to decide. In order for the Constitution to become law, nine out of the thirteen states were required to ratify it, but Federalists knew that nothing less than unanimous ratification was necessary to establish a stable government. Immediately after it was signed, the plan was made public, printed throughout the states in broadsides, posted at church doors and taverns, read aloud on town squares. A torrent of essays and pamphlets rained upon the nation as proponents of the Constitution rushed to publish arguments endorsing its ratification, most notably the eighty-five essays known as the Federalist Papers, written by John Jay, Alexander Hamilton, and James Madison. (At the request of a convention delegate, Webster added his own contribution to this flood of print; his *Examination into the Leading Principles of the Federal Constitution* was published in Philadelphia in October 1787, just a month after the signing.[19]) Meanwhile, opponents of the Constitution, known as the Antifederalists, published their own forceful tracts, disputing the Federalists' claims point by point. The bells that rang in Philadelphia on September 18, 1787, heralded not only the new Constitution but also nearly two years of rancorous debate about America, its people, and the nature of government.

Beginning in December 1787, state ratifying conventions were assembled to debate the Constitution's merits. Everywhere Federalists argued that the Constitution was a necessary reform from the excesses of revolution. At the New York State ratifying convention, Hamilton asserted that in the drafting of the Articles of Confederation, "The zeal for liberty became predominant and excessive," but that the Constitution represented "a principle of strength and stability in the organisation of our government, and vigor in its operations." Antifederalists meanwhile claimed that in the interests of such stability, the Constitution took so much power away from the states as to create a tyrannical national government. In New York, John Lansing denounced the Constitution as "a triple headed monster, as deep and wicked a conspiracy as ever was invented in the darkest ages against the liberties of a free people." Many Antifederalists, like Richard Henry Lee of Virginia, considered the Constitution a reversal of the Revolution. "'Tis really astonishing," Lee declared, "that the same people who have just emerged from a long and cruel war in defense of liberty, should now agree to fix an elective despotism upon themselves and their prosperity."[20]

Among Antifederalists' prime objections to the Constitution was its provision for a small elite to represent the people of a vast nation. Prevailing eighteenth-century political philosophy, most famously articulated by

Montesquieu, warned that a republican government could only exist in a small, homogeneous country. Only where the people were so alike and living in such close proximity as to share common, if not identical, concerns could a representative government work. Antifederalists argued that in establishing a republic so sprawling and heterogeneous as the United States, the people would inevitably fragment into factions, each concerned with its narrow self-interest rather than with the good of the whole.

"Republics are proverbial for *factions*," Noah Webster would write in his definition of *faction,* in his 1828 dictionary. Indeed, this pervasive fear of factions in large republics had influenced the framing of the Articles of Confederation, which essentially created an alliance of small republics, the states, in order to avoid the kind of factionalism that was expected to result from uniting them into a single large republic of peoples with dueling interests.

In Federalist Number 10, James Madison provided the Federalists' most important response to this objection. He began with a definition (which Webster later quoted in his 1828 dictionary): "By a faction I understand a number of citizens, whether amounting to a majority or minority of the whole, who are united and actuated by some common impulse of passion, or of interest, adverse to the rights of other citizens, or to the permanent and aggregate interests of the community." He then proceeded to reverse Montesquieu's argument by declaring that a republic could thrive *only* in a large territory, where there would be so many different people and so many competing factions as to prevent any one faction from becoming tyrannical. "Extend the sphere [of a republic] and you take in a greater variety of parties and interests; you make it less probable that a majority of the whole will have a common motive to invade the rights of other citizens; or if such a common motive exists, it will be more difficult for all who feel it to discover their own strength and to act in union with each other." Moreover, in a large republic, the challenges of leading such a diverse people, and the small ratio of representatives to constituents, would bring only the most talented, most impartial men to Congress. A larger republic, Madison argued, offers "a greater option" of representatives "and consequently a greater probability of a fit choice."

Madison considered factions inevitable. "The latent causes of faction," he declared, "are . . . sown in the nature of man." Everywhere, there will always be "men of factious tempers, of local prejudices, or of sinister designs." Only a large republic could dilute their influence.[21]

While Madison turned factions to his favor, another Federalist strategy was to deny the factiousness of the American people, to argue, in effect, that Americans were already one people, ripe for a political union that would do no more than formalize already existing bonds and a system of government in which their common interests would be ably represented by like-minded citizens. It was here that the question of language inevitably arose. In Federalist Number 2, John Jay gave thanks that "Providence has been pleased to give this one connected country, to one united people—a people descended from the same ancestors, *speaking the same language*, professing the same religion, attached to the same principles of government, very similar in their manners and customs."[22]

Yet writing in 1790, Thomas Paine in *The Rights of Man* seemed to be describing a different nation when he observed: "If there is a country in the world where concord, according to common calculation, would be least expected, it is America. Made up, as it is, of people from different nations, accustomed to different forms and habits of government, *speaking different languages,* and more different in their modes of worship, it would appear that the union of such a people was impracticable." (Only a republican government, Paine believed, could unite such a sprawling, diverse nation: "By the simple operation of constructing government on the principles of society and the rights of man, every difficulty retires, and the parts are brought into cordial union.")[23]

Which was the real America? And how many languages did Americans speak? Was America John Jay's nation of "one united people . . . speaking the same language" or Tom Paine's republic of "people from different nations . . . speaking different languages"?

Part of the answer lies in a happy provision of the Constitution itself: it required the new government to take a census every ten years. At the first national census, in 1790, census takers on horseback counted 3.9 million people: 3.1 million whites, 60,000 free blacks, and 700,000 slaves. Of the white population, at least one-quarter were of non-English European descent, and about one-fifth were non-native English speakers. The census failed to count Indians at all; their population in the thirteen states was probably about 150,000, and if they are added to the total population, it is closer to 4 million.[24]

To put it another way, the total white population of the United States in 1790 was 3.1 million, about 2.3 million of whom were of English descent (the remaining 800,000 whites were principally of German, French, Dutch, Scottish, and Irish extraction) and about 2.5 million of whom spoke English as their first language (the majority of the remaining 600,000 whites were native German or French speakers). Of the 760,000 blacks living in the United States, about one-fifth, or 152,000, were African-born. Free blacks and most slaves born in America probably spoke English (a Virginian observed as early as 1724 that "the *Native Negroes* generally talk good *English* without *Idiom* or *Tone*"), while many of those born in Africa spoke only their native tongues. Meanwhile, the 150,000 Indians living east of the Mississippi spoke a variety of native American languages; very few spoke English as a first language.[25]

The number of non-native English speakers in the United States in 1790, then, was about 902,000 (600,000 whites, 152,000 African-born slaves, and 150,000 Indians), out of a total population of about 4 million. Roughly, nearly *1 out of every 4* people living in the United States in 1790 did not speak English as a first language (though many of these probably spoke English with greater or lesser facility).

Contrast this with linguistic diversity in the United States today. Census takers in 1990 counted 230.4 million Americans, of whom 198.6 million spoke only English. Of the remaining 31.8 million Americans, the largest group was Spanish speakers (17.3 million), followed by French, German, Italian, and Chinese speakers (about 1 million of each). In 1990, then, *1 out of every 6* people living in the United States did not speak English as a first language (though, again, many also spoke English with great facility).[26]

In other words, the percentage of non-native English speakers in the United States was actually *greater* in 1790 than in 1990.

Anecdotal evidence better illustrates the situation that the numbers confirm. Advertisements for runaway slaves and indentured servants placed in the *Pennsylvania Gazette* from 1725 to 1775 include notices for "an Irish servant boy, named *William Wiley*, . . . can talk a little Dutch" (1771); "a likely Negroe Man . . . named Francisco; he speaks Spanish and Dutch well, but not much English" (1762); "A German Apprentice Lad, born in Makuntchi, named George Schwartz . . . Speaks but little English" (1762); "a Dutch servant man named FREDERICK LUDERTZ. . . . As he speaks the French language very fluently, he may try to pass for a Frenchman" (1767); "a Servant Man named *Thomas Robards*, a *Welch* Man, and speaks good *English* and *Welch,* and some *Irish*" (1734); "an English indented servant man, named Edward Davis . . . talks Dutch and Welsh" (1771); and "a Negro Man named JIM . . . speaks Dutch and English plain" (1763).[27]

Pennsylvania was an unusual place: two-fifths of its residents spoke German. In 1751 the Philadelphian Benjamin Franklin famously complained about Pennsylvania's German newspapers, German legal documents, and German street signs and asked, "Why should Pennsylvania, founded by the English, become a colony of aliens, who will shortly be so numerous as to Germanize us instead of our Anglifying them?" Even as late as 1821 the *Niles' Weekly Register* attacked Pennsylvania Germans for their continued loyalty to their native tongue: "It is out of the question that the German can ever be the prevailing language in the United States—the descendants of the Germans should, therefore, learn the English, and mix themselves with the mass of the society in which they live—the common home of us all."[28]

But even outside Pennsylvania the United States housed French- and German-language schools, and many Americans attended non-English church services and read non-English newspapers. The Articles of Confederation were themselves printed in French in 1777, not merely for the eyes of Gallic allies across the ocean, and the Continental Congress printed numbers of its proceedings in German. Benjamin Franklin must have been disheartened to discover that soon after he presented the Constitution to the Pennsylvania Assembly in September 1787, it was printed as *Die Constitution* in no fewer than four German editions. And when, in 1786, Noah Webster proposed giving a series of lectures on the English language in Albany, New York, a resident discouraged him on the grounds that his proposed audience would be uninterested in the topic: "The Inhabitants are all, or principally the descendants of the first settlers from Amsterdam who have been taught to read and write their native language, and as in the case with all nations, are strongly prejudiced in favour of it. The English tongue has ever been disagreeable and the majority of them now speak it more from necessity than choice."[29]

If, for many eighteenth-century Americans, English was not a native tongue, why was Webster so concerned about small differences in pronunciation among English speakers rather than with bigger differences between languages? Because, for him English dialects were the linguistic equivalent of political factions, a kind of "local prejudice" that could rend the Union apart. Foreign languages, especially non-European languages, simply did not concern him; of one thing he was certain: "The English is the common root or stock from which our national language will be derived." Webster would have been the first to admit that John Jay was premature in calling the nation monolingual in 1787, but he believed the extinction of all languages other than English inevitable: all others "will gradually waste away—and within a century and a half, North America will be peopled with a hundred millions of men, *all speaking the same language.*"[30] For Webster, Americans who did not speak English did not belong to the nation. And they could not participate in what Webster and his contemporaries called the republic of letters, the sphere of printed public discourse—of newspapers, pamphlets, and books—that made self-government possible. Webster's business wasn't to teach Americans English; it was to reform the language of those who already spoke it.

There iz no alternativ

In 1785 and 1786 Noah Webster traveled from Boston to Charleston, and back again, selling his spelling book, lobbying for copyright laws, and delivering his tiresome lectures on language.[31] Life on the road was difficult. Outside Baltimore, Webster's stage broke down, forcing him to hire a horse ("I curse all stage Waggons," he scrawled in his diary). Near Bladensburg, Virginia, he beat his "dull horse" so fiercely that he cracked his cane ("a little vexatious matter"), and near Annapolis another hired horse took fright, injuring Webster in the fall. On board the *George,* sailing to South Carolina, he had to fish for his supper—and failed ("Harpoon a porpoise; but in a hurry & confusion, lose both the harpoon & the porpoise"). Arriving in Charleston, he found little comfort ("the weather is hot & the Musketo's troublesome"). But Webster's tour of the new nation wasn't all misery and mosquitoes. In Baltimore he hired a French master and began studying the language, after which he peppered his diary with the very French phrases he had earlier found so pretentious (July 30, 1785—"Finish my last Lecture *avec eclat*"; August 16, 1785—"Ne rien de Nouvelles"). And, everywhere he went, Webster hobnobbed with America's elite. In May 1785, after finishing his business with the Virginia legislature (where, he later claimed, he gave James Madison the idea for a federal government), Webster rode his dull horse "to Genl Washington's seat, 9 miles from Alexandria, down the River Potowmack." Delighted to be "treated with great attention," he enjoyed a pleasant Friday evening playing whist with Washington and his wife ("who is very social").

Everywhere, Webster looked for a wealthy bride. "Take tea with Miss Ray," he wrote from Albany, "a ten thousand pounder." And everywhere, he read his lectures on language—or as many as he could scare up an audience for at two shillings a head. In Williamsburg "6 gentlemen only" showed up for his first lecture. "The Virginians," Webster concluded, "have . . . Great contempt for Northern people." In Baltimore he delivered his lectures to "a crouded audience, whose applause is flattering" ("More taste for science in these States than below"). In Philadelphia in February 1786 his lectures drew as many as "100 reputable characters," and in New York the next month, they were attended by David Ramsay "& many other members of Congress." Among those in attendance at Webster's Philadelphia lectures was one reputable character who was to influence him greatly, Benjamin Franklin.

Intrigued by Webster's interest in orthography, Franklin told Webster about his own "idea of reforming the English alphabet" and showed him a copy of a pamphlet he had written in 1768, *A Scheme for a New Alphabet and Reformed Mode of Spelling,* in which Franklin proposed deleting the letters *c, w, y,* and *j* and adding six new letters.[32]

In his 1783 spelling book, Webster had mocked all proposals "to alter the spelling of words, by expunging the superfluous letters." He had wanted to standardize and Americanize spelling, not simplify it. Writing *favour* f-a-v-o-r seemed to him ridiculous. "This appears to arise from the same pedantic fondness for singularity that prompts to new fashions of pronunciation." Webster didn't dispute the irregularity of English spelling, only the wisdom of trying to change it. "Our language is indeed pronounced very differently from the spelling; this is an inconvenience we regret, but cannot remedy. To attempt a progressive change, is idle; it will keep the language in perpetual fluctuation without an effectual amendment. And to attempt a total change at once, is equally idle and extravagant, as it would render the language unintelligible."[33]

Yet, in reading Franklin's *Scheme,* Webster found himself persuaded. "Your Excellency's sentiments upon the subject," he wrote Franklin in May, "backed by the concurring opinion of many respectable gentlemen and particularly of the late chairman of Congress [David Ramsay], have taught me to believe the reformation of our alphabet still practicable."[34]

Why reform the alphabet? Because, as Webster had admitted in his spelling book, "Our language is . . . pronounced very differently from the spelling." If spelling does not dictate pronunciation, Webster's entire project—to eradicate dialect by standardizing spelling—makes little sense.

Characters.	Sounded [respectively] as in [the Words in the Column below.]	Power of Letters as exprest in the former Sounded and Characters.	[Manner of pronouncing the Sounds.]
o	Old.	o	The first Vowel, naturally, and deepest found; requires only to open the mouth, and breathe through it.
a	John, Folly; Awl, Ball.	a	The next requiring the mouth opened a little, or hollower.
a	Man, can.	a	The next, a little more.
e	Men, lend, Name, Lane.	e	The next requires the *Tongue* to be a little more elevated.
i	Did, Sin, Deed, feen.	i	The next still more.
u	Tool, Fool, Rule.	u	The next requires the *Lips* to be gathered up, leaving a small opening.
y	um, un; as in umbrage, unto, &c. and as in *er*.	y	The next a very short Vowel, the Sound of which we should express in our present Letters thus, *uh*; a short, and not very strong *Affirmation*.
h	hunter, happy, high.	huh	A stronger or more forcible aspiration.
g	give, gather.	gi	The first CONSONANT; being formed by the *Root of the Tongue*; this is the present hard g.
k	keep, kick.	ki	A kindred found; a little more acute; to be used instead of the hard *c*.
ſh	(ſh) Ship, wiſh.	iſh	A new letter, wanted in our language; our *ſh*, separately taken, not being proper elements of the found.
ŋ	(ng) ing, repeating, among.	ing	A new letter, wanted for the same reason;—These are formed *back in the mouth*.
n	end.	en	Formed *more forward* in the mouth; the *Tip of the Tongue* to the *Roof of the mouth*.
r	Art.	r	The same; the tip of the tongue a little loose or separate from the roof of the mouth, and vibrating.
t	Teeth.	ti	The tip of the tongue more forward; touching, and then leaving, the roof.
d	Deed.	di	The same; touching a little fuller.
l	ell, tell.	el	The same; touching just about the *gums* of the *upper teeth*.
ſ	Eſſence.	es	This found is formed, by the breath paſſing *between* the moiſt end of the tongue and the *upper teeth*.
z	(ez) Wages.	ez	The same; a little denſer and duller.
þ	(th) think.	eþ	The tongue under, and a little *behind*, the upper teeth; touching them, but ſo as to let the breath paſs between.
ħ	(dh) thy.	eħ	The same; a little fuller.
f	Effect.	ef	Formed by the *lower lip* against the upper teeth.
v	ever.	ev	The same; fuller and duller.
b	Bees.	b	The lips full together, and *opened* as the air paſſes out.
p	peep.	pi	The same; but a thinner found.
m	ember.	em	The *cloſing* of the lips, while the *e* [here annexed] is founding.

* [N. B. The fix new letters are marked with an afteriſk * to diſtinguiſh them, and ſhew how few new founds are propoſed. E.]

Benjamin Franklin's "Reformed Alphabet." (Courtesy of the Harvard College Library.)

Even if all Americans learned to spell using his speller, they would not all learn to speak alike. Uniform spelling does not produce uniform pronunciation. A New Englander might read *lecture* as *lecter,* but teaching a Virginian to spell it l-e-c-t-u-r-e would not prevent him from pronouncing it *lectyur,* an observation no doubt brought home to Webster night after night on his lecture tour, especially by Virginians with their "Great contempt for Northern people." The problem was not only the absence of American spelling books but also the inexact English system of spelling. So long as the principles behind spelling were flawed, pronunciation would remain variable, no matter how many people bought Webster's books.

In May 1786, inspired by Franklin and newly confident of success in reforming the alphabet, Webster drafted "a plan for the purpose of reducing the orthography of the language to perfect regularity," which he eventually published as an appendix to his 1789 collection of lectures, the *Dissertations.*[35] The basic premise of Webster's "Essay on the Necessity, Advantages and Practicability of Reforming the Mode of Spelling, and of

A sample in Franklin's "Reformed Alphabet," 1768. (Courtesy of the Harvard College Library.)

Rendering the Orthography of Words Correspondent to the Pronunciation," as well as of Franklin's *Scheme,* was to redesign the alphabet "so as to give a distinct character to every distinct sound, and to let no one sound be signified by more than one character."[36]

The lack of a one-to-one correspondence between the alphabet and the sounds of the English language is a problem, of course, with which every schoolchild wrestles. Learning to spell *through* t-h-r-o-u-g-h and *bureau* b-u-r-e-a-u is no mean feat. (The notorious difficulty of English spelling was perhaps most famously deplored by George Bernard Shaw, who observed that English writers might just as well spell *fish* g-h-o-t-i, using the *gh* of *laugh,* the *o* of *women,* and the *ti* of *nation.*)[37]

In early modern Europe, rising literacy rates following the invention of the printing press had highlighted this problem as it exists, to a greater or lesser degree, in all European languages, and English writers had sought to reform English orthography for centuries before the likes of Franklin and Webster tackled the task.[38] Most earlier proposals traced the alphabet's flaws to its foreign origins. The English language is written with the Roman alphabet, a modified version of the Greek alphabet, which in turn is derived from an ancient Phoenician writing system, brought to Greece, according to legend, by Cadmus, the mythological brother of Europa, who also built the city of Thebes. (Recall that the flag carried by the New York Philological Society at the Federal Procession in 1788 depicted Cadmus in a purple robe holding papyrus covered by Phoenician characters.) Europeans considered the Greek-derived alphabet a perfect writing system since it matched each character to a sound (rather than to an idea, a syllable, or a phrase). But the imported Greek alphabet is a poor fit for English or any other language other than Greek since the sounds of the Greek language are different. Some English sounds (like *sh*) require more than one letter, and some letters (like *g*) have more than one sound. To remedy the situation, English spelling reformers hoped to invent a "perfect" or "philosophical" alphabet, one that exactly matched letters with sounds.

As Benjamin Franklin saw it, one problem with using a Greek-derived alphabet to write English was that it was too much like using a nonalphabetic system like Chinese. English writers needed not only to learn the twenty-six letters of the alphabet, and their sounds, but also all the sounds of combinations of letters. Franklin suspected that the Chinese script "might originally have been a literal Writing like that of Europe, but through the Changes in Pronunciation brought on by the Course of Ages and through the obstinate Adherence of that People to old Customs, and among others to their old manner of Writing, the original Sounds of Letters and Words are lost, and no longer considered." Following many English writers, Franklin believed that the situation for the English language was dire: "If we go on as we have done a few Centuries longer, our words will gradually cease to express Sounds, they will only stand for things, as the written words do in the Chinese Language."[39]

From the perspective of many Europeans and Americans, the Chinese system required so much memorization, and was so difficult to learn, that literacy was restricted to a few, and communication and the advance of learning were greatly limited. Later American spelling reformers even argued that the Chinese script condemned the Chinese people to despotic government, suggesting that a republican government required a "perfect alphabet."[40]

By way of remedying English, Franklin prescribed eliminating redundant letters, like *c*, "*k* supplying its hard sound, and *s* the soft," and adding new letters to represent sounds that otherwise require two letters; he proposed, for example, introducing the character ꝺ to replace *th* as in *think*.[41]

Webster's more conservative proposal operated on the same principles. He recommended "the omission of all superfluous or silent letters; as *a* in *bread*," and "a substitution of a character that has a certain definite sound, for one that is more vague and indeterminate" (by which *mean, near, speak, grieve, zeal* would become *meen, neer, speek, greev, zeel*). In a departure from Franklin, Webster eventually argued against the invention of entirely new letters, since "a trifling alteration in a character, or the addition of a point would distinguish different sounds, without the substitution of a new character." (He proposed diacritical marks not unlike those used by the French.) Still, Webster's plan was much like Franklin's, and neither differed greatly from previous proposals.[42]

Webster sent a rough draft of his plan to Franklin in May 1786. Franklin responded with both alacrity and enthusiasm. "Our Ideas are so nearly similar," he replied, "that I make no doubt of our easily agreeing on the plan." Eager to see a corrected orthography put into practice, Franklin asked Webster to return to Philadelphia as soon as possible to discuss the plan in person ("Sounds, till such an alphabet is fix'd, not being easily explain'd or discours'd of clearly upon Paper") and offered him his "Dictionary on his scheme of a Reform." In the hope that Webster would relent on the question of new characters, Franklin offered him a special set of types he had ordered cast in his new alphabet.[43]

Yet, however similar Webster's ideas were to Franklin's and earlier English proposals, for Webster—but not for Franklin—altering orthography was a uniquely *American* endeavor. Franklin's *Scheme*, written in London before the American Revolution, was addressed to all English writers, on both sides of the Atlantic, to whom he proposed a "perfect alphabet" as an improvement in the interests of education and efficiency.[44] Webster's plan was for Americans only, to strengthen their own republic of letters. The day after sending Franklin his "plan of a new Alphabet," Webster listed its six advantages:

1. It will render the acquisition of the language easy both for natives and foreigners. All the trouble of learning to *spell* will be saved.

2. When no character has more sounds than one, every man, woman, and child who knows his alphabet can spell words, even by the sound, without ever seeing them.

3. Pronunciation must necessarily be uniform.

x   P R E F A C E.

me to publiſh them in a volum, with ſuch alter-
ations and emendations, az I had heerd ſuggeſt-
ed by frends or indifferent reeders, together
with ſome manuſcripts, that my own wiſhes led
me to hope might be uſeful.

DURING the courſe of ten or twelv yeers, I
hav been laboring to correct popular errors, and
to aſſiſt my yung brethren in the road to truth
and virtue ; my publications for theze purpoſes
hav been numerous ; much time haz been ſpent,
which I do not regret, and much cenſure incurred, which my hart tells me I do not dezerv.
The influence of a yung writer cannot be ſo
powerful or extenſiv az that of an eſtabliſhed
karacter ; but I hav ever thot a man's uſeful-
neſs depends more on exertion than on talents.
I am attached to America by berth, education
and habit ; but abuv all, by a philoſophical
view of her ſituation, and the ſuperior advantages ſhe enjoys, for augmenting the ſum of ſocial
happineſs.

I SHOULD hav added another volum, had not
recent experience convinced me, that few large
publications in this country wil pay a printer,
much leſs an author. Should the Eſſays here
preſented to the public, proov undezerving of
notice, I ſhal, with cheerfulneſs, reſign my other papers to oblivion.

THE reeder wil obzerv that the orthography
of the volum iz not uniform. The reezon iz,
that many of the eſſays hav been publiſhed before, in the common orthography, and it would
hav been a laborious taſk to copy the whole, for
the ſake of changing the ſpelling.

IN

A sample of Webster's reformed spelling, 1790. (Courtesy of the American Antiquarian Society.)

4. The orthography of the language will be fixed.

5. The necessity of encouraging printing in this country and of man-
   ufacturing all our own books is a political advantage, obvious and
   immense.

6. A national language is a national tie, and what country wants it
   more than America?[45]

In his 1789 "Essay," Webster greatly elaborated on these last two points,
the two that were furthest from Franklin's vision. "A capital advantage of
this reform in these states," Webster argued, "would be, that *it would
make a difference between the English orthography and the American.*
This will startle those who have not attended to the subject," he conceded,
"but I am confident that such an event is an object of vast political consequence." Why create an artificial distinction between English and American orthography? For Webster, distinctive spelling was yet another means
to free the former colonists from the shackles of the mother tongue. Not
only would it require, eventually, "that all books should be printed in

America," but even more significantly, Americans would benefit from knowing, at a glance, whether a writer was an American or an Englishman. "A *national language* is a band of *national union*," Webster insisted, echoing his earlier call for the eradication of dialect. "Every engine should be employed to render the people of this country *national;* to call their attachments home to their own country, and to inspire them with the pride of national character."[46]

In his "Essay," Webster asked of superfluous letters and other irregular spellings, "Ought the Americans to retain these faults which produce innumerable inconveniences in the acquisition and use of the language, or ought they at once to reform these abuses, and introduce order and regularity into the orthography of the AMERICAN TONGUE?" In his *Collection of Essays and Fugitiv Writings*, he answered emphatically, "There iz no alternativ."[47]

Kamyn Ius

After his tour of the nation in 1785 and 1786 and his residence in Philadelphia in 1787, Webster moved to New York to found a Federalist paper, *The American Magazine*. In April 1788, four months before the Federal Procession, he took out a notice in the magazine announcing the formation of the New York Philological Society. "Since the separation of the American States from Great-Britain," Webster declared, "the objects of such an institution are become, in some measure, necessary, and highly important." For much of the spring and summer of 1788, a handful of members of the newly formed society met regularly, on Monday evenings. Their "highly important" work, however, consisted largely of listening to Webster's lectures and promoting his publications. In April the society adopted bylaws and a constitution and listened to Webster read his "Dissertation concerning the Influence of Language on Opinions and of Opinions on Language." In May, Webster visited Connecticut. In June the society heard Webster read "a Philological Dissertation." In July the society chose officers, listened to Webster read his "4th Lecture," prepared for the Federal Procession, and formally endorsed Webster's spelling book, producing a letter recommending it "to the use of schools in the United States, as an accurate well digested system of principles and rules, calculated to destroy the various false dialects in pronunciation in the several states, an object very desirable in a federal republic." In the fall of 1788 the society didn't do much of anything except, in October, appoint Webster "Examiner in Philology." Meanwhile, Webster didn't hesitate to employ the society for promotional purposes, instructing the printers Hudson & Goodwin in September to advertise the spelling book with the notice "The Philological Society in New York recommend this work with a view to make it the *Federal school book.*" In December, Webster left New York for Boston, and bereft of its leader, the society soon disbanded.[48]

Meanwhile, his proposal for spelling reform faltered. In 1768 a friend had warned Benjamin Franklin that his Iŋlis Alfabet would never make it into "kamųn ius." And she was, of course, quite right. Noah Webster, in his 1789 "Essay," insisted that schemes like Franklin's had failed "rather on account of their intrinsic difficulties, than on account of any necessary impracticabilty of a reform." The problem with Franklin's plan, as with all earlier proposals, was the introduction of new characters, an innovation that would always meet resistance. Webster's more modest plan was, he believed, more likely to meet with success. As he saw it, "The only steps necessary to ensure success in the attempt to introduce this reform, would be, a resolution of Congress, ordering all their acts to be engrossed in the new orthography, and recommending the plan to the several universities in America; and also a resolution of the universities to encourage and support it." Eventually, "curiosity would excite attention to it, and men would be gradually reconciled to the plan." Webster's optimism about the prospects of success for his new alphabet in the republic of letters knew no bounds. From his lecture circuit he wrote to a friend, "There is no longer a doubt that I shall be able to effect a uniformity of language and education throughout this continent."[49]

Despite his optimism, Webster's plan was unsuccessful. When he published his lectures and essay on orthography in 1789 as *Dissertations on the English Language,* they did not sell well; as he complained to Timothy Pickering, the paper on which they were printed must "be sold for wrapping paper." Webster also included several essays written in reformed spelling in his 1790 *Collection of Essays and Fugitiv Writings,* but that, too, sold badly. Of five hundred copies printed, priced at $1.67, fewer than two hundred ever left the bookshop. Not many people read the *Fugitiv Writings,* and the few who did were not particularly enthusiastic about Webster's spelling. A review in the *Columbian Magazine* ended on a particularly nasty note: "We shall conclude with two articles of advice to Mr.

Webster. The first is, to reform *his own* language, before he attempts to correct that of *others;* the second, to learn to deliver his opinions with a less dictatorial air."[50]

Nor did Webster's spelling find much private support. In September 1790, after receiving the *Fugitiv Writings,* Ezra Stiles wished Webster well but warned of his spelling, "I suspect you have put in the pruning Knife too freely for general Acceptance." In Boston, Jeremy Belknap wrote to Ebenezer Hazard: "I join with you in reprobating the . . . new mode of spelling recommended and exemplified in the *fugitiv Essays, ov No-ur Webstur eskwier junier.*" In December 1791, Webster glumly reported to Timothy Pickering, "Some of my Essays found a sale, perhaps a third; the remainder will probably be a dead loss."[51]

Publication of the English editions of the *Dissertations* and *Fugitiv Writings* in 1797 must have done little to improve Webster's spirits or fill his purse. The *London Critical Review* wryly observed that "his proposal for a reformation of spelling may rather be called a scheme for the corruption of it." Regarding Franklin's earlier *Scheme,* the reviewer gave thanks that "the Americans, however, have not followed, in this respect, the advice of the deceased philosopher, and of his surviving admirer." And the *London Monthly Review* regretted Webster's "very peculiar and unsightly mode of spelling, founded on a rule of pronunciation adopted by the author, but which, notwithstanding his plausible reasons for it, more mature experience will most probably induce him to abandon." Yet even as Webster matured, his "Essay" haunted him. As late as 1809 a reviewer recalling it scoffed, "The perusal of this essay must strike every reflecting mind with a sense of the mildness of the municipal regulations of this land of *liberty,* which permitted the writer to roam abroad, unrestrained by a strait waistcoat, and a keeper."[52]

Noah Cobweb

The failure of Webster's radical spelling reform may be explained, in part, by his character. Webster was, to say the least, a difficult man. One historian summed up Webster's breathtaking unpopularity among his own contemporaries this way: "Benjamin Franklin Bache called him a 'self-exalted pedagogue' and 'an incurable lunatic.' William Cobbett . . . called him 'a spiteful viper' and a 'prostitute wretch.' . . . Jefferson described him as 'a mere pedagogue of very limited understanding.' " Many of these remarks were partisan, but there are more. A printer Webster worked with called him "a pedantic grammarian . . . full of vanity and ostentation." One Bostonian complained, "I wish . . . he were not so confident in his own merit, but would be content to address the public as though there were some equal to himself."

Moreover, for all his work with language, Webster on paper fails to charm, and apparently he was no more eloquent in person. Jeffersonian orator and Webster's Yale classmate Abraham Bishop said of Webster that his "head is like a vendue master's room, full of other people's goods," and urged, "As Mr. Webster is very apt to give advice to others, I leave him with a word of advice, which is, to prosecute to conviction and sentence of death the man or men who ever told him that he had talents as a writer." A student of Webster's during his schoolmastering days confided to her diary, "In conversation he is even duller than in writing, if that is possible." And William Dunlap, himself a member of the New York Philological Society, wrote a play about the society in which Webster appears as "Noah Cobweb" (a name drawn from Webster's apt phrase "our confederation, a cobweb"), about whom another character remarks, "What a curst boring fellow now that is / You may read Pedant in his very phiz."[53]

Webster's reputation as an arrogant, self-promoting pedagogue may have weakened the New York Philological Society's credibility. In Boston, Ebenezer Hazard wrote to Jeremy Belknap in August 1788: "I do not know all the members of the Philological Society, though I have understood that they are not numerous. The Monarch [Webster] reigns supreme. . . . How they will succeed in establishing a 'Federal Language,' time must determine."[54] Time did determine. Within just a few months after Belknap offered his skeptical appraisal, the New York Philological Society was no more.

Noah Webster, of course, labored on with undaunted enthusiasm. When he published his spelling book in 1783, at the end of the War for Independence, he had declared uniform American pronunciation a proposal consistent with the spirit of the age: "Greater changes have been wrought in the minds of men in the short compass of eight years past, than are commonly effected in a century." When he marched in New York's Federal Procession with his fellow philologists in July 1788, dressed in black and carrying a flag, a scroll, a treatise, and an extraordinary coat of arms, he insisted that a federal language was nearly as necessary to national unity as the new Constitution itself. And when he published his essay on reformed spelling in 1789, the timing, he believed, was equally auspicious. Having recently ratified the Constitution, and having been inspired by the revolution in France, Americans were uniquely positioned to take the bold step of adopting a new way of spelling. "*NOW* is the time," Webster declared, "and *this* is the country."[55]

2

A Universal Alphabet

In 1789, when Parisian sansculottes stormed the Bastille and the National Assembly declared the citizens of France free men, Noah Webster, like most Americans, celebrated. "I exulted in the joyful event, and my heart felt the liveliest interest in the success of their measures," he later recalled. Even the early bloodshed was understandable, given the circumstances: "My belief in the utility of the revolution furnished apologies for the violent measures of the French." Only when Webster became convinced that French revolutionaries were conspiring to "gain a controling [sic] influence" over the U.S. government did he change his mind. In 1794, Webster published *Revolution in France,* in which he argued that the French had gone too far: "Americans! be not deluded. In seeking *liberty,* France has gone beyond her." (Webster's *Revolution* was well received by sympathetic Federalists, although at least one Bostonian, expecting it to be printed in Webster's reformed spelling, replied, "I wont read it or anything else of that Webster's").[1]

However much he came to condemn the French Revolution, Webster was pleased that his own revolutionary work—his efforts to unify the nation through language—constituted "a plan similar to that which has occupied the time and talents of the National Convention in France."[2] In 1794, the year Webster published *Revolution in France,* the French Jacobin Bertrand Barère addressed the French National Convention: "We have revolutionized government, laws, habits, manners, dress, commerce, and even thought; let us now revolutionize language." Echoing Webster's insistence that "a national language is a national tie," Barère declared, "Citizens, the language of a free people must be one and the same for all."

In 1790, speaking before the National Assembly, the comte de Mirabeau had called France "a nation of twenty-four million people speaking the same language." But like John Jay's insistence in Federalist Number 2 that America consisted of "one united people . . . speaking the same language," Mirabeau's estimate, which blithely ignored French patois like Breton and non-French languages like Basque, was more wishful thinking than informed calculation. (In a report submitted to the National Convention, the abbé Henri Grégoire estimated that "at least six million French people are ignorant of the national language.") By 1794 the dangers of language diversity in a free French republic had caused alarm, at least in some quarters, and establishing a single, standard French as the national language, and eradicating all others, became official government policy: "La langue d'un peuple libre doit être une et la même pour tous."[3]

If Webster saw a connection between his work with language and that of French revolutionaries, so too did William Thornton, a new immigrant to the United States and a man far more sympathetic to the French than was Webster. In 1794, the year Barère addressed the National Convention and Webster published *Revolution in France,* Thornton sent a letter to "the Citizen President of France" (at the time, Robespierre), offering support for the revolution that Webster now condemned. "You are not engaged in the mere liberation of a people," Thornton assured Robespierre, "but in the emancipation of the globe." Along with his letter Thornton enclosed a copy of a book he had recently published, titled *Cadmus: Or, a Treatise on the Elements of Written Language,* in which he proposed an alphabet of thirty letters. "If it meet with the approbation of your learned men, and I could conduce any thing towards its application to the language of the regenerated French," Thornton wrote, "I request your commands."[4]

In the 1790s, just as Noah Webster feared, the French Revolution destabilized American politics, polarized the American people, and led the newly United States to the brink of war. Meanwhile, French revolutionaries seriously considered the need to establish a uniform language in their

*William Thornton in 1801, in a
miniature by Robert Field.* (Courtesy
of the National Portrait Gallery.)

new republic (though they never fully implemented Barère's recommendations). Against this backdrop, Noah Webster and William Thornton, Americans with opposing views of the French Revolution, looked hard at the twenty-six letters of the Roman alphabet, and both found something missing.

Tu ÐƆ Sitiznz ov Norø AmƆrika

Two years before he sent a copy of *Cadmus* to Robespierre, William Thornton had submitted the manuscript to an essay competition held by the American Philosophical Society, a learned society in Philadelphia founded by Benjamin Franklin. Echoing Webster's essay on reformed spelling, Thornton addressed "Cadmus" "Tu ÐƆ Sitiznz ov Norø AmƆrika" and claimed that "if this were to be adopted by the AMERICANS, AND NOT BY THE ENGLISH, the best English authors would be reprinted in America, and every stranger to the language, *even in Europe,* . . . would purchase the American editions." Moreover, "Dialects would be utterly destroyed, both among foreigners and peasants." The society, which had denied Webster membership year after year, awarded "Cadmus" the gold Magellan prize, given "for the best discovery, or most useful invention, relating to navigation, astronomy or natural philosophy."[5]

East elevation of William Thornton's design of the Capitol rotunda. (Courtesy of the Library of Congress.)

But William Thornton's flair for invention did not end there. In 1793 he submitted a packet of drawings to a design competition for a capitol building to be constructed in the middle of a large tract of mosquito-infested swampland south of Philadelphia, the planned federal city, Washington. He won that too. (His original design of the rotunda and facade have survived two centuries' worth of changes to the building.) The irony of bringing a new alphabet and a new capitol to the new nation did not escape the inventor. In 1795, Thornton confided to his friend John Coakley Lettsom, "It is odd, but when I baptized my work *Cadmus . . .* I had no idea that, like him, I was to build a city."[6] To Thornton, designing the Capitol rotunda and devising a new alphabet were simply different means to the same end: he would help build the American nation, block by block, letter by letter.

Noah Webster and William Thornton had a great deal in common. They were nearly the same age; Thornton was born on the British West Indian island of Tortola in May 1759, less than a year after Webster was born in Hartford. Both men befriended Benjamin Franklin, both deeply admired George Washington, and both at one time courted positions in Washington's household, Webster as a tutor and Thornton as a private secretary. Both men briefly considered teaching at the University of Pennsylvania, and both lived in Philadelphia in 1786 and 1787, where both hobnobbed with delegates to the Constitutional Convention and courted the affections of young Quaker women (though neither man succeeded in his suit; instead, Webster married Bostonian Rebecca Greenleaf, the wealthy bride he had long sought, in 1789 and Thornton married non-Quaker Anna Maria Brodeau in 1790).[7]

Both men also studied the alphabet. Indeed, Thornton had read much of the same English scholarship on the subject as had Webster. He had also read Webster's "Essay on the Necessity, Advantages and Practicability

Tu ᴅɑ Sitiznz ov Norθ Amɑriᴋa,

Mai diir ᴋuntrimen,

In prizentiɒ tu iu ᴅis smɒɒl uɑrk ai siik les ᴅɑ gratifiᴋeerɑn ov obteeniɒ iur feevɑr, ᴅan ᵍv rendɑriɒ maiself iusfɑl; and if ᴅɑ benifits ai ᴋontempleet rud bi diraivd from mai leebɑr, ai rɑl endjoi a satisfaʟrɑn θitr deθ onli ᴋan tɑrmineet.

Bai ᴅɑ grandjɑr ov ᴋaraᴋtɑr ᴅathaz so loɒ distiɒguird iu, and bai θitr iu hav, in meni instɑnsiz, biin ᴋarrid ovɑr eenrɑnt predjudisiz tu ᴅɑ ful ateenmɑnt ov pɑrfeᴋrɑn, a hoop iz inspaird ᴅat iur egzɑrrɑɒz uil stil bi direᴋtid tu liid ᴅɑ maindz ov ɑᴅɑrz from ᴅi influɑns ov irooniɑs ᴋɑstɑm tu ᴅi adoprɑn ov djɑst prinsiplz. Iu hav ɑlredi tɒɒt a rees ov men tu ridjeᴋt ᴅɑ impoziɑn ov tirani, and hav set a briliɑnt egzampl, θitr ɒɑl uil follo, θen riizn haz asiumd hɑr suee. Iu hav ᴋoreᴋtid ᴅɑ deendjrɑs doᴋtrinz ov Iuropiiɑn pɒuɑrz, ᴋorreᴋt nɒu ᴅɑ laɒguidjiz iu hav importid, for ᴅi opresed ov variɑs neerɑuz noᴋ at iur geets and

Thornton's preface to Cadmus. (Courtesy of the Library of Congress.)

of Reforming the Mode of Spelling," published in his 1789 *Dissertations*, although his admiration for it appears to have been either halfhearted or short-lived: in the manuscript of "Cadmus" Thornton wrote out a reference to "the Dissertations of the ingenious Noah Webster," and then, curiously, he carefully crossed out the words *the ingenious*.[8]

Ingenious or no, any similarity between Webster's "Essay" and Thornton's "Cadmus" turns out to be almost entirely superficial. What led Thornton to devise a new alphabet—at least originally—was altogether different from what inspired Webster. "The cause of my considering the subject at all," Thornton explained, "was the difficulty I had in teaching a negro servant to read."[9]

The Dictates of Conscience

William Thornton owned seventy slaves, most of whom he had never met. Sent to England as a young boy after the death of his father, he did not

The Characters.

William Thornton's alphabet, from Cadmus, 1793. (Courtesy of the Library of Congress.)

return to his native Tortola until 1785, at the age of twenty-six. Before his return, young Will Thornton, touring the great cities of Europe, had found himself increasingly uncomfortable with the knowledge that the income that made his education and his travels possible came from African slaves laboring on his family's Caribbean sugar plantation. Gradually he became convinced that he must free them. ("I am induced to render free all that I am possessed of, by the dictates of conscience," he wrote to Lettsom.) When Thornton visited Tortola in 1785 and 1786, his alarmed mother and stepfather warned him that if he were to emancipate any slaves, he must also immediately remove them from the island. Meeting the challenge, Thornton began planning a venture to settle them in the coastal West African country of Sierra Leone, where English philanthropists proposed to establish a colony of freed slaves. Thornton, who believed that "the minds of many Africans are ripe, and their understandings clear," envisioned a settlement of freeholders farming sugar, cotton, indigo, cocoa, ginger, coffee, rice, and corn, whose commercial success would "bring to industrious lives the ignorant and slothful of the warm country of Africa."[10]

After his visit to Tortola, Thornton's interest in African colonization schemes brought him in October 1786 to Philadelphia, where he immediately became involved with other like-minded Quakers. A month after his arrival, he headed north, to discuss his plans with free blacks and anti-slavery activists. (In February 1787, when Webster delivered his lecture about spelling reform in Philadelphia, Thornton was out of town, meeting with free blacks in Rhode Island to plan the Sierra Leone expedition.)[11]

Noah Webster, too, opposed slavery. He had held abolitionist views at least since 1789, and in 1792, the year Thornton completed *Cadmus*, Webster served as secretary of the Hartford antislavery society, where, in May 1793, he delivered a lecture later published as *Effects of Slavery, on Morals and Industry*. Webster, however, supported neither immediate emancipation nor African colonization, arguing instead for gradual emancipation. African colonization was impractical, he believed, both because of the expense and because of the vulnerability of such settlements to disease and attack from hostile neighbors. Webster also worried "whether even well civilized blacks placed in the torrid zone, where little labor is requisite to procure their necessary food and clothing, would not neglect all arts and labor, . . . and gradually revert back to a savage state." And he suspected, quite rightly, that "it is not certain that the slaves themselves would be willing to risk such a change of situation; as most of them are born in this country and are total strangers to Africa and its inhabitants." To compel them "to quit the country, and encounter the dangers of the sea, an insalubrious climate and the hostile tribes of Africa; together with the risk of starving," Webster insisted, "would be a flagrant act of injustice, inferior only to the first act of enslaving their ancestors." Yet if Webster concerned himself with the matter of slavery, he expressed no interest in African languages. And he never linked his antislavery sentiment to his work on spelling reform.[12]

But the more William Thornton thought about it, the more he came to consider the study of the alphabet critical to African colonization. On the eve of a return voyage to Tortola in 1790, still preparing for the Sierra Leone settlement, he wrote to the antislavery activist Samuel Hopkins, "The reduction of the language to the eye, in the most philosophical and easy manner, has lately engaged very much my attention—by which they [Africans] may be taught to read their own language perfectly in a few weeks." He promised Hopkins, "When I return to the West Indies, I mean to . . . make a vocabulary of the languages by which the blacks of Sierra Leona may have intercourse with the surrounding nations." In Tortola, Thornton made good on his promise, reporting in several letters that he was "learning the language of the blacks of Sierra Leona" (presumably by conversing with his African-born slaves) and "endeavouring to reduce their language to writing."[13]

By July 1791, still on Tortola, Thornton had completed a draft of "Cadmus." By then the essay had expanded from a notational system for

African languages to a treatise on written language more generally. The following October Thornton returned to Philadelphia and submitted the revised manuscript of "Cadmus" to the American Philosophical Society. Ambitiously seeking fame and fortune in the United States, Thornton now addressed his essay "Tu ÐƆ Sitiznz ov Norø AmƆrika" and reframed it as a plan to prop up the new American nation by distinguishing American from English spelling and eradicating local dialects.

Yet despite the opportunistic bow of "Cadmus" to nationalist sentiment, William Thornton was not particularly intrigued by the idea of a distinctive American orthography. On the contrary, his experience on Tortola had convinced him that the greatest orthographical challenge lay not in establishing a distinct American alphabet or even an African alphabet but in devising "an *Universal alphabet.*"

All the World More Nearly Allied

A universal alphabet, as William Thornton explained, "ought to contain a single distinct mark or character, as the representative of each simple sound which it is possible for the human voice and breath to utter"—a "perfect alphabet," that is, for all the languages of the world. Such an alphabet would consist not of one letter for every sound in the *English* language but of one letter for every sound possible in *any* language. With a universal alphabet, the "hundreds of nations whose languages are not yet written" could be transformed into written languages overnight. Unwritten languages, like African and Native American languages, could be rendered in a single notational system, and languages with different writing systems, like Chinese and Arabic, could be adapted to that same system. "If one nation only take this advantage, only one will enjoy this benefit; but were more nations to do it, languages would in time assimilate as knowledge became more diffused by intercourse; . . . and all the world [would] seem more nearly allied."[14]

In this endeavor, Thornton was not alone. In 1786, while Noah Webster delivered his wearying lectures on language in cities along the eastern seaboard and William Thornton sailed from sunny Tortola to friendly Philadelphia, the English scholar and jurist Sir William Jones, in faraway Calcutta, drafted a *Dissertation on the Orthography of Asiatick Words in*

Roman Letters, in which he complained that "every man, who has occasion to compose tracts on Asiatick literature, or to translate from the Asiatick languages, must always find it convenient and sometimes necessary, to express *Arabian, Indian,* and *Persian* words or sentences, in the characters generally used among *Europeans;* and almost every writer in those circumstances has a method of notation peculiar to himself." The pernicious effect of these idiosyncratic, individual notational systems was that comparison of languages was nearly impossible. Regretting the "disgracefully and almost ridiculously imperfect" English spelling, Jones offered a new phonetic alphabet that he hoped would become standard. (Because of the difficulty of casting new fonts in Calcutta, he avoided introducing new letters and settled, like Webster, with adding diacritics to existing letters.)

Jones, who died in 1794, was admired in the United States as a kind of emblematic man of letters. In 1805 the Philadelphia *Literary Magazine and American Register* eulogized him: "There is a kind of competition among his survivors, which shall be most lavish in his veneration." And Jones's work on the *Orthography of Asiatick Words in Roman Letters* made possible the comparative study that led to his revolutionary assertion, in 1786, that Sanskrit, Greek, and Latin shared a common parent language: "No philologer could examine them all three, without believing them to have sprung from some common source." For this observation, and for the careful, prodigious scholarship that followed it, Jones is today widely credited as the father of comparative linguistics.[15]

And his *Orthography of Asiatick Words in Roman Letters* was a critical step toward what eventually became the International Phonetic Alphabet. But it was also part of a centuries-old tradition. The search for a universal alphabet, like the closely related but equally illusive quest for a universal language, dates back arguably to the confusion at Babel. Theologians, philologists, and philosophers all had tackled the problem, with little success. In the eighteenth century, however, the search for a universal alphabet was renewed by prominent philologists like Jones who were interested in establishing a common notational system in order to compare languages and discover their common origins. Meanwhile, Enlightenment thinkers also took up the cause, believing that if the Enlightenment promised to usher in a new age free from disease and intolerance, it also promised a world free of base divisions like those of language, divisions that could only be overcome by first establishing a universal alphabet. If Webster's national spelling reform was explicitly political, the Enlightenment search for a universal alphabet was a self-consciously scholarly mix of philology and philosophy. The philosophical pretensions of the search for a universal alphabet (as opposed to the desire for a distinctive national orthography) explains why Thornton, not Webster, won the American Philosophical Society's gold Magellan prize, given "for the best discovery, or most useful invention, relating to navigation, astronomy or natural philosophy."

Indeed, Thornton believed he had made great strides in this Enlightenment effort. In 1792 he boasted, "There is no language that I cannot write perfectly (with regard to sound I mean), nor indeed is there a dialect that I cannot reduce to writing, provided I can pronounce it," but in the published version of *Cadmus* in 1793 he confessed that he had failed to devise either a universal alphabet or even a set of characters fitted to the West African languages with which he had begun his study. Instead he had found it necessary to confine his study to inventing a "perfect alphabet" of thirty letters for the English language alone.[16]

Then, in 1795, on hearing that the French philosophe Constantin Volney planned to visit the United States, Thornton returned to his earlier and grander ambition: he hoped to collaborate with him on a truly universal alphabet.

The Celebrated Volney

Born in 1757, Constantin Volney rose to fame as a traveler and orientalist in 1787 with the publication of his *Voyage en Syrie et en Égypte* and became widely known as a scholar of languages and of scripts with the publication, in 1795, of his *Simplification des Langues Orientales,* an attempt to reduce Asian and Arabic languages "*à un alphabet universel.*" (For Volney's work in his *Simplification,* Sir William Jones's Asiatic Society paid him the honor of electing him to membership.)[17]

Almost immediately after the publication of *Simplification,* Volney embarked on his journey to the United States. William Thornton was thrilled to hear it. To his friend Lettsom he enthused, "When Volney comes here, we shall try to reduce the Eastern languages to a fixed scale, which will advance towards the completion of an universal alphabet. I think it will not contain more than about fifty characters." Having heard of Thornton's work, Volney was apparently equally eager to make his acquaintance. Thornton boasted to Lettsom, "I am pleased to hear that the first person he inquired for was thy friend Cadmus," while to Thornton Volney wrote, "We have, without knowing it, worked on the same subject and almost with the same views."[18]

During much of Volney's stay in the United States, he lived with William Thornton. How much they actually worked on the universal alphabet is difficult to know. Volney later recalled that his American sojourn improved his English to such a degree as to allow him to read the brilliant work of "l'honorable sir William Jones," which renewed his dedication to the possibility of "*un Alfabet universel*." Spending time with Volney certainly excited Thornton's universalist, Enlightenment passions. In the summer of 1797, flush with the promise he saw before him, Thornton wrote to a friend, "Revolutions *on* the Earth are almost as quick now as revolutions *of* the Earth. Astonishing changes have taken place, but they will not stop yet—more is to be done, and will be done!—mankind have long been imposed on, but the Day of Light and Reason is at hand; a day terrible to tyranny!"[19]

But perhaps the "Day of Light" was not altogether imminent. In June 1798 Constantin Volney fled Philadelphia and the wrath of the U.S. government on board the *Benjamin Franklin,* a ship that Secretary of State Timothy Pickering asked naval authorities to give unmolested passage to France, so eager was he to rid the country of the insidious influence of men like Constantin Volney.[20]

The Mad Work of Factions

The danger Volney posed to the Republic had little to do, at least directly, with his contributions to the search for a universal alphabet. Instead he was despised as a scandalous revolutionary. In 1791 Volney had published *Les Ruines, ou Méditation sur les révolutions des empires,* an investigation of "what causes have erected and overthrown empires; what are the principles of national prosperity and misfortune; what the maxims upon which the peace of society and the happiness of man ought to be founded." *Ruines* proved enormously influential, and controversial, in the United States, where its English translation was begun by Volney's friend and admirer Thomas Jefferson. For his atheism and endorsement of revolution, Volney was roundly attacked by Federalists, one of whom wrote of him that "such a man may with justice be classified with that merciless horde of infidels and cannibals that have destroyed the peace of Europe, spread desolation through the civilized world and entailed so much misery on human nature." Some Federalists even suspected Volney of espionage. "They fancied that I was engaged in a conspiracy (*me*, a single Frenchman) to throw Louisiana into the hands of the directory," Volney scoffed.[21]

Why should Americans, not two decades after their own revolution, despise a man for endorsing revolution? Because Volney was French, and because Federalists linked his ideas to the French rebellion rather than to their own. Ultimately, Volney's fate in the United States was determined by Americans' shifting responses to France's revolution.

The year before Volney's arrival, Webster had published *Revolution in France*, hoping to offer the American people "a just estimate of the Revolution in France and the danger of *faction*." As Webster explained in a letter to Volney (with whom he corresponded regarding Volney's study of the North American climate) in 1796, "My enthusiasm in favor of republicanism was as warm and animated during the revolution in America as that which has distinguished the French people," but "the *mad work* which factions make with free governments, both in Europe and America . . . has somewhat abated the ardor of my enthusiasm."[22] To Webster's mind, faction had ruined the French republic and threatened to ruin the United States through the establishment of dogmatic, scheming political parties.

After the ratification of the Constitution, the earlier split between Federalists and Antifederalists had evolved into a two-party political system dividing Federalists from Republicans. As Webster saw it, France's revolution had further polarized American politics. As the French Revolution became bolder and bloodier, the ideological gap between the two parties became a chasm: Federalists opposed France while Republicans, led by Jefferson, continued to support it. Webster also blamed France for fueling American factionism in the form of so-called Democratic Societies, political clubs organized in support of the French, which Webster called associations "of political Jesuits" that "ought to be avoided like a pestilence": "They are a faction organized . . . to rally and prostrate the government of their country."[23]

Meanwhile, Republicans like William Thornton supported the French Revolution almost as ardently as Webster opposed it. Thornton joined the Democratic Society of Pennsylvania, and in 1793 he wrote to the French Girondist Jacques Brissot admiringly, "The Romans conquered to enslave, the French to liberate mankind." And, when he sent Robespierre a copy of *Cadmus* in 1794, Thornton wrote sympathetically: "We all lament the loss of blood, but such a revolution is not to be effected by ordinary modes. In extraordinary cases you are warranted in the use of extraordinary means."[24] Constantin Volney would have agreed.

Unnatural Aliens

Volney had originally planned a long sojourn in the United States. He had even toyed with the idea of settling permanently. In any event, he had hoped to stay long enough to write a travelogue about the land and its people, in much the same way that he had portrayed the Middle East in his *Voyage en Syrie et en Égypte*. But he was forced to flee the country before completing his work, and eventually he published, in 1803, only a treatise on North America's soil and climate. Nonetheless, in the treatise's preface Volney made clear that had he written of the American people, he would not have had much good to say: "I . . . should have proved, by the plainest facts. . . . That the character and principles of their leaders have deplorably degenerated; that, in 1798, very little more was wanting to one of the parties, but a suitable occasion and favourable means, in order to subvert the whole structure built up by their revolution."[25]

The subversion of the revolution to which Volney referred had largely to do with the actions of John Adams's administration in 1798, especially the passage of the Alien Act (which forbade treasonable conspiracies) and the Alien Enemies Act (which gave the president the power to expel foreigners). This legislation, together with the Sedition Act (forbidding criticism of federal officeholders) and the Naturalization Act (extending the period of residence required for aliens to become citizens from five to fourteen years), was intended to suppress criticism of the Adams administration in Republican newspapers and to protect the United States from the pernicious influence of unwanted (French) immigrants. As Volney suggested, its measures, so repressive of liberties achieved by the Revolution, did indeed threaten the health of the Republic.[26]

Although Volney left the United States before Adams signed either of the Alien Acts into law, Thomas Jefferson was convinced that Volney was their target. As Jefferson wrote James Madison in May, Volney "has in truth been the principal object aimed at by the law." Yet despite Jefferson's suspicions, Volney may have fled the country more out of general concern about the very real possibility of an actual declaration of war between the

United States and France than because of the alien laws. By 1798 France's military expansion in Europe and its perfidious diplomatic dealings with the Adams administration had forced the United States into a quasi war with its former ally to protect American shipping rights. In the wake of the Reign of Terror and the XYZ Affair, American hostility against the French surged. By June 1798 even William Thornton was moved to admit that "the French have acted so unjust a part . . . that I suspect different motives govern them than the emancipation of the human race; and their continued treatment of America is such a proof of wanton aggression that their cause, which filled every humane mind with enthusiastic good wishes, no longer operates."[27]

In such a climate, rage against French visitors and immigrants to the United States was furious. In 1799 Jedidiah Morse foreshadowed 1950s McCarthyism when he preached before his Charlestown congregation: "It has long been suspected that *Secret Societies,* under the influence and direction of France, holding principles subversive of our religion and government, existed somewhere in this country. . . . Evidence that this suspicion was well founded, has since been accumulating, and I have now in my possession complete and indubitable proof that such societies do exist, and have for many years existed, in the United States. I have, my brethren, an official, authenticated list of the names, ages, places of nativity, professions, etc. of the officers and members of a Society of *Illuminati.*"[28]

Webster, who shared Morse's views, used the widespread nativist sentiment of the 1790s and the Alien and Sedition Acts as an opportunity to vent his rage against all foreigners. In 1795 he wrote, "I consider as a matter of infinite consequence the cautious admission of foreigners to the rights of citizenship." Two years later, in a letter to Timothy Pickering, Webster called immigrants to the United States "the convicts, fugitives of justice, hirelings of France, and disaffected offscourings of other nations." And in 1800 he seethed, "The country would be as prosperous and much more happy if no European should set his foot on our shores."[29]

A French Revolution Among the Alphabet

Behind the fierceness of Noah Webster's hostility to immigration lay more than political sentiment. Webster was opposed not only to French infiltrators but to foreigners in general. Often accused of parochialism, Webster once defended himself from the charge by essentially admitting to it: "Yes, I am a native of New-England, and he that would name that fact, to excite a prejudice against my book, must be as devoid of honor as of patriotism." Webster was uncomfortable outside New England, as was made evident during the southern leg of his lecture circuit in the 1780s. And he did not travel abroad until 1825, when he was sixty-seven years old. As a nineteenth-century biographer said of Webster, "he was not so much opposed to foreign culture as he was absolutely ignorant of it." By contrast, William Thornton, born in the Caribbean, educated in Edinburgh, London, and Paris, once wrote of himself, "By having studied in different countries I am become a cosmopolite."[30]

Webster was a provincial New Englander who hoped to isolate the United States from the rest of the world by codifying an American language and barring foreigners from American shores. Thornton was a cosmopolitan, himself an immigrant to the United States, who wanted to devise a notational system for African languages to ensure the success of colonization schemes, and he ultimately hoped to make the world "more nearly allied" by collaborating with Constantin Volney on a universal alphabet. (His claim, in *Cadmus*, that his alphabet would make American spelling distinctive was clearly just pandering to an American audience.)

To some degree, Webster's and Thornton's different ideas about the alphabet were also the consequence of their very different characters. Thornton was worldly; Webster was not. However much they shared, the two were very different men indeed. Thornton was expansive; Webster was not. William Dunlap, the New York Philological Society member who dubbed Webster Noah Cobweb ("What a curst boring fellow now that is / You may read Pedant in his very phiz"), wrote of Thornton, "He was a scholar and a gentleman—full of talent and eccentricity. . . . He was 'a man of infinite humour'—humane and generous . . . his company was a complete antidote to dullness."[31]

In the 1790s pedantic Noah Webster, a Federalist and ardent nationalist who decried the French Revolution and despised immigrants, advocated the adoption of a distinctly American orthography. Meanwhile, witty William Thornton, a Republican committed to the principles of the Enlightenment who, for longer than most, celebrated the French Revolution, worked toward devising a universal alphabet. Neither succeeded.

By the end of the 1790s Noah Webster's ardor for republicanism had "somewhat abated," and even William Thornton had begun to suspect that something other than "the emancipation of the human race" motivated French Revolutionaries. "*NOW* is the time" for spelling reform, Webster had insisted in 1789, "and *this* is the country." "The Day of Light and Reason is at hand!" Thornton had exclaimed in 1797. But both of their schemes were, in the end, quixotic.

By the turn of the century Webster had given up his more radical spelling reforms for smaller marks of national distinction while Thornton's *Cadmus,* despite winning the American Philosophical Society's Magellan prize, was soon forgotten. Although at least a thousand copies were printed, *Cadmus* was little noticed. In 1795 the *London Monthly Review* noted it only with disapproval, and much later the London *Quarterly Review* remembered Thornton's alphabet as "a barbarous murder of English orthography" consisting "in turning the e topsy-turvy, dotting the i underneath, and adding a few pot-hooks and ladles."[32]

William Thornton's youthful plans to send his freed slaves to Sierra Leone also failed. American antislavery activists found Thornton impractical, unreliable, and more interested in fame and forgiveness than philanthropy. He did achieve a certain degree of public prominence as an architect and as an effective, even visionary bureaucrat. In 1794 George Washington appointed him the commissioner of the new Federal District (now Washington, D.C.), and in 1802 Jefferson named him head of what became the U.S. Patent Office, where he served until his death in 1828, the same year Noah Webster published his monumental *American Dictionary of the English Language.*

But by then the idea of any real change to the everyday alphabet could be as easily dismissed as the notion of admiring Robespierre as the emancipator of the globe. In 1814 an American satirist could mock revolutionary innovation in the alphabet as easily as the excesses of the French Revolution itself: "If . . . we should think proper to make a new grammar, alter the spelling and pronunciation, and invent a dozen more letters—in short, to make a French revolution among the alphabet, and, like true republicans, degrade that great aristocrat A. down to the bottom of the set, and put honest Z. in its place, I don't see that any body would have a right to complain."[33]

The Revolution of 1800

Between 1783 and 1800 the new United States constituted itself as a nation. With the war behind them, Americans began the long process of erecting a stable government, drafting and ratifying the Constitution, and the even longer process of discovering—or, rather, inventing—an American character.

Noah Webster believed that language was critical to the integrity of the nation, a nation held together, as he put it, by little more than a cobweb. In the 1780s and 1790s Webster insisted, again and again, that Americans needed to distinguish their spoken and written language from British English. His spelling book, his essays and lectures, and, most of all, his proposal for spelling reform all articulated this conviction.

But Webster's campaign to nationalize spelling was at odds with the prevailing philosophy of his day, the Enlightenment's quest for reasoned, universal truth, a quest well illustrated by William Thornton's pursuit of a universal alphabet that could "reduce" all the world's languages to a single set of characters. Considering Webster alongside Thornton reveals the range, and the limits, of early Americans' ideas about the relationship between letters and nations. Webster believed that the United States needed to be held together by something more than a constitution and that a distinctive way of spelling would help; Thornton was convinced that a universal alphabet could make all the world one.

If Webster abandoned radical spelling reform, he did not abandon the idea of an "American language." On June 4, 1800, he announced to the public a new plan; he published a proposal to compile a "Dictionary of the American Language." At forty-one, he was embarking on what was to become his most important and enduring life's work. "A work of this kind is absolutely necessary," he insisted, "on account of considerable differences between the American and English language. New circumstances, new modes of life, new laws, new ideas of various kinds give rise to new words."[34] For a man dedicated to the reform of the language, compiling a dictionary was the logical, if awesome, final step, the natural conclusion to a life spent urging Americans to recognize that their language was different from that of the mother country.

But Webster's dictionary proposal was roundly attacked in all quarters. Federalists hated it for its departure from tradition (one critic, signing himself "An Enemy to Innovation," linked it to the French Revolution by declaring, "These innovations in literature are precisely what Jacobinism is in Politics"), and Republicans simply hated Webster, labeling him a "pusillanimous, half-begotten, self-dubbed patriot," a "quack," and, most memorably, a "dunghill cock of faction."[35]

However innovative (and unpopular), Webster's decision to compile an American dictionary spelled the end to his more radical innovation, a revolution in orthography. In 1806 printers told him they would not publish his books unless they "could add the ours [as in *honour*] and k's [as in *frantick*] &c." By 1813 Webster had conceded the inevitable. He informed subscribers to his proposed dictionary that it would not follow his earlier spelling, "as any considerable changes must prevent the sale and use of a work of this sort": "If any persons are solicitous about the orthography proposed, they may make themselves very easy on that score. Established orthography will not be disturbed, and changes will not be admitted, except in a very few instances, to correct most palpable errors."[36]

By the time Webster announced his plan to compile a dictionary, the Federalist Party, which had controlled the national government since Washington's inauguration, was about to be voted out of office. Webster campaigned hard against Thomas Jefferson, in large part, as he put it, "because the French wished him elected."[37] But despite zealous Federalist opposition, Jefferson won the presidency and the Republicans took over Congress. With this election and inauguration, the so-called Revolution of 1800, Americans participated in one of the world's most important transitions of power, a transition that, however bitterly opposed by the defeated Federalist Party, remained peaceful and seemed to prove the wisdom of the Constitution, the strength of the Union, and the virtue of its people. Americans had not descended into the French madness of factions; they had created a stable two-party system.

At Jefferson's inauguration he declared, "We are all Republicans, we are all Federalists." Nonetheless, the new government was quick to undo the work of the old one. Once in office, the Republican Congress repealed the Naturalization Act, the remaining Alien and Sedition Acts were allowed to expire at the end of their two-year terms, and Jefferson pardoned everyone still in prison under the Sedition Act. William Thornton's Washington was transformed overnight. "To call the city of Washington the *Federal* City is quite obsolete," one Federalist newspaper editor snickered. "It would be more accurate to call it the *Anti-Federal* City."[38]

William Thornton was at home in that antifederal city, a city he had helped build. He was also at home in Jefferson's administration, as commissioner of patents. But he dreamed of a different kind of federal city. In 1800, while Noah Webster announced his plans to compile an American dictionary and Thomas Jefferson gained the presidency, William Thornton drafted a constitution "for a United North and South Columbia," in which he proposed unifying the governments of North and South America into a single federal republic. Just as the U.S. Constitution had united the sprawling confederated North American states under a strong federal government, so too could the sprawling countries of the

Western Hemisphere find peace in union. "Columbia," Thornton argued, was in effect already a nation, "a country whose bounds are measured but by the poles and the ocean." Under his proposed constitution, the two continents would be divided into thirteen states and a new capital city built in Darién, on the Isthmus of Panama (closer to Tortola than to Washington). If this were done, Thornton argued, and his Columbian constitution adopted, Columbia would form "the grandest system that has ever been forced by the most expanded mind of man: a system that would secure to the remotest ages the tranquillity and peace, the virtue and felicity of countless millions!"[39]

Even as Noah Webster scribbled words he considered distinctly American into a draft of a new dictionary, to make sure the people of the United States remained as separate as possible from the rest of the world, William Thornton imagined breaking down national boundaries to unify the nations of the whole of the Western Hemisphere, with a constitution and an alphabet.

B

Heathens

B′ARBAROUS, *a.* Uncivilized; savage;
unlettered . . .

—NOAH WEBSTER,
An American Dictionary, 1828

3

A National Alphabet

On May 1, 1828, President John Quincy Adams met with a delegation of Cherokee Indians to discuss the terms of a delicate treaty by which the administration hoped to acquire a great deal of Cherokee land in Arkansas. During the meeting Adams was particularly intrigued by the delegation's most famous member, an aging Cherokee named George Guess, who stood out from the rest of the delegation in more ways than one. Unlike his companions, he "was dressed in all respects like an Indian," wearing a "tunic and robe, leggings . . . —moccasins instead of shoes,—and a turban," a costume well captured by a portrait of him painted during his visit to Washington. But Guess's fame had nothing to do with his dress. Instead, as Adams noted in his diary, "George Guess is the inventor of the Cherokee alphabet, by which, I told him, he had rendered a great service to his nation, in opening them to a new fountain of knowledge."[1]

George Guess, better known as Sequoyah, proved a sensation in Washington that spring. Journalists rushed to interview him; city folk craned their necks to catch a glimpse of him. Sequoyah's invention, "this greatest

Henry Inman, Sequoyah, *c. 1830, after Charles Bird King.* (Courtesy of the National Portrait Gallery.)

effort of genius of the present day," newspaper editor Samuel Lorenzo Knapp reported, "has excited the astonishment of the philosopher in this country and in Europe." All marveled, as Knapp did, that "the Indians themselves are becoming philologists." And most wanted to know: How had he done it? How had this unschooled Indian who spoke only Cherokee invented an altogether new way of writing? Jeremiah Evarts, secretary of the Boston-based philanthropy the American Board of Commissioners of Foreign Missions, managed to sit Sequoyah down and ask him. "In answer to my inquiry," Evarts reported, "Guess replied; —that he had observed that many things were found out by men & known in the world, but that this knowledge escaped & was lost for want of some way to preserve it; —that he had observed white people write things on paper, & he had seen books, & he knew that what was written down remained & was not forgotten; —that he attempted therefore to fix certain marks for sounds; —that he thought if he could make things fast on the paper, it would be like catching a wild animal & taming it."[2]

It was a wonderful tale. Perhaps a bit too wonderful. Adams ultimately dismissed the tale as fanciful and the man as mercenary. "I found afterwards that he had sent me a copy of this alphabet, with a letter intimating that it was thought the United States ought to give him a gratuity of six thousand dollars for his invention." Sequoyah left Washington in the spring of 1828, no richer than when he arrived and, by some calculations, considerably poorer. His party concluded negotiations on May 6 and signed a treaty on May 28, ceding territory in Arkansas in exchange for territory in Oklahoma.[3] Sequoyah and the rest of the Cherokee delegation left the city soon afterward, to return to Arkansas and pack for Oklahoma.

In Washington, Jeremiah Evarts had asked Sequoyah how he had developed his writing system. But the question of why remains. Did Sequoyah believe, like Noah Webster, that languages define nations, that distinctive writing marks a people *as a people*? And if he believed that, did his invention succeed?

The White Man Is No Magician

Sequoyah is remembered by most Americans, if at all, as the man after whom the redwood tree is named. Even historians find his life mysterious. A man who literally reinvented writing, Sequoyah nonetheless managed to leave very few written documents behind. Most of what is known about him is taken from accounts written by whites, and much must be viewed with suspicion.[4] Consider this: all accounts agree that Sequoyah's mother was Cherokee, but they variously report that his father was a Scotsman, a Revolutionary War soldier named Nathaniel Gist, or a Dutch or German peddler named George Gist. Since Cherokee society is matrilineal, Sequoyah's mother's heritage mattered more, at least in the world in which he lived, but white writers had a stake in how they described his father. "See-quah-yah is not a full Indian," the *New England Magazine* insisted in 1831. "The invention, therefore, is not Indian."[5]

However biased the sources, it is possible to learn a good deal about Sequoyah's life by relying on claims for which there is corroboration. Sequoyah, it seems, was born about 1760 or 1770 in the village of Tuskegee on the Little Tennessee River in Cherokee territory.[6] Early in his life he moved to Willstown, Alabama. He was lame, possibly from "disease when young" but most likely from a wound sustained when he served in the Creek War. In any event, his condition confined him to stationary pursuits, and he became a skilled silversmith. He had at least one wife, Sally Benje, and several children, among them a daughter, Ayokeh. Sequoyah spoke only Cherokee. He never learned to read, write, or speak English. As a boy he may well have met Moravian missionaries, who had been teaching and preaching to the Cherokees since the 1740s, but he received no formal schooling.

Sequoyah began working on a writing system for the Cherokee language in 1809. When he began, he had no idea how writing worked, but he knew what it was. It was often reported that Sequoyah had "seen books," and he may even have "had an English spelling-book in his house" (if so, it was very likely Noah Webster's, which was widely used in Cherokee mission schools). No doubt he had also heard Cherokee tales explaining how white people came by writing in the first place. According to one Cherokee tradition recorded in the 1820s, "It is said among their principal or 'beloved' men, that they have it handed down from their ancestors, that the book which the white people have, was once theirs; that, while they had it, they prospered exceedingly; but that the white people bought it of them, and learned many things from it; while the Indians lost credit, offended the Great Spirit, and suffered exceedingly from the neighboring nations."[7]

But Sequoyah found this just-so story ridiculous. In poring over the strange marks on the pages of books, he was awed but by no means humbled by these "talking leaves." A narrative written in 1828 and informed by "a particular friend of Mr. Guess, who lived near him at the time he made his invention," asserted that Sequoyah once heard several men "making remarks on the superior talents of the white people": "One said, that the white men could put a talk on paper, and send it to any distance, and it would be understood by those who received it. They all agreed, that this was very strange, and they could not see how it could be done. Mr. Guess, after silently listening to their conversation for a while, raised himself, and putting on an air of importance, said, 'you are all fools; why the thing is very easy; I can do it myself.' "[8]

Apparently, Sequoyah never believed that there was anything "so very wonderful and difficult" about writing. George Lowery, a prominent Cherokee leader and a relative of Sequoyah's (Lowery's wife, Lucy Benje, was half sister to Sequoyah's wife, Sally Benje), reported that Sequoyah once declared: " 'The white man is no magician. It is said that in ancient times when writing first began, a man named Moses—made marks upon a stone. I, too, can make marks upon a stone. I can agree with you by what name to call those marks and that will be writing and can be understood.' "

It wasn't as simple as that, of course. Sequoyah's invention took him many long years of study and experiment. In an interview with Knapp,

Sequoyah described the painstaking process: "The thought struck him to ascertain all the sounds in the Cherokee language. . . . When he thought that he had distinguished all the different sounds in their language, he attempted to use pictorial signs, images of birds and beasts, to convey these sounds to others, or to mark them in his own mind. He soon dropped this method, as difficult or impossible, and tried arbitrary signs, without any regard to appearances."

In effect, Sequoyah began by experimenting with an ideographic system (one character for every idea) and then proceeded to logographic characters.

Each character stood for a word. He had made considerable progress; he had invented a great number of characters for words, when he discovered that the number of separate signs required for a complete set of words, would be so great that no one could ever learn or remember them. He now changed his plan. By making one character to represent one sound, and another to represent another sound, he saw that they would combine so as to form words. A few trials satisfied him that this plan would enable him to succeed. After vast labor and study he had completed eighty-six characters and with these began to frame sentences.[9]

Sequoyah began making "marks upon a stone" in 1809. He completed his eighty-six-character syllabary in 1821 (one character was later omitted), after which he presented it to the Cherokee National Council. But in the 1810s and early 1820s, even while Sequoyah wrestled with the problem of putting his language down on paper, Cherokee missionaries were also hard at work on a "perfect alphabet" for Cherokee—in order to save the souls of "heathens" like George Guess.

Reducing the Language

Beginning in the 1810s, Americans were swept up in millennialist movements that promised the return of Christ to earth once all the world's peoples had been converted to Christianity, a development many considered imminent. American Protestants believed reading the Scriptures was

The Cherokee syllabary, signed by Sequoyah, 1839. (Courtesy of the Gilcrease Museum, Tulsa, Oklahoma.)

essential to conversion, and that belief, coupled with the missionary fervor of the age, gave new momentum to reformed spelling schemes, since the difficulty of teaching heathens to read and write was exacerbated by the imperfections of the alphabet. In 1807 Noah Webster made this point himself, in defending his plan for reformed spelling. "The friends of the Christian religion," Webster declared, "have an interest of vast moment in the improvement of our language, as an instrument of propagating the gospel." Missions "in the remotest parts of the earth . . . in Asia, Africa, and the South Seas," he believed to be eminently admirable, "but the diffusion of their language among foreigners will be greatly retarded by the difficulty of learning it. . . . A language, in which a large part of its words are so written, that the characters are no certain guides to the pronunciation, a language which may be called a compound of alphabetical writing with hieroglyphics, can never make its way extensively among foreigners."[10]

Websterian spelling, designed for Americans and not for "foreigners," never really exerted an influence on American missionaries, who found themselves more interested in proposals for a universal alphabet. As American missionaries saw it, ushering in the millennium required either teaching all the world's peoples to read English or translating the Bible into all of the world's languages. Eventually most missionaries opted for the latter, believing it the quicker path to salvation. But all too often that option required inventing alphabets for languages, like most Native American and African languages, that had none. Experience soon proved that devising a new, particular writing system for each unwritten language, one at a time, was akin to reinventing the wheel. In time missionaries came to realize that the wiser course by far was to develop a truly global writing system, and in the first half of the nineteenth century, missionary organizations increasingly worked with philologists to develop a universal alphabet. What had been, for men like William Thornton, a vehicle of reason in an Enlightened world became, for missionaries, a tool for universal Christian conversion.

Early Christian missionaries among the Cherokees had at first hoped to teach them English. The mission of the Congregationalist, Boston-based American Board of Commissioners of Foreign Missions, as stated in 1816, was "To make the whole tribe English in their language, civilized in their habits, and Christian in their religion." But teaching the Cherokees English proved daunting and inevitably slowed the process of conversion. If Cherokees had difficulty learning English, missionaries had just as much, if not more, difficulty learning Cherokee. After living among the Cherokees for twenty years, Moravian missionary John Gambold admitted in 1824, "I can hardly purchase a Venison from an Indian without an interpreter."[11]

It wasn't simply that Gambold found Cherokee difficult to learn; he found it unworthy. "Their language," he wrote in 1817, "is incapable of conveying any Idea beyond the sphere of the senses." Gambold's was a common sentiment: Americans had long viewed Indian languages with disdain. But in the early part of the nineteenth century prevailing ideas about the inferiority of Indian languages were beginning to change. Under the influence, in part, of Rousseau's theory about the nobility of savages and, in part, of Americans' quest for a national character and a national heritage, many Americans came to embrace Indian languages and, most especially, Indian oratory. Indeed, the celebration of Indian poetic eloquence became a kind of American fetish.[12]

It was in this spirit that in the 1810s the Baptist missionary Evan Jones countered Gambold and others by arguing that the Cherokee language, far from being limited, was entirely capable of incorporating abstract concepts. The "native fertility of the language," Jones claimed, "compensates in a great measure for the paucity of ideas familiar to the natives of the forest." Jones set about studying Cherokee and "reducing the language to writing." His colleague Thomas Roberts reported from a Baptist mission in Cherokee territory in 1822, "We have collected all the sounds and then fixed characters to represent them."[13]

Meanwhile, the American Board missionary Daniel Butrick, at the Congregationalist mission at Brainerd, pursued the same end. In 1819 Butrick collaborated with his star student, a seventeen-year-old Cherokee named David Brown, to compose *Tsvlvki Sqclvclv,* a Cherokee spelling book. Of his orthography, Butrick boasted, "In writing I am not confined to the Eng. Alphabet & give to no letter (either vowel or consonant) more than one sound; as there is one vowel sound in Cherokee, which is not found in Eng. I have 15 distinct vowels. I have no silent letters." By 1822 Jones and Roberts had learned of Butrick's work and had begun collaborating with him, so that by 1824 Roberts could report, "We have, in conjunction with the Rev. Butrick of Brainerd, selected from the Roman characters an alphabet which comprehends all the sounds in the language."[14]

Nor were missionaries Jones, Roberts, and Butrick and the Christian convert Brown the only people attempting to "reduce" the Cherokee language to writing in the 1810s and 1820s. Hundreds of miles from Cherokee territory, in Salem, Massachusetts, the eminent philologist John Pickering tackled the problem too.

A Perfect Alphabet

In 1783, when John Pickering was six years old, his father, Timothy Pickering, sent his wife a copy of Noah Webster's newly published spelling book, instructing her, "Let John take it to his master . . . ; for I am determined to have him instructed upon this new, ingenious and at the same time easy plan." The elder Pickering's interest in his young son's education bore fruit: John turned out to be a language prodigy, learning, beginning at a very young age, French, Spanish, Portuguese, Italian, Turkish, Hebrew, Latin, and Greek. As an adult, Pickering undertook philological research that rivaled that of America's most eminent scholars: in 1806 he was elected Hancock Professor of Hebrew at Harvard; in 1812 he was offered the chair of Greek literature. He turned both offers down and instead, throughout his life, earned his living as a lawyer. "Nothing is more pleasing to me than the study of languages," Pickering wrote in 1799, "but a person cannot devote all his life to that alone."[15]

Among John Pickering's most passionate philological projects was his effort to thwart Noah Webster's plan to develop an "American language." While living in London from 1799 to 1801, Pickering became fascinated by Americanisms, which he came to despise, and began compiling a list of such "barbarisms" in an effort to stamp them out. Perhaps he had got-

C LE TV TSV LV KL.

TSU NV TA C'LI.

Te ko whe li. Marks.	Tsɪ Na pv Ki. Sounds.	Tu nv ta v. Names.
C c—a	as in hate or c qa	c
A a—a	- - hall wa' kv	a
A ʋ—a	- - part A mv	ʋ
E e—e	- - mete E kv	e
ᶐ ɔ—ɔ	- - met kɪ hɔ	ɔ
J j—i	- - pine J yv	j
I i—i	- - pin i tsɔ	i
O o—o	- - note o ni	o
Ꞇ ꞇ—o	- - prove ꞇ sv	ꞇ
U u—u	- - duke tse U	u
V v—vᵘ	- - duck v nv	v
I ꞇ—u	through the nose kɪ nv.	ꞇ

NU NA PV KI NV.

Tc ko whc li. Marks.	Tsɪ Na pv ki. Sounds.	Tu nv ta v. Names.
G g—g	as in go	gi
H h—h	- - ho	hv
K k—k	- - ko	kv
L l—l	- - lo	li
M m—m	- - mo	mv
N n—n	- - no	nv
Q q—qᵘ	- - queen	qi
T t—t	- - to	tv
W w—w	- - wo	we
Y y—y	- - yo	ye
P p—hy	- - p i	p j
S s—s	- - so	si

The orthography proposed by Daniel Butrick and David Brown in Tsvlvki Sqclvclv, *1819.* (Courtesy of the American Antiquarian Society.)

ten wind of Webster's announcement, in 1800, of his plans to compile a "Dictionary of the American Language" and found it distasteful. In any event, upon his return to the United States, Pickering positioned himself as Webster's chief adversary. In 1814 he delivered a lecture attacking Americanisms—and, implicitly, Webster's dictionary—before the American Academy of Arts and Sciences and soon after published both his address and his compiled *Vocabulary, or Collection of Words and Phrases which have been supposed to be Peculiar to the United States*. Not surprisingly, Pickering's *Vocabulary* inspired a long, vituperative public response from Webster, about which Pickering calmly wrote to his father in 1817, "W. wants to make an American language, and will of course feel hostile to those who take the opposite ground." But even before this bitter exchange, both Pickerings had developed "a low idea of Mr. Webster," who, in some circles, was increasingly considered a crank: "When they hear Webster say that he has more knowledge than any European they are rather disposed to laugh than to admire."[16]

In 1819, not long after battling with Noah Webster, John Pickering met with Hiram Bingham, a student at the Andover Theological Seminary who had agreed to become the American Board's first missionary to the

Sandwich Islands, along with a young Hawaiian, Thomas Hopoo, a graduate of the Foreign Mission School in Cornwall, Connecticut, founded in
1816 by the American Board as a school for American Indians and other
"heathens."[17] As a service to the board, Pickering attempted to teach
Bingham Hopoo's language. The experience, however, proved immensely
frustrating and convinced Pickering of the need to turn from his campaign against Websterian Americanisms to a more urgent philological
project: establishing a uniform orthography for the unwritten languages of
the world's heathens. In October 1819 Pickering wrote Bingham, "As various nations of Europe are engaged in the work of foreign missions, and
have already written and will continue to write and publish books, both for
the instruction of the heathen and for the information of the learned, it is
desirable that some common orthography should be adopted." The next
year Pickering published *An Essay on a Uniform Orthography for the
Indian Languages of North America,* explicitly modeled on Sir William
Jones's *Dissertation on the Orthography of Asiatick Words* and, as Pickering placed it, in the tradition of the celebrated Constantin Volney's *L'Alfabet européen appliqué aux langues asiatiques.* On reading Pickering's
Essay, Thomas Jefferson, himself a student of Indian languages, wrote
him, "It would be fortunate could it become the commencement of an
uniform orthography for the world; but I supposed we are to despair of
seeing such a sacrifice by any one generation for the good of all succeeding ones."[18]

Not long afterward, in the summer of 1823 (the year Samuel Morse
painted Noah Webster's portrait), Pickering met David Brown, the young
Cherokee who had collaborated with Daniel Butrick on the Cherokee
spelling book. In 1819 Brown had left Cherokee territory and traveled to
Cornwall to attend the Foreign Mission School, where he was Thomas
Hopoo's classmate. At Cornwall, Brown's teachers had seen in him great
promise and, to further his education, had sent him to the Andover Theological Seminary. In the summer of 1823, Brown traveled to nearby Salem
during a break from his studies to seek support for the work of Cherokee
missionaries by speaking publicly and meeting privately with "persons
interested in his cause"—among them, John Pickering.

On meeting David Brown, Pickering became persuaded of the need to
employ his uniform Indian orthography in the making of a customized
alphabet for the Cherokee language, to be used by both missionaries and
their students. Brown seemed the perfect collaborator. "I retain the language of my nation perfectly," Brown boasted. He was also a fluent and
elegant English speaker, knew Hebrew and Greek, and was learning

French. Soon Brown and Pickering began work on a Cherokee alphabet and grammar book. Even after Brown returned to his classes at Andover in September, he continued reviewing Pickering's drafts. Still, he was distracted both by his studies and by his public speaking and fund-raising obligations. In 1824, David Brown left New England entirely, to resettle in Cherokee territory, where he translated the sermons of missionaries and preached to his unconverted brethren "in the sweet language of Tsu-saw-ya-wa-sah," his native tongue.[19]

In spite of the loss of David Brown's assistance, John Pickering's work progressed, and in February 1825 he sent the first forty typeset pages of his *Cherokee Grammar* to Thomas Jefferson, reporting, "You will perceive, sir, that I have been obliged to form an alphabet." Pickering claimed to have reduced all the sounds of the Cherokee language to a perfect alphabet, nineteen customized characters based on the Roman alphabet, one character for every sound in the Cherokee language.[20]

He would soon throw it all away. Even as the first forty pages of his *Cherokee Grammar* were at the press in Boston, Pickering suddenly abandoned the project entirely. The final pages of the *Cherokee Grammar* were never even printed.

Why? Because, as Pickering later explained, in the midst of his work he had received astonishing news: A native Cherokee, "whose name is Guest, and who is called by his countrymen 'The Philosopher,' was not satisfied with the alphabet of letters . . . which we white people had prepared for him. . . . Strange as it may appear," Pickering marveled, this man, "The Philosopher," had instead invented his own Cherokee "national alphabet," which his people had enthusiastically adopted.[21]

Very Unphilosophical

The first time most non-Cherokees learned of Sequoyah's work was in September 1825, when David Brown sent a copy of the syllabary to the Bureau of Indian Affairs in Washington reporting "the philological researches of one in the nation, whose system of education had met with universal approbation."[22] It only became more widely known in February 1826, when the invention of the syllabary was reported in the *Panoplist, and Missionary Herald,* published in Boston for the American Board by

Jedidiah Morse. Before then even people familiar with the Cherokees were utterly unaware of the syllabary's existence. David Brown, after all, seems to have known nothing of it before returning to Cherokee territory in 1824, even though Sequoyah was a relative of his (Brown was married to Rachel Lowery, the daughter of George Lowery; in other words, Sequoyah was Brown's wife's uncle). Jedidiah Morse, who, along with his son Richard, traveled through Indian Territory between 1820 and 1822, failed to mention the syllabary in a report issued to the U.S. War Department in 1822.[23] Elias Boudinot, another Cherokee graduate of both the Foreign Mission School and the Andover Theological Seminary, recalled that the Cherokee chief John Ross mentioned the syllabary to him as the two rode by Sequoyah's cabin in the winter of 1822–23, but he took no notice of it until 1824. The Baptist missionary Evan Jones did not hear of it until 1826, and as late as August 1826 the *United States Literary Gazette* reported that Pickering's *Cherokee Grammar* was "now in the press," making no mention of Sequoyah's invention.[24]

But once Sequoyah's work became known, it was almost immediately clear that he had succeeded where Pickering, Brown, Butrick, Evans, and Roberts had failed. The Cherokee people were learning to read, it seemed, almost overnight. As early as 1824 a visiting missionary reported that "a great part of the Cherokees can read and write in their own language." In 1826, Cherokee John Ridge reported that Sequoyah had "succeeded in a few months . . . to educate a Nation." Ridge estimated that "there is a large majority who read and write in George Guess' syllabic character." In 1835 a U.S. War Department census reported that more than half of all Cherokee households had at least one literate member. A visitor in 1838 offered a still-higher estimate: "About three-fourths of the entire population can read in their own language."[25]

John Pickering was astonished. In a letter to the German linguist and philosopher Wilhelm von Humboldt in 1827, Pickering scoffed that Sequoyah "was not satisfied with the alphabet of letters or single sounds which we white people had prepared for him . . . , but he thought fit to devise a new syllabic alphabet." Pickering admitted that "the use of the new characters had spread among them in the most inconceivable manner, and they learn with great rapidity, both the old people and the young." Indeed, the syllabary was famously easy to learn. The American Board missionary Samuel Austin Worcester, who graduated from the Andover Theological Seminary in 1823 and began his mission among the Cherokees in 1825, reported in the *Panoplist* in 1826, "Young Cherokees travel a great distance to be instructed in this easy method of writing and reading. In three days they are able to commence letter-writing, and return home to teach others." As Pickering himself acknowledged, "An active Cherokee boy may learn to read his own language in a day, and not more than two or three days are ordinarily requisite. To read is only to repeat successively the names of the several letters; when a boy has learned his alphabet, he can read his language."[26]

Compare this speed—learning to read their own language in a day, or even three—with the time it took for Cherokees to learn to read English. Catherine Brown, David Brown's sister and the first Cherokee baptized at the Brainerd Mission, was considered a prodigy because she was able to read the Bible after sixty days of study and "could read as well as most persons of common education" after ninety days. John Arch, another Brainerd convert, was held up as an extraordinarily proficient student since "in ten months he could read and write well." From the missionaries' point of view, the syllabary was a godsend. Evan Jones wrote that Sequoyah's syllabary was "more beneficial to his people than a gift of ten thousand dollars." By 1827 Jones had proposed using it in day schools: "One, two, or three months in each town would be sufficient to teach the whole population . . . to read and write the new characters."[27]

Yet largely because it challenged Pickering's orthography, Sequoyah's invention was, at least initially, a blow to the American Board and to Pickering in particular. Samuel Austin Worcester clearly felt compelled to defend the syllabary against charges that it was inferior to Pickering's alphabet. "I am not insensible of the advantages which Mr. Pickering's alphabet . . . possesses above the English, by being so much more nearly a perfect alphabet," Worcester conceded in 1827. "But in point of simplicity, Guess has still the pre-eminence; and in no language probably can the art of reading be acquired with nearly the same facility." As late as 1835 Worcester was still being pressured by his superiors at the American Board to use Pickering's alphabet. "I do not know what is to be gained by the experiment of printing Cherokee in Pickering's alphabet with the syllables divided," Worcester wrote in exasperation. "I have no doubt that the Cherokees could pretty readily learn to read in that manner . . . ; yet it would be inferior to an alphabet strictly syllabic."[28]

Why, if the syllabary was so successful in promoting literacy, did Worcester need to defend it? Because a syllabary, according to prevailing theories, was a grossly imperfect, even savage form of writing.

Pickering, in a letter to Humboldt, called Sequoyah's syllabary "very unphilosophical" and "quite contrary to our notion of a useful alphabetic system."[29] Since men like Pickering and Humboldt understood types of writing as stages in the development from savagery to civilization, a perfect alphabet, with its one-to-one correspondence between sounds and characters, was the marker of an advanced civilization. In a series of lectures on language in 1762, for instance, the English writer Joseph Priestley classified writing systems into four categories: pictographic, hieroglyphic, Chinese, and alphabetic. These four categories represented four stages of progress, from the most primitive to the most civilized. The earlier the stage, the more characters one needed to learn to employ the art of writing. Writers using more primitive writing systems had to memorize a vast archive of symbols, a task that restricted literacy to a few. And those few, alas, were not likely to write much that mattered since primitive writing systems were considered incapable of expressing abstract ideas (what pictogram could represent "liberty" or "salvation"?).

To illustrate his point, Priestley considered the Chinese, who, he believed, had gone so far as to refine hieroglyphs but had failed to take the final, civilizing step to an alphabetic system, and as a result,

> we need not wonder that, contrary to what hath happened in other nations, arts and sciences should have been so early invented by those people, and yet have been at a stand for upwards of a thousand years: and till they remove this impediment, and introduce *alphabetical writing,* it is no difficult matter to foresee, that they never can make much greater progress than they have already made in the sciences, and that all the improvements they will henceforward receive they must derive from *European* philosophers, and *European* languages.[30]

In 1798 the American spelling reformer James Ewing explained in *The Columbian Alphabet* that a syllabary emerged when hieroglyphic writers observed "that notwithstanding the words in use were many, yet the articulate sounds composing those words were comparatively few," upon which "signs were instituted for those articulate sounds." The problem with a syllabary, however, was the same as with Chinese: "The number of the syllabic signs or marks necessary for writing must be great, and the labor of acquiring a competent knowledge of them would be sufficient to damp the ardor of the most enterprizing genius."[31]

As reports of Sequoyah's invention circulated, it appeared that in reinventing writing, he had recapitulated its evolution. As the actor, dramatist, and Cherokee advocate John Howard Payne reported, after declaring that "the white man is no magician," Sequoyah had begun by drawing hieroglyphs and proceeded to designing ideographs, but "when he discovered that the number of separate signs required for a complete set of words, would be so great that no one could ever learn or remember them," he "changed his plan" and eventually settled on a set of characters that would represent the syllables of the language. What bothered John Pickering was that Sequoyah had stopped there. "His alphabet accordingly consists of eighty-three arbitrary characters, instead of sixteen or eighteen Roman letters," he complained to Humboldt. "It wanted but one step more," Albert Gallatin observed in 1836, "and to have also given a distinct character to each consonant, to reduce the whole number to sixteen, and to have an alphabet similar to ours."[32]

This distinction between alphabets and syllabaries was central to Pickering's, Gallatin's, and Humboldt's understanding, yet it turns out to be rather sloppy. Our alphabet is composed of consonants (*b, c, d*) and vowels (*a, e*); a syllabary is composed of syllables: vowel sounds (*ae, ee*) and consonant/vowel combinations (*ba, dee, cad*). If *b* and *e* are the elemental units of the sounds of human speech, then our alphabet may be said to be an (imperfect) system of one symbol = one sound. But if *ae* and *ba* are those elemental units, then the syllabary actually is the one symbol = one sound system, and the alphabet is constituted of symbols representing something other (and smaller) than elemental sounds.

The ambiguity hinges on what constitutes a sound. Eighteenth-century thinkers believed that an alphabet was a refinement of a syllabary because it broke sound into smaller units (as it does). But a script could be invented that breaks sound into even smaller units. Here we arrive at the problem described recently by the British linguist Roy Harris as placing "the alphabetic cart before the phonetic horse." How many sounds make up the word *dog*? One, two, three, or more? And if three, are they really the sounds we say when we speak the letters *d, o, g*? In other words, to say that the unit to which the alphabet reduces speech is the smallest possible unit of sound is to make an altogether arbitrary judgment. (As Harris puts it, "sounds are not discrete segmental units. Or if they are, there must be an infinite number of them in even the 'shortest' spoken word: for the same reason that there is an infinite number of sequential divisions in an inch.")[33]

All this is not to say that the alphabet isn't brilliant and elegant. The problem lies in our simply assuming that the alphabet is wholly phonetic, that it is or should be an exact mirror of the way we speak (in just the way Noah Webster hoped it could be). As Harris has written, "The notion that in speaking we select the individual consonants and vowels which somehow emerge from our mouths threaded in the right order like beads on a string is simply the image of alphabetic orthography projected back on to speech production." This image is so pervasive in alphabetic societies that we teach children pronunciation by asking them to look at how words are spelled. (As Saussure said of spelling, "It is rather as if people believed that in order to find out what a person looks like it is better to study his photograph than his face.")[34]

However arbitrary, the notion that syllabaries were more savage than alphabets mattered. Most philologists would have expected that reliance on a syllabic form of writing would confine the Cherokee people to a system of government less democratic than a republic, in the same way that Chinese writing was understood to condemn the Chinese to despotic government. The less perfect the script, the fewer the people who could learn it, and the less democratic their system of government.[35]

Sequoyah's syllabary, however, turned all this logic on its head. His eighty-five characters were astonishingly easy to learn, and rather than restrict literacy to a few and consign the masses to ignorance, his syllabary brought the Cherokees to literacy rates unheard of in native communities, rates that compared well with white America's. Some American educators even suggested that a syllabary be developed for English by which white American schoolchildren could learn to read and write as fast as Cherokee boys and girls.[36]

Meanwhile, other missionaries eyed the syllabary with envy. Even American Board missionary Hiram Bingham eventually proved ungrateful for the aid John Pickering had given him. In *A Residence of Twenty-one Years in the Sandwich Islands* (1847), Bingham suggested that the success of his extraordinary mission to the Sandwich Islands had been compromised by the great difficulties he had encountered in teaching Hawaiians to read, difficulties that he attributed in part to the inadequacy of Pickering's alphabet. "Is not our anomalous, intricate, and ever dubious orthography a prominent cause of failure?" For vowels (but not for consonants), he had relied on Pickering's "uniform orthography," but in truth, he had found much of it useless. Not so Sequoyah's syllabary, about which Bingham wrote with admiration: "The philosophical, syllabic alphabet of the sagacious Choctaw [*sic*], GUESS, enables the men, women and children of his tribe to read their own language with facility."[37]

In the end, Pickering, too, came to admire Sequoyah's syllabary. In 1829 he called it "much more convenient than our alphabet would have been" for the Cherokee people. And in 1831 he declared that "the true sounds" of the Cherokee language "cannot, in every instance, be perfectly expressed by any other than the national *syllabic alphabet.*" What fascinated John Pickering most about Sequoyah's alphabet was that "strange as it may appear," Cherokees preferred it. Pickering attributed this preference to either "their national pride (for which we cannot blame them), or . . . the greater convenience of their syllabic alphabet."[38]

No doubt the syllabary was easy to learn. But to what extent was it, as Pickering put it, the Cherokees' "national alphabet"? To what extent did Sequoyah's syllabary help nationalize the Cherokee people in the way that Noah Webster hoped to Americanize Americans?

A National Alphabet

During Sequoyah's young adulthood, Cherokee political culture underwent a series of major transformations. At the time, some sixteen thousand Cherokees inhabited 20,000 square miles across North Carolina, Tennessee, Alabama, and Georgia. (The Cherokees had once ranged much farther, but in the century before Sequoyah's birth, they had lost nearly 50,000 square miles of territory to their English and Spanish neighbors.) Previously subject to faction, political intrigue, and frontier skirmishes under clan leadership, the tribe was unified in 1794 under a National Council and a principal and second principal chief, with a set of laws enforced by the Cherokee mounted police. Especially after 1800, Cherokee leaders began, self-consciously, to frame a European-style national government, largely in response to the U.S. government's attempts to persuade, and later to force, Cherokees to "remove" from their homeland to lands west of the Mississippi River. Although the United States had previously pledged the Cherokees permanent occupancy of their lands, that policy was reversed when, in 1802, Georgia persuaded the federal government to agree to remove all Cherokees from the state. Other states pursued other means of removal, and in 1806 Cherokee tribal delegates accepted bribes to sign two treaties ceding 8.6 million acres in Tennessee to the United States for less than two cents an acre.

The nefarious treaty of 1806 redivided the Cherokee Nation, half of which now proposed to separate itself and remove to the West voluntarily. Government agents were happy with this proposal, urging only that it be adopted by the entire nation. In 1808, addressing the Cherokee chiefs, the

U.S. agent Colonel Return J. Meigs encouraged voluntary removal as the best solution for the nation by appealing to a nascent cultural nationalism: "I wish to excite in yourselves a just pride, that is to have you value yourselves as *Cherokees;* the word *Cherokee* or *Cherokees* should always convey an idea of Respectability to your people and to preserve your nation from being lost, to keep up your National existence as a distinct people, you must not let your people straggle one or two at a time or in small parties [to the West] because small parties cannot support the character of the Nation."

But in 1809, instead of removing as a group, the two halves of the Cherokee Nation formed a new coalition determined to remain on the ancestral lands. One chief wrote to Meigs, "We have . . . become as one. You will now hear from us not from the lower towns nor the upper towns but from the whole Cherokee nation." The nation defined the two thousand mostly traditional Cherokees who had already left for Arkansas as expatriates; the Cherokee National Council declared that citizenship in the "Cherokee Nation" required residence in the ancestral homeland, a declaration intended both to unify Cherokees living within Cherokee territory and to exclude from the rights of citizenship those Cherokees who had voluntarily moved to the west.[39]

It was at this important juncture, in 1809, that Sequoyah began working on a writing system for the Cherokee language. Not long afterward, in 1813, the nation became involved in the Creek War, during which many eastern Cherokees, including Sequoyah, served as allies to U.S. government troops forcing the Creeks from their land. Meanwhile, the Cherokee Nation's quest for nationhood continued. In 1817 the Cherokee National Council declared the nation a republic and established a national bicameral legislature, much of whose attention was devoted to resisting removal. In 1826 a capital city was founded at New Echota; in 1827 the National Council ratified a written constitution and a tripartite system of government modeled on that of the United States.

In 1828 gold was discovered on Cherokee territory, just fifty miles from New Echota. The same year the Tennessee native Andrew Jackson was elected president, having campaigned in part on an aggressive policy of Indian removal. These two developments were to prove disastrous for the Cherokee people. In 1830 Jackson pushed his Indian Removal Act through Congress and sided with Georgia in its efforts to force the Cherokees out of the state. Eventually, the fight over removal would lead, in 1831, to the landmark Supreme Court case *Cherokee Nation v. State of Georgia* and, in 1838, to the infamous Trail of Tears.

After 1821 the Cherokees' bid for nationhood was advanced by Sequoyah's syllabary. In 1824 the Cherokee National Council voted to award Sequoyah a medal as a reward for his contributions to the nation, and the next year it voted to establish a national printing press, with special fonts in Sequoyah's syllabary, to be used to publish a national newspaper, the *Cherokee Phoenix*. In 1826 David Brown and George Lowery were appointed to translate the nation's laws "into the Cherokee language, written in characters invented by George Guess," to be published in the *Phoenix*. Meanwhile, the Cornwall graduate Elias Boudinot was sent on a trip to eastern cities to deliver lectures to raise funds for the printing press.

On his lecture tour, Boudinot was quick to invoke the syllabary in his pleas for the sympathy (and donations) of whites. "There are three things of late occurance, which must certainly place the Cherokee Nation in a fair light, and act as a powerful argument in favor of Indian improvement," Boudinot argued:

First   The invention of letters.

Second   The translation of the New Testament into Cherokee.

And third   The organization of a Government.[40]

It was an effective plea. Like David Brown, Boudinot found much sympathy in the North. Even John Pickering, much as he disliked the syllabary, was moved by the plight of the Cherokees. Noah Webster, too, sympathized with them and listened to a lecture by Boudinot with rapt attention in 1832. As Pickering, Webster, and other Cherokee sympathizers observed, the Cherokees were, in many ways, exactly the civilized Indian people government agencies and Christian missionaries had long hoped to meet or to make, a civilized, lawful, literate people. And their civilized status hinged on their astonishing literacy.[41]

By the early nineteenth century the Cherokee people had adopted many of the trappings of "civilization" (not for nothing were the Cherokees one of what came to be called the Five Civilized Tribes). A census taken in 1835 revealed that the Cherokees' social and economic world was very little different from that of their white neighbors: they had hundreds of mills, schools, manufactories—and thousands of African slaves. As John Howard Payne wrote in a letter bemoaning the Cherokees' treatment at the hands of the state of Georgia, "When the Georgian asks—shall savages

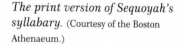

The print version of Sequoyah's syllabary. (Courtesy of the Boston Athenaeum.)

infest our borders thus? The Cherokee answers him—'Do we not read? Have we not schools? churches? Manufacturers? Have we not laws? Letters? A constitution? And do you call us savages?' " Literacy was but one of these "improvements," but the one that, most of all, marked the line between savagery and civilization. "Never has a tribe of the aborigines made such advances in civilisations," argued Payne. "They have even produced from among themselves an alphabet and letters of a fashion entirely original and they have books among them printed with their own language; and with this alphabet they daily communicate from one end of the nation to the other."[42]

Cherokees used literacy not only to gain sympathy from northern whites but also to build a national culture. In February 1828 the Cherokee printing press with the special syllabic fonts arrived at New Echota, and the *Cherokee Phoenix* (with the motto "I Will Arise") began printing that same month, with Boudinot as its editor. In the first issue, Boudinot declared: "As the Phoenix is a national newspaper, we shall feel ourselves bound to devote it to national purposes. 'The laws, the public documents of the Nation,' and matters relating to the welfare and condition of the Cherokees

Cherokee Phoenix, 1828. (Courtesy of the American Antiquarian Society.)

as a people, will be faithfully published in English and Cherokee." This kind of remark has led one historian to hold up the *Phoenix* as "a supreme expression of Cherokee Nationalism."[43]

But just how much the syllabary, especially through the printing press, promoted Cherokee nationalism is difficult to say. To begin with, the printing press served the purpose of missionaries as much as it served the National Council. After meeting Sequoyah in the fall of 1824, John Arch began translating the third chapter of John into Cherokee, after which hundreds of copies of his manuscript were made and "widely and wonderingly read by Cherokees who were eager to learn all that the white men knew." In September 1825 David Brown began translating the New Testament from Greek into Cherokee, using the syllabary. From the beginning the syllabary was used to promote the Christian religion. When the National Council approved the commissioning of a printing press, the American Board fronted the funds for it (it was repaid by the proceeds of Boudinot's lecture tour). Samuel Austin Worcester himself traveled to Boston to supervise its construction, and the syllabary first appeared in print in December 1827, when the Boston *Panoplist* printed the first five verses of Genesis, translated by Brown and Lowery, before the fonts were shipped south. After the press, and Worcester, had returned to New Echota in 1828, Boudinot edited the *Phoenix,* but he also worked closely with Worcester to print thousands of copies of Bibles, catechisms, and religious tracts in Sequoyah's syllabary.[44]

Worcester's enthusiasm for Sequoyah's syllabary, in preference to Pickering's alphabet, was no doubt largely due to the immediate audience for these publications. "If books are printed in Guess's character, they will be read; if in any other, they will lie useless." John Pickering might consider this a loss ("So strong is their partiality for this national alphabet," he told Humboldt, "that our missionaries have been obliged to yield to the impulse, and consent to print their books in future in the new characters"), but clearly the immediate readability of material printed in the syllabary advanced Worcester's work.[45]

Much printing in the syllabary, in short, was religious, rather than political. Moreover, the Cherokees' forum for national political discourse, the *Cherokee Phoenix,* never lived up to its promise of printing in both English and the syllabary. As it turned out, no more than 16 percent of the *Phoenix*'s articles were translated into the syllabary, in large part because Boudinot had at best a tenuous command of Cherokee. Educated from a young age at Cornwall and Andover and married to a white woman, Boudinot once complained to his brother-in-law that "one can't write first in Cherokee." The *Phoenix*'s editor found the work of translation difficult, as suggested in a plea he published in the paper in 1828:

> If any of our Cherokee readers think we have slighted them, we can assure them that it has not been through neglect. . . . We have a heavy task, & unless relieved by Cherokee correspondents, a greater amount of Cherokee matter cannot reasonably be expected. We hope those of our correspondents, who take a lively interest in the diffusion of intelligence in their mother language, will lend us aid in this department . . . [which is] the most arduous part of our labors.[46]

Two facts compromise the supposition that Sequoyah's syllabary acted as a nationalizing force for the Cherokee people: its use by missionaries and its disuse in the nation's newspaper. That the syllabary was used by missionaries does not mean that it was not a national alphabet. It might well have served both purposes, aiding the Cherokees' path both to Christianity and to nationhood. Certainly many whites and most members of the Cherokee National Council saw these as parallel paths, and indeed, most prominent Cherokee leaders were Christians. But the vast majority of Cherokees were not Christian. Indeed, this division, between a Christian Cherokee elite and a non-Christian Cherokee majority, is central to any understanding of the prospects for Cherokee national identity.

The national newspaper, as it turns out, really served only the 20 to 25 percent of the Cherokee population who were of mixed ancestry, spoke only English, and embraced Christianity. These men and women, the best-educated and wealthiest Cherokees, had powerful personal and political ties to whites and identified the future of the nation in adopting the trappings of white society—right down to the Constitution. The *Phoenix* mouthed their political sentiments: vigorous opposition to removal. But the *Phoenix* was of little use to full-blooded Cherokees who had not learned English and whose only other avenue to reading works printed in the syllabary was mission schools. Yet this was reading that most traditional Cherokees found distasteful. As Evan Jones discovered, his efforts to establish mission schools where Cherokees could study the Bible in the syllabary failed largely because "having learned to read and write in Cherokee, they lost interest in the school." As one historian has aptly put it, "The Cherokee most interested in the syllabary were not the most interested in acculturation."[47]

In other words, the leaders of the Cherokee Nation—those Anglophones who ran the government and who opposed removal and hoped to build the nation as an American-style republic—generally did not even speak Cherokee, much less need, or even know how to read, Sequoyah's syllabary. Meanwhile, full-blooded Cherokees who used the syllabary had little voice in the nation's politics.

Marks upon a Stone

But what of Sequoyah himself?

Sequoyah, alone in his cabin, speaking only Cherokee, is not easy to connect with intellectual currents in Europe and the United States. He may have stumbled upon a copy of Webster's blue-backed speller, but we can be certain that he never read William Thornton's *Cadmus* or Constantin Volney's *Simplification des langues orientales*.

What were Sequoyah's ideas? Did he believe, like Webster, that "a national language is a national tie"? Did he, like Webster, propose a new kind of writing, at the birth of his nation, in order to unite his people and shore up their national boundaries?

Early in his period of experimenting with different writing systems, Sequoyah was accused, by turns, of being a witch and a lunatic. When told his plan was foolish, he replied, "It is not our people that have advised me to this and it is not therefore our people who can be blamed if I am wrong. What I have done I have done from myself."[48] In at least this narrow sense, Sequoyah denied that his project was "for his people." But this of course is a slender reed on which to rest an argument about his motives. Since his ideas are so difficult to reconstruct, perhaps his actions reveal more.

Sequoyah began his work in 1809, during a crisis of national unity. In 1813 he fought in the Creek War. In 1816 and again in 1817 he signed treaties by which Cherokees traded land in Alabama for land to the west, thereby clearly violating the policies of the National Council that forbade individuals to sell land without explicit authorization from it. His actions might well have been considered treasonous. In 1818 Sequoyah moved to Arkansas. In so doing, under the laws of the council, he forfeited his citizenship in the Cherokee Nation. In 1821 he perfected his invention and returned east to present it to the council, which, however much its members considered Sequoyah a traitor (and a non-Cherokee), decided to welcome him back to the fold. Nevertheless, in 1822 Sequoyah went back to Arkansas, where he shared his syllabary with western Cherokees. In 1828, newly famous as "the Cadmus of his race," Sequoyah again returned east and visited Washington, accompanied by none other than David Brown, who acted as his interpreter. In Washington, Sequoyah met with John Quincy Adams, had his portrait painted, and signed yet another treaty ceding Cherokee land, this time exchanging territory in Arkansas for lands in Oklahoma. Soon afterward he moved with other Arkansas Cherokees to these new lands.

At every opportunity, Sequoyah defied the efforts of the National Council to resist removal by involving himself in negotiations that pushed the Cherokees farther and farther from their eastern homelands. And he voluntarily moved west himself again and again. With every step, he backed farther and farther from whites and from the eastern, elite, Christian,

English-speaking Cherokees. He also explicitly and repeatedly rejected acculturation. In Arkansas, Sequoyah is said to have frequently visited Dwight Mission, but not out of any desire to experience Christ; instead he came to pick up the latest issue of the *Phoenix*. As U.S. Army Major General Ethan Allen Hitchcock reported from Oklahoma in 1841, "Though the Missionaries in the Country have been successful in converting many Cherokees to Christianity by the aid of the invention of Cherokee writing, they have failed to make an impression upon the inventor, who is not friendly to their cause."[49]

Sequoyah was a traditionalist who resented the influence of whites and probably believed his people were better off voluntarily moving as far away from them as possible. Why, then, did he invent the syllabary?

One approach to answering this question is to ask to what use Sequoyah himself put his invention. According to one report, "The first composition he put together was on the subject of the boundary line between his own country and Georgia and Tennessee. After that, he had a suit in the Indian Court. He wrote down a statement of his case." These uses are consistent with how most Cherokees used the syllabary: to write letters, keep records, and file lawsuits. One rare set of records in the syllabary from a Cherokee community in the 1850s consists almost entirely of internal, official records—tax lists, loans, decrees, and other civic and legal records. U.S. Army Captain John Stuart reported from Arkansas in 1837 that in the western half of the Cherokee Nation, among those who had voluntarily removed, "the new language was extensively learned by the people, and applied by them to the purpose of writing letters, keeping accounts, &c." Sequoyah also kept a journal to record a history of his people and their language: "He has been in the habit, ever since he could apply his language in that way, of keeping a journal of all the passing events which he considered worthy of record: and has, at this time (it is said), quite a volume of such matter." This, too, is consistent with other recorded uses. Cherokees also commonly used the syllabary to preserve traditional lore, including herbal recipes and folksongs.[50]

All these uses realize John Pickering's worst fear: Cherokees used the syllabary among themselves. Much as he was annoyed that Sequoyah's syllabary was more popular than his alphabet, and less perfect, Pickering most worried about its separatist implications. The Cherokees' preference for the syllabary, he believed, "is much to be regretted as respects the facility of communication between these Indians and the white people."[51] The syllabary isolated Cherokees from whites, very few of whom (including

Samuel Austin Worcester) could read it. Perhaps that, in the end, was exactly what Sequoyah had in mind when he first set about making marks upon a stone.

East Meets West

No doubt Sequoyah suspected that removal was inevitable. Perhaps he was right. Ultimately, of course, the Cherokee Nation lost its bid for sovereignty. When Georgia threatened to remove Cherokees from the state by force, the case ended up in the Supreme Court, where, in *Cherokee Nation v. State of Georgia,* Chief Justice John Marshall declared the Cherokees a "domestic, dependent nation" and forbade the state of Georgia from taking its lands. Despite that ruling, and despite the support of New Englanders, who were overwhelmingly opposed to the forced removal of the Cherokees, President Andrew Jackson continued to support Georgia.

In December 1835 Boudinot and a handful of other eastern Cherokees, none of them members of the National Council, signed the Treaty of New Echota, ceding all Cherokee territory east of the Mississippi in exchange for five million dollars and new lands in Indian Territory. Signing this treaty violated national law and constituted treason. For selling Cherokee lands without the approval of the council, Boudinot and the other signers of the Treaty of New Echota had committed crimes punishable by death.

Protesting the Treaty of New Echota, the council continued to resist removal, but to no avail. In the spring of 1838, U.S. troops invaded Cherokee territory. (As Noah Webster remarked to his son William in April, "Now a military force is to be employed to drive the Cherokees from their native soil, in consequence of a treaty with a part of the tribe, who had no authority to make it. Was there ever a govt so conducted?"[52]) American soldiers forced some sixteen thousand Cherokees from their homes at gunpoint and marched them thousands of miles to Indian Territory. One in four men, women, and children died along the road.

Sequoyah, of course, didn't march on what came to be called the Trail of Tears; he had long since been living at the other end of the trail. But when the eastern Cherokees moved west, Sequoyah helped reunify the two halves of the nation. In 1839 he signed the Act of Union between the eastern and western Cherokees, all of whom now inhabited the new lands in Oklahoma. Sequoyah signed as president of the western Cherokees; his brother-in-law George Lowery signed as president of the eastern.

That reunification could not have taken place if the two halves of the nation had not been able to remain in close contact, over long distances, during the 1820s and 1830s. And that contact had been made possible only by the use of the syllabary.

Ever since the first voluntary migrations to the west, the Cherokee Nation had been, in a sense, falling apart. Without communication between the east and the west, the two groups would have grown increasingly distant had it not been for the syllabary. Beginning in about 1824, "a regular correspondence was opened and kept up between the Cherokees of Wills Valley and their country-men located five-hundred miles away." John Ridge reported in 1826: "With the Cherokees of Arkansas they correspond regularly by letter in Guess' character." According to John Howard Payne, Sequoyah himself served as a messenger: "Gist brought letters from Arkansas, written by Cherokee whom he had taught in the native character; and when he emigrated to Arkansas, he took back answers of the same description; and when the Indians found they were thus able to talk from a distance, their astonishment and delight were greater than ever."[53]

If Sequoyah's syllabary held his people together, he himself abandoned the "nation" time and again. In the end Sequoyah was a separatist more than a nationalist. For Sequoyah, being Cherokee wasn't about living on the ancestral homeland, as decreed by the laws of 1809, but about speaking, reading, and writing Cherokee. For him, the future of the Cherokee Nation lay not in resisting removal but in resisting acculturation, a resistance that included rejecting the West's own notion of what constitutes a nation.

As Moses Did

In 1841 Sequoyah headed west once again. He left Oklahoma on a journey to Mexico. He had heard of a lost band of Cherokees west of the Rocky Mountains and was eager to discover them and to share with them the syllabary, to reunite them with their fellow Cherokees. As he traveled with a small band of followers, Sequoyah "busied himself with writing descriptions of the country through which they passed." He had brought his journal with him, along with all his notes and papers. As a companion reported, "While sick, and at other times, when not traveling, he was constantly writing."[54]

But Sequoyah was sick more often than not. Two years into his travels, in Tamaulipas, Mexico, he asked his companions to go ahead while he rested in a cave to gain strength. Days later the party returned to the cave to find an animal skin hanging at its entrance, with directions for how to find the old man. When they finally discovered him, Sequoyah was dead. George Guess died alone in Mexico in 1843, the same year Noah Webster died in his home in New Haven.

In 1809, when Sequoyah first announced his plan to reinvent writing, he had declared, "There can I make characters, as Moses did, which every one of you will understand." Perhaps, during one of his visits with missionaries, Sequoyah had learned the story of Moses and found it inspiring. Perhaps he had never intended, like Noah Webster, to build a nation. Perhaps, instead, he had hoped to codify the language so that it might survive the diaspora and hold his scattered people together as they wandered in the desert. Perhaps, in the end, Sequoyah understood his syllabary as the script of a people in exodus.

When Sequoyah's companions first found his body, they returned it, together with his papers, to the cave and "marked the place so that it would without difficulty be found." But Sequoyah's body, and all his writings, were never seen again. In 1845, after hearing rumors that Sequoyah was still alive and living in Mexico, the U.S. secretary of war authorized two hundred dollars to fund an expedition to find him. The expedition returned with confirmation of his death but without having located the body.[55] And so it can be said of Sequoyah, as it was said of Moses (Deuteronomy 34:6): "To this day, no one knows the place of his burial."

4

Natural Language

On February 16, 1828, two and a half months before John Quincy Adams was to meet with Sequoyah during his visit to Washington, the president shortened his morning walk in order to attend a demonstration at the Capitol. There, Thomas Hopkins Gallaudet, the principal of the American Asylum for the Deaf and Dumb in Hartford, Connecticut, exhibited three deaf students before assembled members of Congress. After watching the students for several hours, Adams reported in his diary, "Their language of gesticulating is twofold: one consists of spelling words, each letter of the alphabet being marked by the sign of a distinct collocation of the fingers; the other is by motion of the arms and hands, and of the whole body, and by significant expressions of the countenance." Adams found the demonstration compelling and was annoyed when Vice President John Calhoun quizzed the students on abstruse rules of the Senate (for which Adams mocked him, in his diary, as that "political puritan who proposes to the deaf and dumb to define the distinction between power and right"). Piqued, Adams posed a question of his own: "I asked Mr. Gallaudet if he could make them understand the difference

Thomas Hopkins Gallaudet. (Courtesy of the Gutman Library, Harvard Graduate School of Education.)

between irrefragable and incontrovertible." After Gallaudet begged Adams first to enlighten *him* on the distinction, he managed to convey it to his students with considerable success. Adams was impressed.[1]

The next day, when Gallaudet preached his "Sermon on the Duty and Advantages of Affording Instruction to the Deaf and Dumb" before a large audience at the Capitol, Adams attended. In an impassioned sermon, Gallaudet repeated the refrain *"But who are the heathen?"*: "My heart sinks within me while giving the reply. Millions, millions of your fellow-men. Europe, Asia, Africa and America contain a melancholy host of immortal souls who are still enveloped with the midnight gloom of ignorance and superstition."

Gallaudet mourned for these souls and gave thanks for "the missionary who has taken his life in his hand and has gone to fight the battles of the cross against these powers of darkness." He had no wish to divert his audience's "charities from so noble an object." But, he asked, *"are there still other heathen?"*

Yes, my brethren, and I present them to the eye of your pity, an interesting, an affecting group of your fellow-men;—of those who are bone of your bone and flesh of your flesh; who live encircled with all that can render life desirable; in the midst of society, of knowledge, of the arts, of the sciences, of a free and happy government, of a

widely preached gospel; and yet who know nothing of all these blessings; . . . who are lost in one perpetual gaze of wonder at the thousand mysteries which surround them.

Who were these wretched "long-neglected heathen"?: "the poor deaf
and dumb, whose sad necessities have been forgotten, while scarce a corner of the world has not been searched to find those who are yet ignorant
of Jesus Christ." Insisting that deaf (white) Americans, "bone of your bone
and flesh of your flesh," were in every way as heathen as Cherokees, or
Sandwich Islanders, Gallaudet argued that they equally deserved his audience's sympathy: "I only crave a cup of consolation, for the deaf and
dumb, from the same fountain at which the Hindoo, the African, and the
savage are beginning to draw the water of eternal life."[2]
The president found the Hartford minister "fervent in manner and
cogent in reasoning," a man who could, "without imputation or arrogance,
compare his own condition and services to his fellow-mortals with those of
the apostle of the Gentiles." Three days later Adams dined with Gallaudet
and his companions, after which the delegation lobbying for support of
deaf education left town and Gallaudet returned to Connecticut.
In meeting Gallaudet and his students, President Adams had been
struck by the "great resemblance between the gestures of all the unin-
structed deaf and dumb." No doubt Gallaudet had suggested such a
resemblance to him. What Adams called the deaf's "language of gesticulating" Gallaudet liked to call the "natural language of signs." He believed
it was the natural, universal language of all humankind, God's gift to His
people. As a young man just beginning to learn sign language Gallaudet
had written an essay in which he wondered: "Before the millenium
arrives, will *one* language prevail and swallow up the rest, or will mankind
agree to form a universal language? What shall this universal language
be? Is there already one provided by Nature herself, easy of acquisition,
universal in its application, which demands neither types nor paper?"[3]
Sign language, he came to believe, was that language. Could it be that the
search for a perfect, philosophical alphabet was misguided? Could it be
that a form of universal communication, one that could not be written,
already existed? Yes, Thomas Hopkins Gallaudet might have replied. Yes,
my brethren, yes!
Yet the language Gallaudet heralded as universal turned out to be particular, a language that some Americans came to believe isolated its deaf
users from the hearing world just as powerfully as it "rescued" them from
"heathenism." For teaching the deaf to sign rather than to speak, Gal-

laudet was later accused of creating a nation within a nation, entirely cut off from American social and political life, almost as profoundly separate from the Republic, and the republic of letters, as were the Cherokees. Eventually, and in a time of rising sectionalist and secessionist tensions, some Americans came to see sign language as just another strain on what many considered the weak and already fraying bonds tying the nation together.

A Sad Monopoly

Thomas Hopkins Gallaudet was born in Philadelphia in December 1787, not long after the close of the Constitutional Convention. Reared in Hartford, Gallaudet graduated from Yale in 1805. He pursued careers in law and business before professing his faith and enrolling in the Andover Theological Seminary in 1811 to train for the ministry. Like Samuel Austin Worcester and Hiram Bingham, Gallaudet was soon swept up in the millennialist missionary movement of the early nineteenth century (what Bingham called the Age of Missions), in which impassioned American missionaries anticipated the imminent return of Christ to earth—specifically, to the United States—as a consequence of the imminent conversion of the world's peoples to Christianity. Yet much as Gallaudet was compelled by the work of foreign missionaries, his poor health discouraged him from traveling to the far reaches of the globe.[4]

Instead he found a mission in his very own backyard. During a vacation from Andover, he watched Alice Cogswell, the young daughter of his next-door neighbor, playing in his father's garden. At the age of two Alice had contracted spotted fever (cerebrospinal meningitis) and had lost her hearing; by the age of four she had lost her speech. Encouraged by Alice's father, Dr. Mason Fitch Cogswell, Gallaudet attempted to teach Alice to communicate. Gallaudet, Cogswell, and no doubt Alice most of all were startled and deeply gratified by his success. Cogswell soon convinced Gallaudet to "visit Europe for the sake of qualifying himself to become a teacher of the deaf and dumb."[5]

At the time there were no schools for the deaf in the United States, and very few elsewhere. For most of human history, in most parts of the world, children born deaf, or those who became deaf at a young age, received no formal education, acquired little language, and lived in often excruciating isolation. Most were considered mentally deficient, and indeed, because they had little language, their intellectual lives were vastly circumscribed. (In many parts of the world, this remains true today.)

For centuries before Gallaudet set about his work, philosophers had debated whether the deaf, lacking language, were truly human, a question that especially occupied Enlightenment thinkers. By way of experiment, some had attempted to teach the deaf to speak. Philologists, too, contemplated the problem of deafness and, more, the muteness that was usually its consequence. But serious efforts to educate the deaf were unknown before the sixteenth century, when a Spanish Benedictine monk, Pedro Ponce de León, developed a method for teaching the deaf to speak and read. Ponce de León was followed by other pioneers, nearly all of whom served as private tutors to the deaf children of wealthy or royal families. It was not until the mid-eighteenth century that educational institutions for the deaf were founded. The first was the abbé de l'Épée's Institution des Sourds et Muets in 1755, followed by the Scottish elocution teacher Thomas Braidwood's academy in Edinburgh in 1764; Samuel Heineke's school in Leipzig, Germany, in 1778; and the London Institute, started by Joseph Watson, Braidwood's nephew, in 1792.[6]

When Gallaudet traveled to Europe in 1815 "for the sake of qualifying himself to become a teacher of the deaf and dumb," he went first to London and then to Edinburgh, seeking to learn how to teach the deaf to speak.[7] In Britain all the schools he planned to visit emphasized articulation, or speech training, and rejected the use of sign language. This emphasis reflected Thomas Braidwood's expertise; before he began working with the deaf, he had taught elocution to hearing children. But more, it reflected the preference of hearing parents of deaf children, who were anxious that their children learn to speak, and to read lips, in order that they might appear in society as undeaf as possible. Yet although the British "oral schools" reported great success, much of it was exaggerated. These schools tended to disproportionately admit students who were hard of hearing, rather than profoundly deaf, and who had become deaf only after having already acquired language. With years of painstaking tutoring, many of these students were able to retain what speech they had before becoming deaf and to vastly improve their pronunciation. When these "talking deaf" students were exhibited before a credulous public, they could prove extraordinarily inspiring. And profitable.

Fearing competition, Britain's oral schools jealously guarded their methods. Everywhere he went, Gallaudet met with a frigid reception. Joseph Watson promised to allow him to visit the London school and learn its methods only if Gallaudet would agree to stay on as an assistant for three years. After a month and a half of frustrating and ultimately failed negotiations, Gallaudet left London for Edinburgh and the Braidwood school. There he met with the same evasions. "Sad monopoly on the resources of Charity!!!" he exclaimed in his diary. Braidwood, like Watson, was unwilling to share what he considered a proprietary method of instruction with someone who would set up a competing school in the United States, not least because Thomas Braidwood's grandson John Braidwood was himself attempting to found a school for the deaf in the United States. (The younger Braidwood soon failed largely because of his dissipated habits.)

Meanwhile, Gallaudet had managed to discover that the oral schools succeeded in teaching only students who were partially and especially postlingually deaf. Teaching the congenitally and profoundly deaf to speak, he observed, is an altogether different matter. Lacking the ability to hear even their own voices, the deaf must be taught to associate particular minute movements of the lips, tongue, throat, and lungs with the utterly abstract units of language that we call sounds and that we imperfectly represent with the alphabet.

Indeed, in the view of many early educators and observers, the difficulties of teaching the deaf to speak were compounded by the imperfections of the alphabet. In 1793, William Thornton published an appendix to *Cadmus,* an essay titled "On Teaching the SURD, or DEAF and Consequently DUMB, to Speak." Thornton believed the Roman alphabet's imperfect representation of the sounds of the English language posed a special challenge to deaf students: "The written and spoken languages are so different, that they become to such pupils two distinct studies." (John Pickering later made this same observation, arguing that "two classes of . . . men" especially illustrate how "our *written* and *spoken* languages [are] entirely distinct in their nature": "on the one hand, the illiterate of our own people, and the savage nations on our frontiers, all of whom express their ideas perfectly well without knowing a letter of any alphabet; and, on the other, the deaf and dumb, who can do the same thing by means of letters, without having any ideas of the sounds of a *spoken* language.") Thornton proposed his "perfect" thirty-character alphabet as the solution. But beyond advocating his new alphabet, Thornton's essay merely repeated common assumptions about helping the deaf control their organs of speech by using mirrors, holding their throats, and manipulating their mouths. (The London estimation of *Cadmus*'s appendix by the *Monthly Review* was rightly dismissive: "The subjoined essay on a subject so important appears to contain nothing of any material consequence.")[8]

Another solution to this dilemma was to employ a perfectly phonetic manual alphabet, an alphabet spelled with the fingers. In the seventeenth century the Spanish philologist Juan Pablo Bonet, in *Reducción de las Letras y Arte para Enseñar a Hablar los Mudos,* proposed an alphabet of twenty-one hand shapes. These, he asserted, not only corresponded exactly to the twenty-one sounds he counted in the Castilian tongue but also, in their shapes, conveyed the position of the lips, tongue, and throat necessary to articulate them. Bonet himself had not invented the manual alphabet. It was derived from a manual alphabet published in the Franciscan monk Melchor Yebra's sixteenth-century book of prayers; Yebra in turn had taken the hand shapes from St. Bonaventure, who devised them not for the deaf but to help the dying, too weak to speak, to communicate prayers.

In the eighteenth century Bonet's manual alphabet was adapted by the French oralist educator Jacob Rodrigues Pereire. After reading Bonet's book, Pereire designed a manual alphabet of thirty hand shapes that he claimed was perfect for French in just the same way that Bonet's was perfect for Castilian: "Each handshape designates simultaneously the position and movement of the speech organs suitable to produce the sound and also the letter or letters that normal writing requires to represent this very sound." Pereire then employed his manual alphabet as a means of teaching the deaf to read and, most of all, to speak. At public exhibitions he would finger-spell words to his students, who would then pronounce the sentences he dictated.[9]

In the hands of oralist educators like Pereire, the manual alphabet differed little from mirrors and physical manipulations of the mouth. It simply offered another means by which the deaf could be taught to speak, but not necessarily to understand what they were saying. The real revolution in deaf education came only when Pereire's rival the abbé Charles-Michel de l'Épée left speech behind.

Natural Language

All deaf people naturally communicate by gesture. A deaf child born to a hearing family will develop "home signs," a repertoire of signs used within the family. Such children may develop a prodigious vocabulary of signs, which can be combined in useful, meaningful ways. But their communication will not be a true language, a system of signs with syntax and grammar. Only when enough deaf people live together and, especially, when deaf children are born to deaf parents will the children naturally, and then inevitably, develop a true language, one as expressive and eloquent as any spoken language. Indeed, armed with what Noam Chomsky calls universal grammar and Steven Pinker calls the language instinct, deaf children living in a community of signers cannot help developing a true language.[10]

Sign languages have spontaneously evolved in deaf families and communities all over the world throughout human history. Yet none were recorded—or even, astonishingly, really noticed—by anyone in the hearing world until the abbé de l'Épée began working with the deaf in bustling, pre-Revolutionary Paris. When, in the 1750s, de l'Épée decided to make it his life's mission to teach the deaf, he had the amazing good sense to observe that the deaf men, women, and children he met in Paris already had a language. Instead of attempting to teach them to articulate speech in the French language, which would have required teaching them both a new language (French) and an entirely new kind of language (spoken), de l'Épée learned the signed language of the deaf. Their language was visual, rather than aural, and altogether unrelated to French or to any other spoken language. But once de l'Épée was able to communicate with his students, he was able to teach them how to read his language, French, and since he wasted no time in teaching them to articulate sounds, he was able to concentrate his efforts on teaching them about the world and, as was his main goal, about the Catholic Church.

Unlike Pereire, who used the manual alphabet to teach his students to articulate speech, de l'Épée communicated with his students using their own copious language of signs. He employed the manual alphabet, which is infinitely more cumbersome than signing, only to teach reading or to translate between signing and written French.

In Paris, de l'Épée achieved extraordinary success. Schools modeled after his were soon founded throughout France. Unlike his British counterparts, de l'Épée was eager to share his methods; beginning in the 1770s, he elucidated them in a series of essays. (Mason Fitch Cogswell gave Gallaudet an English translation of one of them in 1817.) Moreover, almost from the beginning, de l'Épée welcomed scholars and other visitors to public demonstrations of his students.[11]

It was at just such a demonstration in London in 1815 that Thomas Hopkins Gallaudet met with de l'Épée's successor, the abbé Roch-Ambroise Sicard, who was at the time touring Britain exhibiting his star students, Laurent Clerc and Jean Massieu. On visiting Sicard, Clerc, and Massieu, Gallaudet received warm assurance that "every facility would be granted me at Paris, and that I could regularly attend the school of the deaf and dumb, and also receive the private instructions of the Abbé." While he idled away his time in Edinburgh negotiating with Braidwood, Gallaudet read Sicard's treatise and studied French. He also attended philosophical lectures and became very much influenced by the Scottish commonsense philosopher Dugald Stewart, who had written with effusive admiration of Sicard's methods. In an address to the Royal Society of Edinburgh in 1815, Stewart expressed his regret at the emphasis on articulation in English and Scottish schools and applauded Sicard, whose priority was "not to astonish the vulgar by the sudden conversion of a dumb child into a speaking *automaton;* but . . . to convert his pupil into a rational and moral being" by teaching him a standardized sign language.[12]

After Gallaudet arrived in Paris in March 1816, he began meeting with Sicard for private instruction. He also received daily lessons from Massieu. When he began his study, Gallaudet was skeptical and agreed with critics who found signed language primitive and animalistic. Only gradually did he change his mind, writing to Cogswell in April, "I am now convinced of the utility of their language of pantomime to a *certain extent,*" and assured him, "Don't be alarmed at this system of signs[.] I shall learn and practice just as much of it as I think best."[13]

Eventually Gallaudet determined to employ sign language as the primary means of instruction at his American school. Amazed by the copiousness of the language and humbled by his efforts to learn it, Gallaudet persuaded Sicard that the success of the American school would depend on a signer far more fluent than himself. At Gallaudet's urging, thirty-one-year-old Laurent Clerc, a brilliant deaf man who had been Sicard's pupil and was now a teacher at the institute, agreed to accompany Gallaudet to Hartford, to continue educating him in sign language, and, upon his arrival, to serve as the new school's first teacher. Sailing across the Atlantic in the summer of 1816, Clerc taught Gallaudet sign, while Gallaudet taught Clerc English.

A Universal Language

In 1817, soon after Gallaudet and Clerc had returned from France, the newly founded American Asylum welcomed an entering class of thirty-one students. Fifteen of them were over nineteen years old; one was forty.

Eighteen had been born deaf; nine had been deafened before the age of four. One of them, Sophia Fowler, nineteen years old and deaf since birth, was to become Gallaudet's wife. That Gallaudet had been turned away from the British oral schools was fortunate indeed, for almost none of these students would have excelled in learning to speak. But they all could sign.[14]

In replicating Sicard's methods, Clerc was adamant that sign language remain the language of instruction. Through sign language, his students were able to study other subjects and eventually to learn to read and write. Proponents of the asylum marveled at Clerc's dramatic results: he had put these students "in use of faculties of mind, of the possession of which, they had before been unconscious; and thus,—from being objects of pity, shut out from the intellectual world and its inhabitants,—they can be admitted to a participation of most of the pleasures of science and letters." Yet the most important goal of their education remained, as it had always been for Gallaudet, acquainting them "with the all-important truths of religion."[15]

Again and again Clerc, Gallaudet, and their supporters opposed critics of the asylum's use of sign language and insisted that oral instruction confined deaf students to ignorance and isolation. Instruction in articulation is ridiculous, Gallaudet argued in 1819, since the deaf "can know nothing of the powers of letters, nor of the syllabic division of words, so far as sound is concerned." As J. A. P. Barnard observed in the *North American Review,* the alphabet is "founded on no analogy, which they can comprehend. To the deaf and dumb, there are neither vowels, consonants, nor silent letters." But sign language seemed to Barnard fully capable of expressing all human thought and emotion: "This beautiful language is their own creation, and is a visible testimony to the activity of their intellect. It is a language of action, full of force, full of animation, full of figurative expression, oftentimes full of grace."[16]

Gallaudet agreed. Initially convinced of the utility of sign language by the writings of Dugald Stewart and his experiences in Paris, Gallaudet found himself, through his friendship with Clerc, his encounters with his students, and perhaps especially his marriage to Sophia Fowler in 1821, moved by the grace, beauty, and expressiveness of sign language. In an essay written in 1819 he described the "natural language of signs" as "significant and copious in its various expressions," capable of denoting "the invisible operations of their minds and emotions of their hearts."[17]

What Gallaudet found most compelling about sign language was its seeming universality. The set of signs "spontaneously employed by the

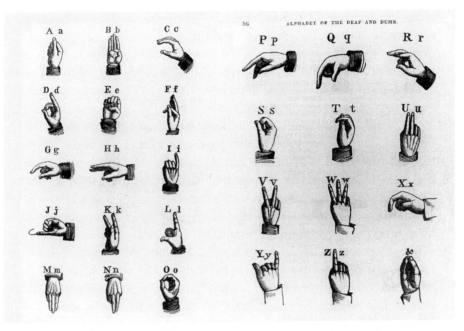

Manual alphabet used in the United States in the early nineteenth century. (Courtesy of the Gutman Library, Harvard Graduate School of Education.)

deaf-mute" seemed to him to be the same in every family. "Its similarity is so great that two uneducated deaf-mutes, who have never had any intercourse with others in a similar condition, can, at their first interview, communicate with each other, on a considerable number of common subjects." Moreover, "The universality of this natural language of signs is manifested also, in the striking fact that the instructors of the deaf and dumb, who have become familiar, by their habitual and long continued intercourse with their pupils, with this language in all its varieties and peculiarities, find it easy, as they meet, in different parts of the country, with the uneducated deaf and dumb, to converse with them on a considerable variety of subjects."[18]

Laurent Clerc made the same point. Interviewed by the New York legislature in an exhibition with Gallaudet in 1816, Clerc was asked, "Is there any universal language founded upon the principles of human nature? If so in your opinion, what is it?" Gallaudet signed the question to Clerc, who answered by writing on a chalkboard: "The language of signs is universal, and as simple as nature herself."

By calling sign language universal, Clerc and Gallaudet meant partly that pantomime (not actual sign language) is an extremely useful means

of communication. "I think those who gesticulate can be understood
everywhere they go," Clerc remarked. But Gallaudet meant something
more. For him, sign language was the first language of children, the first
language of humankind. The language of signs was our natural language,
given to us by God at the time of creation. It was, for Gallaudet, the language that had been lost at Babel, the restoration of which would herald
the return of Christ to earth. De l'Épée himself had hinted at this: "The
universal language that your scholars have sought for in vain and of which
they have despaired, is here; it is right before your eyes, it is the mimicry of
the impoverished deaf. Because you do not know it, you hold it in contempt, yet it alone will provide you with the key to all languages."[19]

But where de l'Épée hinted, Gallaudet experimented. Almost as soon as
he returned to Hartford from Europe, Gallaudet began testing his theory
of the universality of the language of signs. Whenever a foreigner came to
town, Gallaudet attempted to converse with him by signs. In 1819 Gallaudet and Clerc conversed with a visitor from China "who was quite ignorant of the English language, and also of the language of signs and
gestures." When Clerc signed to him, this man "was at first lost in amazement; but not one half hour had elapsed before a rapid conversation
ensued between them, in which Mr. ——— ascertained many interesting
circumstances respecting the birthplace, parentage, occupation, and life
of the stranger, and also learned the import of nearly twenty Chinese
words, some of which denoted quite complex and abstract ideas." When it
was reported that Indians beyond the Mississippi used sign language as a
lingua franca, Gallaudet undertook a comparison and determined that
their language and the language used by students at the American Asylum
were extraordinarily similar. When, in 1841, fifty West Africans took control of the Spanish slave ship *Amistad,* on which they were being carried
to the Caribbean, and ended up in New Haven, Gallaudet and Clerc
served as their translators. Each of these experiences confirmed Gallaudet's belief that he had discovered the natural language of all the
world's peoples.[20]

The handiest subjects for Gallaudet's experiment were conveniently
local: at the Foreign Mission School in nearby Cornwall, Connecticut. In
May 1819 Gallaudet visited Cornwall to attend the students' semiannual
exhibition, during which "members of the school gave a specimen of their
talents and improvements in speaking." Some spoke in their native
tongues; the more advanced students spoke in English. To Hiram Bingham, who also attended, Gallaudet declared that "the exhibition was more

interesting to him than a hundred college commencements." When the Hawaiian Thomas Hopoo recited the first chapter of Genesis in Hebrew, Bingham and, undoubtedly, Gallaudet were extraordinarily impressed. "I could not but be filled with admiration," Bingham wrote, "to see these youth, the sons of the forest and pagan isles, appearing on a public stage, in the bosom of this Christian land, with as much propriety as students in college."[21]

As Gallaudet told Bingham, he made a point of visiting Cornwall often. He found the students inspiring—and useful. During one visit Gallaudet had "gathered round him several of these interesting strangers, from the islands of the South Sea, and from different tribes of the North-American Indians" in order "to ascertain how far a conversation could be conducted with them merely by signs and gestures." Believing that "savages, whose language is very poor and imperfect, make up its deficiency by signs" or gestures, he expected that the students "would of course be acquainted in some degree with the language of signs." He asked them a host of questions, which they answered, demonstrating "a peculiar aptitude, both in comprehending the signs, which were proposed to them, and in inventing such as were necessary for a reply." Gallaudet reported: "For example, Thomas Hoopoo [sic], a native of Owhyhee [Hawaii], was asked if his parents were living; how many brothers and sisters he had; when he left his native shores; whether his countrymen worshipped idols, and sacrificed human victims . . . all of which he well comprehended, and to many of which he replied by signs."

So impressed was Gallaudet with Hopoo's aptitude for signing that he invited him to visit the American Asylum, "in the way of experiment." When Hopoo arrived, Gallaudet asked him "to endeavour to converse with his pupils." Apparently, Gallaudet's deaf students almost immediately understood Hopoo's sign language, and he theirs; "in less than an hour they became quite familiar. . . . They understood each other perfectly." The proof? When Hopoo described "the idolatrous rites and wretched superstitions of his countrymen," the deaf students "looked on with intense interest, and at length a large number burst into tears of compassion for their fellow creatures involved in such deplorable ignorance." Gallaudet then conducted the experiment in reverse, bringing Laurent Clerc to visit Cornwall, where, "after an hour's intercourse, [he] conversed by signs without difficulty, on any ordinary topic, with the young heathen there."[22]

At Cornwall in May 1819, Gallaudet told Bingham all about his work with the deaf and his experiments with Hopoo; perhaps he even repeated them for Bingham's benefit. Hopoo's facility with signs, Gallaudet told Bingham, suggested that Sandwich Islanders used signs "to supply the deficiency of, or to give emphasis to, their own comparatively barren language." Gallaudet told Bingham that "the knowledge of natural signs might greatly facilitate intercourse between the missionaries and the heathen to whom they are sent." Bingham found Gallaudet persuasive: "I have in my acquaintance with Mr. Gallaudet become so far acquainted with the language of signs as to [be] fully convinced that it must be of immense importance to the missionary to the unlettered heathen." Of Gallaudet's invitation to visit the asylum, Bingham wrote, "This would certainly be desirable if there were time."[23]

Whether Bingham ever found the time to visit the American Asylum for the Deaf and Dumb is uncertain, but he did study "natural signs" before his departure. And not long after arriving in the Sandwich Islands, Bingham put that knowledge of sign language to good use. He met a deaf man and found that he was easily able to communicate with him by signs. Moreover, as Bingham reported to the American Board, "the signs employed by that *Deaf-mute Sandwich Islander, were substantially the same with those employed by the teachers and pupils in the American Asylum.*"[24] Gallaudet was thrilled to hear it.

A Foreign Language

But Thomas Hopkins Gallaudet was wrong. Signed languages are as particular to their communities of users as are spoken languages. In Hartford the French Sign Language that Clerc and Gallaudet brought with them on board ship was quickly creolized when deaf students in the American Asylum added to it their own home signs, as well as syntax and vocabulary from local sign languages, like that used by a large congenitally deaf community on Martha's Vineyard. Not unlike parent and child spoken languages, like British and American English, French Sign Language and American Sign Language (ASL) today are mutually intelligible. A deaf American can manage to converse with a deaf Frenchman in much the same way that a hearing New Yorker can talk with a hearing Yorkshireman; it can be done, although not without effort. But a deaf American cannot understand a deaf Englishwoman or a Nicaraguan, just as that hearing New Yorker cannot be expected to understand a Russian without first learning the language. There are many different sign languages, and dialects within them, just as there are many different spoken languages and dialects.[25]

If Gallaudet erred in thinking sign language universal, he did correctly perceive that it was more natural to the deaf than was spoken language. Indeed, he took pains to remind the hearing community that to the deaf, English—or any other spoken language—was a foreign language. Over the course of his years as the principal of the American Asylum (1817–30), Gallaudet always rejoiced and marveled at how whenever a new pupil arrived at the asylum, "He finds himself, as it were, among his countrymen. They use his native language." The "mother tongue" of the deaf, Gallaudet argued, "is their own native language of signs. . . . The fact is, our language, so far from being their mother tongue, is to them a foreign language." Laurent Clerc agreed. "The language of any people cannot be the mother tongue of the deaf and dumb born amidst these people. Every spoken language is necessarily a learned language," Clerc wrote in 1818. "The English language must be taught to the deaf and dumb, as the Greek and Latin are taught in the colleges."[26]

But, as Noah Webster might have asked, if the deaf cannot speak the mother tongue, the national language, what ties them to the nation? Does the manual alphabet belong in the republic of letters?

To Gallaudet, the idea that the deaf had their own mother tongue, their own native language, by no means implied their isolation since he believed the language of the deaf was universal. But for some deaf Americans, and for many later critics of the American Asylum, sign language spelled separatism. A people whose mother tongue was not English (or, as Webster would have said, *American*) were not only socially isolated—even from their nearest relatives—but also politically excluded from the nation and denied the ability to participate in the republic of letters. That "our language, so far from being their mother tongue, is to them a foreign language" constituted the chief source of opposition to sign language in the United States. Although the American Asylum enjoyed extraordinary success in its first decades and spawned dozens of similar institutions across the country, sign language instruction came under attack in the 1840s. In 1844 the Boston educator and reformer Horace Mann issued a report to the Massachusetts Board of Education in which he strongly argued against manual instruction. Mann, along with Samuel Gridley Howe, the director of Boston's Perkins Institute for the Blind, had toured schools for the deaf in Europe (including those that had refused Gallaudet entry) and had determined that oral instruction was far superior to manual instruction. "With us, the deaf and dumb are taught to converse by signs made with the fingers. There, incredible as it may seem, they are taught to *speak* with the lips and tongue."

While Mann acknowledged, "It is a great blessing of a deaf-mute to be able to converse in the language of signs," he saw sign language instruction as a deal with the devil since it condemned signers to lifelong isolation from the hearing world. "It is obvious," he concluded, "that, as soon as he passes out of the circle of those who understand that language, he is as helpless and hopeless as ever. *The power of uttering articulate sounds—of speaking as others speak,—alone restores him to society.*"[27]

Gallaudet emerged from retirement to express his outrage at Mann's report. "Without the language of Natural Signs," he wrote Mann, "the teacher can have, at first, no ready and adequate means of free communication with his pupils." Moreover, all that deaf students needed to know they could learn "without being able to articulate and understand what is being said to them":

The development of the intellectual & moral faculties of deaf-mutes; their intellectual & moral training, their government by moral influences, the imparting to their sense, religious and other knowledge; their participating understandingly in the social and public devotional exercises of the Institution; the furnishing of their minds with the idea, the facts . . . which are necessary to prepare them to understand a vast number of the words which must be taught them, their becoming acquainted with our social and civil institutions, with arithmetic, grammar, geography and history, with the history, simple doctrines, and the precepts of the Bible, with their duties to God, to their fellow men & themselves; their acquiring a trade, or some means of gaining a livelihood; and especially their being taught to write the English language correctly, and to read books intelligently.[28]

For Mann, the purpose of educating the deaf was to teach them how to communicate with the hearing world. For Gallaudet, its purpose was to teach them to communicate with God.

Gallaudet never fully reckoned with the core of Mann's criticism, his attack on sign language as fundamentally isolating. Instead, Gallaudet and his supporters argued that teaching articulation was ineffective, delaying (and all too often preventing) the acquisition of language and therefore of all knowledge. Since most deaf education was inspired and conducted by missionaries, with the principal aim of Christian conversion, and since oral methods were, in truth, generally less successful than sign language instruction, Gallaudet's defense of his own methods in the 1840s was largely successful. Mann and Howe formed a tiny minority. The deaf at manual schools did learn language; they did read the Bible; they did become Christians. In the 1840s and 1850s deaf educators stayed the course and continued to teach their students to sign. For the moment, the question of how to "restore" the deaf to the hearing world, rather than only to God, went unanswered.

Manifest Destiny

Meanwhile, some deaf Americans were experiencing firsthand just the kind of isolation Mann had predicted. Gallaudet believed that because the language was universal, any hearing person who tried hard enough could understand a deaf person's signs, but in practice such exchanges proved frustrating at best. Often, written communication was no easier. "There is not a hearing man, that, except for occasional novelty and to while away a *tedium,* would like to hold written converse with any of us," wrote John J. Flournoy, a deaf man who had briefly attended the American Asylum. "It is too irksome," he pointed out. "And such hearing people as know the sign language, or alphabet of our class, [n]ever make it a point to convey to us one ninety-ninth of the information they constantly impart to each other by oral converse." As Flournoy saw it, this all too real intellectual isolation spelled virtual political disenfranchisement.

Flournoy, who came from a prominent slaveowning family, had long sought political appointment in his native Georgia. He ran for state legislature three times, and three times he failed, never gaining more than a handful of votes. Frustrated at his inability to participate politically in the hearing world, Flournoy proposed, in 1855, the establishment of a deaf-only state in the West, to be named Gallaudet. It was a radical, even preposterous proposal, one that violated nearly everything Gallaudet, before his death in 1851, had stood for. But Flournoy saw a deaf state as deaf

Americans' last best hope for full citizenship. "The prevailing idea of rulers and of people, is, that mutes are not capable of *any* political accomplishment," he complained. While in a deaf state, "many of us also could act as governors and legislators." As Flournoy insisted, "It is a political independence, a STATE SOVEREIGNTY, at which I aim." A deaf state, he argued, is "the manifest destiny of our people": "We will have a small republic of our own, under our sovereignty, and independent of all hearing interference." In this "Deaf-mute Republic," none but the deaf would be eligible to hold political office.[29]

Flournoy's proposal occasioned energetic discussion in the pages of the *American Annals of the Deaf and Dumb* and, no doubt, in the corridors and parlors of deaf schools and social clubs. Most printed responses opposed the plan. In general, deaf and hearing critics alike acknowledged the discrimination to which deaf Americans were subjected. "We are far from affirming that every deaf man is always treated by every body, with that consideration which is due to his infirmity, or with that which is due to him as a man, in spite of his infirmity," wrote the editors of the *Annals*. But they recoiled from Flournoy's aggrieved attitude toward the hearing community. "The deaf man can not expect that all the world will give up speech and use only the language of signs."[30]

During several years of debate, Flournoy and his critics explored the limits of deaf participation in a republic of hearers. William W. Turner, a hearing man who was then the president of the American Asylum, agreed with Flournoy that the deaf possessed the talent to govern themselves— "That educated deaf-mutes are capable of self-government and of managing the affairs of a State of their own there can be no doubt"—but he argued that the deaf should not expect to participate in government: "You would not think it wise to give the command of an army to a blind man. . . . For a similar reason, you would not send a deaf and dumb man to Congress or to the Legislature of a State; not for the reason that he was deficient in intelligence and education, but because his want of hearing and speech unfits him for the place." Similarly, Edmund Booth, a deaf newspaper editor from Iowa, argued that not being able to hold public office was a small loss in the face of the real political power the deaf wielded: "We have already the full enjoyment of the rights, common to all, of voting at elections."[31]

To these arguments, Flournoy replied that the deaf should settle for nothing short of full political participation, whatever means must be taken to ensure their ability to conduct government business: "Place *me* for an example in any Capitol with Legislative sanctity, and I will move for an *aid*, a hearer and amanuensis, to reveal to me what is said, what to be done, what to do, and to read my speeches. And by this way I can get along supremely well, as Legislator."[32]

Flournoy's plan to found a deaf-only state named Gallaudet was, to say the least, poorly developed. Beyond a general outline, he offered few specific proposals. The land, he supposed, might be bought "from the Cherokees, or other red men, West of Arkansas, and *very cheaply*." What kind of constitution the state would adopt, he couldn't say. In any case, the intriguing debate his proposal inspired ended abruptly in 1858, when Laurent Clerc made clear that he opposed the plan, calling it "the offspring of a disordered imagination." Gallaudet himself had died in 1851, though in all likelihood he also would have bitterly opposed any proposal for the deaf to live separately. Meanwhile, his son Thomas, who also worked as a teacher of the deaf, "said he regarded the plan of Mr. Flournoy as a result of a morbid state of feeling, a dislike to the society of hearing men."[33]

In truth, John J. Flournoy was at best a visionary and at worst a lunatic. Historian Barry Crouch has called him "fascinating, eccentric, and bizarre," a man who "rarely cut his hair or beard, wore an Indian rubber overcoat in all seasons, and rode a small donkey." Flournoy lived a life of considerable personal isolation (he was married and divorced three times, an especially unusual life course in nineteenth-century America) and was alienated from the most basic social bonds, a characteristic his critics were quick to point out. When Turner and others raised the question of the perpetuation of the state's population, given that most children of the deaf are hearing, asking, "How will you keep it a mute community?" Flournoy replied, "If our children hear, let them go to other States. *This Government is to be sacred to the Deaf alone*." The idea of deporting their own children naturally horrified his readers. "I do not know whether Mr. Flournoy has a family," Edmund Booth wrote. "It would appear not, from the way he talks of sundering the ties of parent and child."[34]

Booth's point illustrates how Flournoy's ill-conceived and unpopular project overlapped with, and departed from, other more successful separatist schemes of the mid-nineteenth century. Flournoy's plan didn't involve isolating people of a particular religion (like closed Shaker or Mormon settlements), who might pass that tradition on to a new generation. Nor was its chief goal to purify the nation racially, like the movement to send American blacks to Africa (although, as the son of a slaveowner and a racial separatist, Flournoy intended Gallaudet to be a whites-only state).[35]

Nor was it a political secession from the Union, like the threatened secession of the slaveowning South. Deaf Americans shared neither a religion,
which they might pass on to their children, nor a racial affiliation, which
their children would inherit (only about 10 percent of deaf couples have
deaf children), nor even a common set of political beliefs.

What Flournoy proposed was a sovereign state of men and women who
were distinct from their countrymen—indeed, in most cases, from their
parents and siblings—only in their language. However ill conceived, his
plan for the state of Gallaudet reveals how Gallaudet's millennialist, universalist vision contained within it the seeds of separatism.

5

Strange Characters

On May 20, 1828, a notice appeared in the Washington, D.C., *Daily National Intelligencer:* "We are requested to state the Prince Abdraman, of Timboo, will attend, in Moorish Costume, at the Panorama of the Falls of Niagara, today, from 10 o'clock A.M. 'til 6 P.M.—Where the public will have an opportunity of seeing this interesting Personage, who has been the subject of singular and extraordinary vicissitudes." That day Washingtonians paid twenty-five cents each to see the "Prince of Timboo," Abd al-Rahman Ibrahima, a "tall, sedate, sable son of Africa," before a five-thousand-square-foot painting of Niagara Falls, on display not far from the White House. The painting was heart-stopping; the "Prince," magnificent. Dressed in "a white muslin turban topped with a crescent, a blue cloth coat with yellow buttons, white pantaloons gathered at the ankles, and yellow boots," and carrying a scimitar, Abd al-Rahman stood for eight hours, signing ladies' autograph albums and writing out passages of the Koran from memory. "He is a fine Arabic scholar," one spectator reported, "and even now, at his advanced life, 66, writes an elegant hand."[1]

Abd al-Rahman Ibrahima had other stops to make during his visit to Washington. On May 15, and again on May 22, he met with President John Quincy Adams. "Abdel Rahman is a Moor, otherwise called Prince or Ibrahim, who has been forty years a slave in this country," Adams noted in his diary. "He wrote, two or three years since, a letter to the Emperor of Morocco, in Arabic," an act that set into motion his eventual emancipation from plantation slavery in Natchez, Mississippi. Now the "Prince" had come to ask Adams "how and when he should be dispatched to his home . . . , Timbuctoo." Adams had little to offer by way of reply. And when the "Prince" returned for a second audience with the president, Adams was as uncharitable as he had been with Sequoyah's request for "a gratuity of six thousand dollars": "Abduhl Rahahman brought me a subscription book to raise a fund for purchasing the freedom of his five sons and his eight grandchildren, to which I declined subscribing."[2]

John Quincy Adams was a busy man. In early 1828 he was greatly distracted by the increasingly vitriolic campaign being waged against him by Andrew Jackson, his challenger for the presidency. Although unwilling to engage in mudslinging, Adams, who before assuming the presidency had been a professor of rhetoric and oratory at Harvard, was eager to expose Jackson as coarse, ill spoken, and unqualified for the office. With James Barbour, his secretary of war, Adams spent more time than was wise attempting to publicize what he considered an incontrovertible (or was it irrefragable?) stain on Jackson's character: Jackson was a terrible speller. A series of letters penned by Jackson and found in Barbour's files contained egregious errors: he even spelled *government* wrong (forgetting the first *n*). Adams was certain that this kind of ignorance, if made public, would "produce an explosion in the House of Representatives." But on April 1 Barbour informed Adams that in preparing to publish Jackson's letter, the printers had automatically "corrected all the spelling, which they say is according to an established rule in the printing of all public documents."[3] So much for that plan.

Despite the distraction of his campaign against that infamously bad speller Andrew Jackson, Adams found time, in the winter and spring of 1828, to meet with three strange characters: in February, Thomas Hopkins Gallaudet, educator of the deaf; in early May, George Guess, Cherokee philologist; and, in mid-May, Abd al-Rahman Ibrahima, freed slave. Adams had a scholar's interest in Gallaudet's work and a diplomat's concern with Sequoyah's treaty negotiations. His relationship with the "Prince" was purely political; by some calculations it had a good deal to do with his campaign against Jackson. Adams's secretary of state, Henry Clay, had worked for Abd al-Rahman's emancipation, an act that later subjected Adams to the criticism of southern slaveholders. An editorial in the *Louisiana Advertiser* in October 1828 even accused Adams of using Abd al-Rahman as a campaign tool: "A negro who can read and write the Arabic language with facility, thirty years in slavery among the 'barbarians of Mississippi,' himself a king, liberated by John Q. Adams—what an irresistible appeal is this to the sympathies and prejudices of the people of the free states!"[4]

While the accusation was at best grossly overstated and at worst entirely unfounded, it's nonetheless revealing: "a negro who can read and write the Arabic language with facility." Why should such a man be particularly threatening or particularly appealing? Because of the letters in which he wrote. Abd al-Rahman Ibrahima secured his freedom and, aided by Gallaudet himself, eventually secured his passage to Africa, by demonstrating his ability to write in "strange characters": the Arabic alphabet. Indeed, the "Prince's" plea was inseparable from his penmanship; even Henry Inman's 1828 portrait included a "Fac simile of the Moorish Prince's writing."

Abd al-Rahman's tale borders on the bizarre. But in its very strangeness it exposes the conventions of what was becoming a cliché of the republic of letters: the slave who gains his freedom by learning to read and write— in English. For American-born slaves like Frederick Douglass, who learned his ABCs by poring over the pages of Noah Webster's spelling book, literacy was a step on the path to freedom and, they hoped, to citizenship. English literacy Americanized slaves as much as it emancipated them, in much the same way as, Webster hoped, it Americanized white Americans.

Not so for the "Prince of Timboo," hence his curious appeal, his strange threat. In his "elegant hand," on display before the Panorama of the Falls of Niagara, in the Oval Office, and everywhere he went, Abd al-Rahman Ibrahima attempted to write his way not into but *out* of the nation, in a script few Americans had ever seen before.

A Facsimile

"His life appears like a romance," Thomas Hopkins Gallaudet said of Abd al-Rahman, "and the incidents would be incredible if the evidence was

Henry Inman, Abduhl Rahhahman, *1828.* (By permission of the Houghton Library, Harvard University.)

not so undeniable."[5] The incidents may be incredible, but the evidence is not altogether undeniable. Abd al-Rahman's life is fairly difficult to reconstruct, partly because his story was put to such propagandistic uses and partly because of the quality of the evidence itself.

Pieced together by Terry Alford in his 1977 biography, *Prince among Slaves,* the best-corroborated version of the story goes like this: Abd al-Rahman Ibrahima was born around 1762 in Timbo, Futa Jallon, in what is now Guinea. He was the son of Ibrahima Yoro Pate Sori, a powerful Fulbe chief, who, beginning in the 1720s, led a violent jihad against lax Muslims. Young Abd al-Rahman was educated at the centers of Islamic learning in Sori's empire, in Timbo, and in Timbuktu. He studied the Koran and learned to speak Bambanakan, Mandika, and Jallonke fluently (all are from the Mandakan language family) and to read and write Arabic. After completing his education, he married and took command of an army of his father's forces ("at twenty-four they made me Colonel," he is said to have recalled). In 1788 (the year Noah Webster marched in New York's Federal Procession), Abd al-Rahman was returning from a victorious military expedition, when he and fifty of his men were captured by a group of non-Muslim enemies and taken to the Gambia River. Through a series of middlemen, he was eventually sold to a British slaving ship. After a year of miserable, sickening travel, with stops at the West Indian island of Dominica and the port of New Orleans, he arrived in Natchez,

Mississippi, where he was purchased by Thomas Foster, a cotton farmer. When told by a Mandika translator that Abd al-Rahman was the son of a king, Foster decided to name his new slave Prince.

In Natchez, Abd al-Rahman tried to escape, just once, and then, realizing the futility of his hope of returning to Africa, resigned himself to his fate. In later years advocates of his emancipation boasted that during his time as a slave Abd al-Rahman "submitted to his fate without a murmur, and has been an industrious and faithful servant." He learned to speak English and married Isabella, an American-born slave, in 1794 or 1795. Year after year, he toiled. No doubt Futa Jallon became a distant, hazy memory, another world. Then, in 1807, after nineteen years of bondage, "Prince" was conducting business in Natchez when he had an unexpected encounter: he ran into John Coates Cox, a white man, the only white man, he had known in Timbo. As Abd al-Rahman recalled, "I said to a man who came with me from Africa, Sambo, that man rides like a white man I saw in my country." When Cox spotted him, "He said boy, where did you come from? I said from Col. F's. He said, he did not raise you. Then he said, you came from Teembo? I answered, yes, sir. He said, your name Abduhl Rahahman? I said, yes, sir."[6]

Thirty years before, Cox, an English doctor, had been shipwrecked and injured, and Abd al-Rahman's father had restored him to health and guided him back to the coast. In Natchez that day, Cox met the son of the man to whom he owed his life. Astonished to find Abd al-Rahman in such straits, Cox attempted to secure his release. His efforts met with no success ("my master was unwilling to sell me," the "Prince" recalled), but Cox told his astonishing tale to everyone he met. Over the next few years Foster's aging slave became a local celebrity, a status even Foster eventually acknowledged by reducing his workload. ("Thirty years I laboured hard," Abd al-Rahman remarked in 1828. "The last ten years I have been indulged a good deal.")[7]

Abd al-Rahman's almost unbelievable story, authenticated by the white man Cox, was a tale of a prince brought low, with all the tragedy of a Shakespearean play or a Walter Scott romance. It gained him a bit of fame and a welcome release from the most arduous physical labor. But it did not secure his freedom. That would require a demonstration of his Arabic literacy.

Some dozen years after his encounter with Cox, around 1820, Abd al-Rahman's story captured the interest of a Natchez newspaper editor, Andrew Marschalk. Invited to visit Marschalk's printing shop (perhaps to dictate the story of his life), Abd al-Rahman expressed his interest in a book of fonts, whereupon Marschalk "produced to him a Printer's Grammar, containing among other specimens of type, from a type Foundry, one in Arabic." Abd al-Rahman, "very much pleased, (remarking that it was the first of his country writing, he had seen, since he left home), requested to copy it, which he did in a very neat and handsome style, producing a facsimile." Marschalk was both impressed and intrigued.[8]

For Marschalk, and for all who sympathized with "Prince," his romanticized plight—a nobleman reduced to slavery—was made both more poignant and more credible by his literacy: a scholar reduced to working in the fields. In the early 1820s Marschalk urged Abd al-Rahman to write a letter, in Arabic, to his relatives in Africa, which Marschalk pledged to deliver one way or another. Eventually Abd al-Rahman agreed, and Marschalk sent his letter through his state senator to the State Department, where it caught the attention of Adams's Secretary of State Henry Clay.

In a note introducing Abd al-Rahman's letter, Marschalk erroneously referred to him as the prince of Morocco. How Marschalk came to commit this error is unclear. Probably, since he always considered Abd al-Rahman a "Moor," a swarthy—and not necessarily "negro"—Arab native of North Africa, Marschalk simply assumed that he was from Morocco. Abd al-Rahman may even have encouraged him in this misconception. In any event, the mistake had significant consequences: while the United States had little interest in Futa Jallon, Abd al-Rahman's homeland, it did have commercial ties and diplomatic relations with Morocco. Acting on Marschalk's misinformation, Clay determined that Abd al-Rahman was of potential use to the State Department and applied himself to securing his release. In 1826, the secretary, with President Adams's approval, managed to convince Foster to manumit "Prince"—without compensation—on the condition that the freed man would immediately leave the country. To Foster, no doubt, "Prince" had become just the kind of troublesome, unexploitable slave he believed he was well rid of.[9]

And so it was that on February 22, 1828, forty years after leaving Africa, Abd al-Rahman was freed. But there was a hitch. "The poor old man, when the news was communicated to him that he was to be free and return to his country, . . . looked at the old companion of his slavery—the mother of his nine children—he could not agree to part without her."[10] Foster, however, valued Isabella highly, not least because she served as the plantation's midwife. Fortunately, Natchez residents, inspired by Abd al-Rahman's much-publicized plight and by his refusal to leave without his wife, raised $293 to purchase Isabella's freedom. On April 8, 1828,

Isabella and Abd al-Rahman Ibrahima headed to Washington, the latter dressed in a "Moorish costume" bought by Marschalk. Traveling east, the "Prince" practiced his penmanship.

Many to Become Christians

"Since I have been in Washington," Abd al-Rahman reported in May 1828, "I have found a good many friends." Under the terms of the agreement forged by Clay and Foster, Abd al-Rahman was to leave the country immediately and to sail to Morocco courtesy of the State Department. But he and Isabella determined to first secure the freedom of their five sons and four daughters, a determination "Prince" made clear in his meeting with President Adams when he presented him with his subscription book. Abd al-Rahman is reported to have said, "I desire to go back to my own country again; but when I think of my children, it hurts my feelings. If I go to my own country, I cannot feel happy, if my children are left."[11]

In Washington, Abd al-Rahman was snubbed by Adams, possibly because it had become clear that he intended to travel to his "own country," which turned out not to be Morocco after all. But the "Prince" was welcomed elsewhere in the city, by "a good many friends" at the headquarters of the American Colonization Society, the organization that, as he shrewdly saw it, provided both the surest means of raising funds quickly and the best available destination, Liberia, just a fifteen-day journey from Futa Jallon.

The American Colonization Society, founded in 1816 for the purpose of sending free American blacks to Africa, followed in the footsteps of the movement led by English antislavery activists in the 1790s (in which William Thornton participated) to send freed slaves to Sierra Leone. But the American experiment held a slightly different appeal, attracting both southern slaveholders, like Henry Clay, who were eager to send free blacks out of the country, lest they incite revolt among slaves, and northern abolitionists and social reformers, like Thomas Hopkins Gallaudet, who headed the Connecticut Colonization Society and who worried that immediate emancipation would reduce Africans in America to poverty. Free blacks themselves largely opposed colonization; they believed they had little to gain by leaving a country they had helped build, and they were insulted, time and again, by the movement's rhetoric, like that of an 1828 circular: "The population which we would remove is injurious to the morals, the industry, and the strength of our nation."[12] By 1822 the American Colonization Society had raised enough funds, and enough emigrants, to purchase a tract of land in western Africa and found the first settlements of what came to be called Liberia.

To the Colonization Society, Abd al-Rahman was a publicity gold mine. Beginning by putting the "Prince" on display in "Moorish costume" at the Falls of Niagara, the organization agreed to support him on a speaking (and *writing*) tour of northern cities and to conduct its own publicity campaign on his behalf. By funding his tour, by parading this elegant exotic before the American public, the society hoped to generate enthusiasm for the larger project of colonization.

As the colonizationists saw it, Abd al-Rahman's picaresque tale was wonderfully compelling, and the "Prince" himself personally impressive. "He is intelligent, modest, and obliging," the organization reported. "Though he has been in slavery forty years, his manners are not merely prepossessing, but dignified." And his cause—raising funds not for himself but for the emancipation of his children and grandchildren—appealed to the family values of middle-class white reformers. Moreover, Abd al-Rahman appeared utterly without personal ambition: "He proposes to have no other desire than to fix himself as a colonist at Liberia; to live and die under American protection; and to render this country what aid he can in promoting an intercourse between our colony and the interior."[13]

Most of all, perhaps, this "Unfortunate Moorish Prince" promised to fulfill the Colonization Society's religious mission. Playing to its northern reform constituency, the society hoped Abd al-Rahman might hold the key to the conversion of Africa: "Is it impossible—is it *improbable* that Abduhl Rahhahman may become the chief pioneer of civilization to unenlightened Africa—that, armed with the Bible, he may be the foremost of that dark band of pilgrims who shall roll back the mighty waves of darkness and superstition, and plant the cross of the Redeemer upon the furthermost mountains of Kong!"[14]

When Thomas Hopkins Gallaudet read about Abd al-Rahman in the *African Repository,* the national journal of the American Colonization Society, his sympathy and missionary zeal were profoundly aroused. At his home in Hartford, Gallaudet's attention was caught, in particular, by the remark that "Prince," while still *"nominally* at least, a Mohamedan," seemed "friendly disposed toward the Christian religion" and was "extremely anxious for an Arabic Testament." Gallaudet knew that the

American Board of Commissioners of Foreign Missions had recently printed the New Testament in Arabic, and he set about to oblige Abd al-Rahman's request. He immediately wrote to the "Prince," enclosing with his letter "a small book in Arabic," which "shows very clearly the truth of the Christian religion," a volume by the Dutch jurist Hugo Grotius. Although he didn't have an Arabic Bible, Gallaudet promised to make arrangements for one to be sent by way of a friend, a former missionary to Palestine. "I beg you," he urged, "to read the Arabic Bible carefully. . . . I beg you at the same time, to pray to Almighty God, that he would guide you by his wisdom into the knowledge of the true religion."[15]

In June, Gallaudet received a gratifying reply. "At the time I left my country," Abd al-Rahman assured the Hartford minister, "they wished to have an Arabic Testament. After I take this book home, I hope I shall get many to become Christians." It was, of course, exactly what Gallaudet wanted to hear, as the "Prince of Footah Jallo" well knew.[16] Gallaudet, along with many other northern reformers involved in the colonization movement, hoped that the "Prince" would spearhead a missionary effort by which freed American blacks would convert native Africans to Christianity.

When Abd al-Rahman reached Hartford in October 1828 on his speaking tour, Gallaudet greeted him warmly. Inspired, Gallaudet preached a rousing sermon about the Muslim's plight at Hartford's Center Church. Believing that he could better serve Abd al-Rahman in his presence, Gallaudet temporarily abandoned his duties at the American Asylum for the Deaf and Dumb and left Hartford with Abd al-Rahman on October 4, 1828, to spend a month with him on the road. In New York two weeks later, Gallaudet delivered an address before a rapt audience in the Masonic Hall, arguing that the Prince's plight constituted "one of the strongest cases that can be presented to our feelings." He later had the sermon printed, to raise funds for the release of the children and grandchildren.[17]

As told by Gallaudet, Abd al-Rahman's story was a parable of Christian salvation. Preaching before northern whites, Gallaudet argued that sending Abd al-Rahman back to Africa not only was the right thing to do but also would provide untold benefits. It might aid commercial relations. It might aid diplomatic relations. And, "as christians we must especially rejoice that an opportunity will be afforded for diffusing the blessings of christianity to that dark and benighted region. . . . The finger of God seems to point to great results arising from the return of Prince. . . . We see why Prince was not permitted to return with his Moorish disposition and his Moorish sword; that Providence continued him here so long until grace had softened his heart"—softened his heart, that is, to Christianity.

In the rousing, emotional crescendo of his sermon, Gallaudet prophesied:

> Methinks I see him like a Patriarch crossing the Atlantic, over which he was taken a slave 40 years since. . . . I think I see benighted Africa taking her stand among the nations of the earth. . . . I think I see Africa, one hand pointing to the tablet of eternal Justice, making even us Americans tremble, while the words are pronounced, "Vengeance is mine; I will repay saith the Lord;" and with the other hand pointing to the golden rule of the gospel, . . . : "Whatsoever ye would that men should do unto you, do ye even so unto them."[18]

Paraded before gawking northern whites in city after city, the subject of Gallaudet's utterly fantastic African vision, the "Unfortunate Moorish Prince" easily might be seen as a simple tool of the Colonization Society, this strange coalition of southern slaveholders and northern missionary reformers. But Abd al-Rahman had much to gain by allying with men like Gallaudet and by pledging his conversion to Christianity. Not only did his speaking tour promise to raise funds to secure the emancipation of his children and grandchildren, but Liberia was as close to home as he was likely to get by American ship. Abd al-Rahman may well have had more in mind than "to fix himself as a colonist at Liberia." Most of all, it seems, he had every intention of remaining loyal to Islam, a faith he had maintained through forty years of bondage, partly by exercising the very literacy that made him so appealing to men like Gallaudet as a potential Christian.

Strange Characters

Some twelve million Africans were sold into the Atlantic slave trade between 1450 and 1850. Of these, two to three million were Muslims, about thirty thousand of whom ended up living as slaves in antebellum America (the rest, like the overwhelming majority of African slaves, were sent to the Caribbean or South America). Many of these Muslim slaves were literate to one degree or another since reading the Koran is a fundamental practice of Islamic faith. Eighteenth-century European visitors to Muslim regions of West Africa were astonished by the emphasis local rulers placed on literacy, for both boys and girls. By the end of the nineteenth century, Futa Jallon, Abd al-Rahman's homeland, boasted three thousand Koranic schools.[19]

In the New World, enslaved Muslims' literacy could be dangerous. Marked as educated, Muslim slaves may have been subject to special persecution and punishment, designed to crush any possibility of rebellion in much the same way that antebellum slave codes forbade teaching slaves to write in English. Yet enslaved Muslims labored to preserve their Arabic literacy, bartering for pen, ink, and paper, trading for copies of the Koran. Such efforts, of course, were not always successful. However much such men and women employed their literacy, it was often not enough to sustain it. Abd al-Rahman practiced by writing with a stick in the sand during breaks in work at Foster's plantation in Natchez, but after forty years in slavery, when he toured northern cities, he felt compelled to spend his evenings practicing to improve his penmanship. When the African-American Muslim Omar ibn Said set about to write his autobiography in 1831, he complained that his Arabic had greatly deteriorated: "I cannot write my life because I have forgotten much of my own language, as well as of the Arabic."[20]

Yet Omar ibn Said did manage to write his autobiography in Arabic letters. Some Muslims, moreover, even succeeded in acquiring copies of the Koran. Since an Islamic education required memorizing the entirety of the Koran, some slaves were able to produce Korans for themselves. Jamaican slave Benjamin Larten wrote out a complete copy of the sacred text. Job ben Soloman, in England, reproduced three identical copies of the Koran from memory, much to his patrons' astonishment.[21]

Having managed to retain their literacy, a handful of Muslims employed it to secure their freedom. Enslaved in 1731 and brought to Maryland, Job ben Soloman "wrote a letter in *Arabick* to his father [in Africa], acquainting him with his Misfortunes, hoping he might yet find Means to redeem him." The letter was intercepted in London and sent to an Oxford professor for translation, after which an English philanthropist purchased his freedom. Like ben Soloman, Omar ibn Said also improved his lot through literacy. A fugitive from a South Carolina rice plantation, he was captured and put in prison in Fayetteville, North Carolina. While in jail, he used coal ash to write on the walls of his cell, to the astonishment of his jailers. "The strange characters, so elegantly and correctly written by a runaway slave, soon attracted attention, and many citizens of the town visited the jail to see him." Omar ibn Said was eventually bought by a man who was curious about this strange writing and who, although he did not emancipate him, relieved him of physical labor.[22]

For Abd al-Rahman too, Arabic literacy was central to his appeal to whites. Beginning with the day Andrew Marschalk marveled at Abd al-Rahman's pleasure at seeing Arabic printer's fonts, white Americans were fascinated by Abd al-Rahman's alphabet. Everywhere he went, the "Prince" displayed his Arabic literacy: he signed autographs, wrote out passages from the Koran from memory, took dictation, and sold as souvenirs small scraps of paper on which he had written the Lord's Prayer in Arabic. Famed orator Edward Everett reported, "The education which Abdul had received in his youth . . . was, no doubt, very limited compared with the standard of European or American education. But when I saw him at Washington, after a long life passed in slavery, he was able to read the Koran with fluency, and wrote the Arabic character with great elegance." On meeting the "Prince," Thomas Hopkins Gallaudet too found himself especially impressed with his literacy: "During all his trials, Prince has not forgot his Arabic, but reads it fluently, and writes it with neatness."[23]

What was, for Abd al-Rahman, a marker of his Muslim faith became, for men like Gallaudet, a signal of his promise as a missionary. As Gallaudet saw it, this educated man, with a scholar's interest in studying the Bible, had a unique ability to convert his countrymen. After all, the lack of white missionaries who could speak, read, and write African languages had long paralyzed efforts to Christianize Africa and threatened to compromise the colony at Liberia, whose success depended on peaceful relations with neighboring natives. Abd al-Rahman, Gallaudet believed, had been singled out to become "a Patriarch crossing the Atlantic," bringing the good news of the Gospel to "the furthermost mountains of Kong."

Much as it underscored his promise as a missionary, Abd al-Rahman's literacy had, for most whites who flocked to see him on display in northern cities, a simpler function: it made them believe him. "There is no doubt of the truth of his story," the *New England Palladium* reported, "as he writes and speaks the Arabic language."[24]

The Pathway from Slavery to Freedom

Abd al-Rahman wasn't the only former slave in antebellum America who could read and write. Nor was he the only one for whom literacy was a ticket to freedom. Indeed, when former slaves wrote about their experiences under slavery, they rarely failed to cite the moment of acquiring literacy—and of learning that books "talk"—as the key to their emancipation. Henry Louis Gates has labeled this convention in the republic of letters the "trope of the talking book" and argues for its centrality to the African-American literary tradition, a tradition already well established by the time Abd al-Rahman began to speak in public, through the writings of freed slaves like Olaudah Equiano.[25] For Equiano, whose autobiography was first published in 1789, writing was a means—as Gates argues, the *only* means—of insisting on his own humanity. In the age of Enlightenment, letters alone could mark a man as a creature capable of reason.

Kidnapped from his home in what is now Nigeria, Equiano labored as a slave in North America before being taken to England. On board a ship bound for London, Equiano, as he told it, came to view whites no longer "as spirits, but as men superior to us": "I could now speak English tolerably well," he recalled, and "had long wished to be able to read and write; and for this purpose took every opportunity to gain instruction." Equiano hoped to "resemble" whites, "to imbibe their spirit, and imitate their manners." This he accomplished by learning to write and, most of all, by publishing his autobiography, illustrated with a portrait in which he holds an open Bible and below which appears his signature, all testimony to his newly acquired status as a literate and hence rational and *human* being, who, by imitating his master's literacy, has become master of himself.[26]

Established in early slave narratives like Equiano's, this convention is most famously and perhaps best illustrated in the autobiography of the American slave Frederick Douglass, first published in 1845. In his *Narrative of the Life of Frederick Douglass, an American Slave, Written by Himself,* Douglass drew on conventions not only of earlier European and Enlightenment-influenced slave narratives but also of the very American autobiography of Ben Franklin, who had himself reckoned his acquisition of literacy as the turning point of his young life, the moment when he had found a voice that allowed him to participate in the republic of letters. As historian David Blight has remarked, writing of Douglass's narrative, "To be judged truly human and a citizen with social and political recognition, a person had to achieve literacy. For better or worse, civilization itself was equated with cultures that could *write* their history."[27]

In Douglass's tale, one every bit as self-consciously fashioned and artfully constructed as Franklin's, Douglass tells of how, as a boy growing up in the 1820s, he learned the ABCs from the wife of his master, Auld, until Auld found out about it and "at once forbade Mrs. Auld to instruct me further, telling her, among other things, that it was unlawful, as well as unsafe,

Olaudah Equiano. (By permission of the
Houghton Library, Harvard University.)

to teach a slave to read. 'Now,' said he, 'if you teach that nigger . . . how to read, there would be no keeping him. It would forever unfit him to be a slave. He would at once become unmanageable, and of no value to his master. As to himself it could do him no good, but a great deal of harm. It would make him discontented and unhappy.' " Listening to these words, Douglass experienced an epiphany: "I now understood what had been to me a most perplexing difficulty, to wit, the white man's power to enslave the black man," he writes. "From that moment, I understood the pathway from slavery to freedom."[28]

Committed to taking that path, to becoming fully literate, Douglass eloquently related his struggle to acquire the tools with which to read and write, emphasizing his Franklinesque hardscrabble ambition and streetwise resourcefulness: he learned the names of letters by observing marked timbers in a shipyard; he tricked a white boy into teaching him the alphabet by challenging his knowledge; he bartered with hungry white boys living on the street to trade bread for reading lessons. "During this time, my copy-book was the board fence, brick wall, and pavement; my pen and ink was a lump of chalk," Douglass recalled. "With these, I learned mainly how to write. I then commenced and continued copying the Italics in Webster's Spelling Book, until I could make them all without looking on the book. . . . Thus, after a long, tedious effort for years, I finally succeeded in learning how to write."[29]

Douglass's tale of triumph over adversity emphasizes a very particular obstacle: legal statutes that made it illegal to teach slaves. In forbidding his wife to teach Douglass to read, his master, Mr. Auld, admonished "that it was unlawful, as well as unsafe, to teach a slave to read." But before about 1820 it had not in fact been illegal to teach slaves to read in most places. Most slaveowners wished their slaves to be Christian (in order that they learn of the biblical justification for slavery and learn to submit to their masters as Christians submit to God's will), and reading was considered essential to conversion. Writing, however, was another matter entirely. Beginning in South Carolina in 1740, teaching slaves to write was declared criminal and punishable by a fine of a hundred pounds, on the grounds that "the having of slaves taught to write, or suffering them to be employed in writing, may be attended with great inconveniences"—mainly, that those who could write could forge passes and plan rebellions.[30]

After about 1820, teaching slaves to read too became illegal. As the abolitionist movement grew and more and more abolitionist literature was smuggled into the South, slaveowners came to see reading as fostering not submission but subversion.

Even under such conditions, a small number of southern slaves, probably about 5 to 10 percent, managed to learn to read. Fewer still learned to write, but those few, like Douglass, had a profound impact on the abolitionist movement and the eventual end of American slavery. Free blacks who could read and write often employed their literacy in the service of abolitionism. David Walker, born free in North Carolina, published an *Appeal . . . to the Colored Citizens of the World* in Boston in 1829, calling for "the entire emancipation of your enslaved brethren all over the world." When copies of Walker's incendiary pamphlet reached Georgia, it almost immediately inspired the state legislature to pass a newly restrictive slave code "to prevent the circulation of written or printed papers within this State calculated to excite disaffection among the coloured people of this State, and to prevent said people from being taught to read or write."[31]

By the time Abd al-Rahman Ibrahima began his speaking tour, in other words, the association between black literacy and liberation was becoming quite marked in the eyes of both blacks and whites. Specifically, black literacy was closely linked to abolitionist agitation. By learning to read and write, a slave gained intellectual independence and access to ideas that would encourage his escape from slavery and his subsequent advocacy of full and immediate emancipation.

To Douglass and other American slaves, the arduous process of learning to read and write spelled intellectual emancipation, the "pathway from slavery to freedom." But comparing Frederick Douglass with Abd al-Rahman reveals that for Douglass acquiring literacy also spelled entry into the national political sphere. He and other slave autobiographers commonly cited Webster's ubiquitous spelling book in their tales of learning to read and write, a reference that explicitly linked them with the process of Americanization. And Douglass's tale of "An American Slave, Written by Himself," made this claim even more explicitly than most. By imitating the English language and American spelling of white American citizens, Douglass entered the United States' republic of letters, its public, civic community of political discourse. Indeed, he even modeled his rhetorical style after Caleb Bingham's 1797 nationalistic tract *The Columbian Orator*. For Douglass, who staked his future in the United States and ardently rejected colonization, literacy was a means not only of insisting upon his humanity and securing his freedom, but also of establishing his Americanness.

Abd al-Rahman's literacy operated very differently. Because he could never use his Arabic to forge a pass, slaveowners perceived it as less dangerous. And the "Unfortunate Moorish Prince" had no interest in imitating whites' language or writing. He had no interest in entering the republic of (American) letters or even in remaining in the United States. He was interested instead in maintaining his own, quite foreign, language, religion, and alphabet. Abd al-Rahman presented specimens of his writing to the American public not to persuade them of his Americanness and to insist on a place for himself in their world but to argue for his differentness, embodied in the very letters with which he wrote.

A Negro Who Can Read and Write

Americans who met Abd al-Rahman Ibrahima generally concluded that he was more "civilized" than most American-born slaves by virtue of his Arabic literacy. "It must be evidence to everyone that the Prince is a man superior to the generality of Africans whom we behold in this country," the *Freedman's Journal* reported in August 1828. "His education is also superior."[32]

Like Andrew Marschalk's insistence that the "Unfortunate Moorish Prince" came from Morocco, such remarks reveal native Americans' complicated (and confused) attitudes toward Africa itself, which made much of the distinction between northern and sub-Saharan Africa, between darker- and lighter-skinned Africans, and between coastal and interior societies. To the extent that any European-Americans in the United States were even vaguely familiar with the African languages spoken by newly arrived slaves, they generally reviled them. The languages of sub-Saharan Africa, according to the *United States Literary Gazette* (1826), "comprehend many sounds scarcely articulate; some that are very strange, sometimes howlings, sometimes hisses, contrived in imitation of the cries of animals, or intended as watchwords to distinguish hostile tribes from one another."[33] Such languages, that is, were considered not really languages at all and were taken as further proof of the animalistic nature of blacks.

But a competing scholarly tradition that, to some degree, celebrated Arabic literature and culture thereby elevated Arabic-speaking and Arabic-writing American slaves to a wholly different status: as civilized (and therefore not black). Thus American geographer and linguist Joseph Emerson Worcester (a lexicographical apprentice and a later rival of Noah Webster as well as a cousin of Samuel Austin Worcester, Cherokee missionary) declared that the Arabic literacy of some slaves in the United States should be taken as evidence not of the intelligence of blacks but of "the superior civilization of the negroes in the interior over those near the coast."[34]

These attitudes are in evidence in the American Colonization Society itself. Just behind the colonizationists' embrace of Abd al-Rahman as "intelligent" and "dignified" lay their belief that he was also somehow not "negro," a belief that required explaining away all his apparently "negro" features, displayed in his person or in Inman's portrait. In 1828 the *African Repository* reprinted a letter by a Natchez newspaper editor, Cyrus Griffin, in which he explained Abd al-Rahman's "superiority" to American blacks. "When he arrived in this country," Griffin began, "his hair hung in flowing ringlets far below his shoulders," like a white man's. After his long hair was cut by his master, Foster, Abd al-Rahman's hair soon fell into a state of neglect and since that time "has become coarse, and in some degree curly," like a black man's. Griffin continued, "His skin, also, by long service in the sun, and the privations of bondage, has been materially changed," making him look more like a "Foolah" than a Moor. These changes, according to Griffin, explained why some might mistake Abd al-Rahman for a "negro." "But," Griffin insisted, "Prince states explicitly, and with an air of pride, that not a drop of negro blood runs in his veins. He places the negro in a scale of being infinitely below the Moor."[35]

At a time when racial distinctions were only beginning to be buttressed by racist scientific discourse, Griffin was quick to employ such explanations. In his Natchez newspaper, the *Southern Galaxy,* he wrote more particularly of Abd al-Rahman's racial features: "It is true his lips are thicker than are usually those of the Moor; but the animal frame is not that of the negro; his eyes, and, in fact, his entire physiognomy is unlike that of any negro we have ever seen. And if the facial angle be an infallible criterion the point is established, his being equal and perhaps greater, than most of the whites."[36]

Griffin's advocacy of Abd al-Rahman's emancipation was dependent on his belief that the "Prince" was, first, not "black" and, second, literate in Arabic, not in English. To be "black" and literate (in English) was a frightful thing to slaveowners like Griffin and his Natchez readers. By being "black" and literate in English (or in Websterian, American English), men like Douglass insisted not only on their humanity but also on their right to citizenship in the Republic. Indeed, Abd al-Rahman's far more palatable—and, to northerners, even appealing—literacy reveals just how tenuous the place Douglass staked out actually was.

In allying with the Colonization Society and therefore at least partly accepting the depiction of himself as a "Moor," who was, in some sense at least, not "black" (if not wholly "white" either), Abd al-Rahman played on the prejudices of white American audiences. But that is not to say that he agreed with them. Much as Cyrus Griffin insisted that Abd al-Rahman also embraced racial distinctions ("Prince states explicitly, and with an air of pride, that not a drop of negro blood runs in his veins. He places the negro in a scale of being infinitely below the Moor"), he apparently rejected it.[37] Instead, and rather astonishingly, even as he courted the American Colonization Society, attracting the sympathy of both slaveowners and missionaries, Abd al-Rahman also successfully allied with free blacks in the North (the very "negroes" Griffin despised). In many of the cities he visited on his speaking tour, Abd al-Rahman met with black abolitionists, as well as colonizationists, often to great fanfare.

In August 1828 the "coloured inhabitants" of Boston "gave a public Dinner to their fellow countryman, the Prince ABDUHL RAHHAMAN," who had recently arrived in town to raise funds for his children's emancipation. The festivities began with a procession from the African School House, at four o'clock, that ended at the African Masonic Hall. There black leaders of Boston's abolitionist community offered toasts to the "Prince," to the Manumission Society, to Liberty and Equality. David

Walker, author of the famous *Appeal,* toasted "our worthy Guest, who was by the African's natural enemies torn from his country, religion, and friends . . . , may God enable him to obtain so much of the reward of his labor, as may purchase the freedom of his offspring." George B. Holmes sang a miserably rhymed song he had specially written for the occasion: "All hail to the Chief from Old Africa's shore, / Who forty years' bondage has had to deplore. . . ." Near the end of the evening, C. A. de Randamie, who presided over the festivities, wished Abd al-Rahman well in his journey back to Africa: "May the evening of your days be like the rising sun which illuminates Footah Jallo."[38]

But Abd al-Rahman's increasingly close ties to northern black abolitionists came at the cost of southern support. The Boston reception and others like it were reported in Natchez newspapers by Andrew Marschalk, who had come to regret his role in securing the "Prince's" release from bondage. Of the Boston reception, Marschalk reported, "The slaves of the south are openly invited to revolt and to murder their masters. . . . For what purpose has Mr. Clay given the emancipated slave Prince a passport to visit the northern cities and to get up negro dinner parties, and give inflammatory toasts against the slave states," Marschalk asked, other than to excite anti-Jackson sentiment?[39]

By violating the terms of the initial agreement he had made with his former master, Thomas Foster—that is, to leave the country immediately upon being freed—Abd al-Rahman lost the sympathy of many of his Natchez supporters. In October 1828, Foster himself declared "that I consider the contract . . . entirely violated and that I would not have entered into it for two thousand dollars, if I had known that the business would be conducted as it has been."[40]

In New Orleans, Foster's claim and Marschalk's alarm were echoed, and amplified, by P. K. Wagner, writing in the *Louisiana Advertiser* in the weeks before the November presidential election. "Be it known," Wagner told his readers, "that J. Q. Adams, President of the United States, procured while President, a negro man named Prince, a native of Africa, from a Mr. Thos. Foster near Natchez, with the avowed object of sending the said negro home to Africa":

What did Mr. Adams do? Did he comply with his contract and send the negro to Africa? No—What then? He gave the negro a passport and sent him in triumph through the free states, where he is now travelling, and has been since last May, arousing wherever he goes the prejudices of the people against slavery and against the slave holders of the South, thereby making a political diversion in favor of Mr. Adams, and preparing the way for the ulterior object—emancipation on a large scale. A negro who can read and write the Arabic language with facility, thirty years in slavery among the "barbarians of Mississippi," himself a king, liberated by John Q. Adams—what an irresistible appeal is this to the sympathies and prejudices of the people of the free states! What a powerful argument this is, in favor of re-electing that *humane man* J. Q. Adams to the presidency, and excluding the slave holder Andrew Jackson![41]

A Negro who could read and write. What an irresistible appeal. "If Mr. Adams had sought the world over he could not have found a better instrument than this negro to work upon the prejudices of the people of Pennsylvania, New Jersey, New York and New England," Wagner concluded, "the negro himself being well educated in English and Arabic, shrewd, sensible, ambitious, deceitful and daring."[42]

Nor did the outrage end with mere editorials. Four days before the election a handbill distributed in Louisiana (and probably written by Wagner) continued to call attention to Adams's alleged use of Abd al-Rahman:

LOUISIANANS! Remember that ANDREW JACKSON IS A MAN OF THE SOUTH, A SLAVE HOLDER, A COTTON PLANTER. Recollect the iniquitous and profligate PLOT of ADAMS and CLAY to excite the prejudices of your Northern brethren against the SOUTH by employing an emancipated NEGRO TO ELECTION-EER FOR THEM. Yes! They thought they could not be withstood when they had
AFRICA AT THEIR BACK!
But we WILL withstand them and their COADJUTORS OF THE HOUSE OF TIMBOO, and conquer them too. TIMBOO AND QUINCY! QUINCY AND TIMBOOO! . . . What a coalition of Royalty to bamboozle the NORTH and destroy the SOUTH![43]

The southern response to Abd al-Rahman's alliance with northern black abolitionists now placed the "Prince" in a position not *less* threatening than that of free blacks literate in English, but *more* threatening. In effect, by dining with men like David Walker, Abd al-Rahman Ibrahima had transformed himself yet again. This time, he had changed from a "Moor" to a "negro."

Saith the Sheikh to Mecca

At least part of Gallaudet's vision of the "Patriarch crossing the Atlantic" came true: Abd al-Rahman, a slave for forty years, did return to Africa. In February 1829, having raised adequate funds, he and Isabella set sail for Liberia, along with 160 colonists. They landed in April, considerably weakened by the journey. In May, Abd al-Rahman wrote to Washington, reporting his arrival, and announced his plans to travel to his homeland "as soon as the rains are over." But he never made the voyage. Taken ill "with the coast fever," Abd al-Rahman died in Liberia on July 6, 1829, just a few hundred miles from Futa Jallon.[44]

At his death it was reported that "Abduhl Rahhahman has left some writings, which he desired to be transmitted to his relatives." A countryman who had visited him before his death read these Arabic writings and "appeared to be much affected" by them, but "as the native spoke but little English," he couldn't tell any of the Americans what was in them.[45]

What became of these tantalizing papers is uncertain; possibly they were held in Liberia and given to the eight children and grandchildren who immigrated to Liberia the following October to join Isabella. But what of Abd al-Rahman's other writings? Although he was celebrated for his fine Arabic hand, very few of his writings survive today (or at least very few are cataloged under his name and hence available to scholars). This is a legacy, ironically, of the fact that Abd al-Rahman could not write in English or with the Roman alphabet; most documents attributed to him are either unreliable translations of his written Arabic or unverifiable transcriptions of his spoken English.

Consider the "Prince's" two "autobiographies." The first was recorded by American Colonization Society secretary Ralph Randolph Gurley during Abd al-Rahman's visit to Washington in April and May 1828. According to Gurley, "At our request, Prince has written a concise history of himself, and we have penned a translation of it from his own lips. The only liberty we have taken, is to correct those grammatical inaccuracies, which resulted from his imperfect knowledge of our language." The original written Arabic of this account has not survived, but Gurley's version of Abd al-Rahman's spoken translation was published in May 1828. It begins, "I was born in the City of Tombuctoo," relates, in some detail, Abd al-Rahman's capture in Africa, and ends with his eventual encounter, in Natchez, Mississippi, with Dr. John Coates Cox, around 1820.

Gurley's version of Abd al-Rahman's autobiography, "from his own lips," tells a story consistent with other accounts, like those recorded by Marschalk and Griffin. It provides little new information, nothing about the period from 1820 to 1828, and no evidence at all about Abd al-Rahman's faith, his education, his ideas about race and slavery, or his intentions in returning to Africa.[46] Since these matters were probably on Abd al-Rahman's mind in the spring of 1828, their absence from Gurley's account suggests that either Abd al-Rahman or Gurley tailored the story for purposes of publication in the *African Repository*. It is a source of limited value at best.

Abd al-Rahman's second "autobiography" was written by him in October 1828 in Arabic and "translated" at the time to read:

> Abdul Rahhahman son of Ibrahim—I born in the city Timbuctoo (oo)—[?] I lived there till I was five years old—I moved to country Foota-Jallo—I lived in the capital Timbo (Teembo) I lived there till I was twenty five year old—I tooking prisoner in the war—I sold to River Gambia—they took me to Dominique (W[est]. I[ndies].) took me to New Orleans—took me to Natchez—I sold to Mr. Thomas Foster—I lived there forty year—I get liberate last March-1828—October 10-1828.

But this "translation," made in New Haven in 1828, is poppycock. In truth, Abd al-Rahman's writing begins: "His name is 'Abd al-Rahman Ibrahim' may God bless Muhammad his Prophet and his people and companions," after which follows not an autobiography but standard, if somewhat mangled, Islamic invocations.[47]

The New Haven "translation" of Abd al-Rahman's second "autobiography" was undoubtedly not so much a translation as a transcription. Abd al-Rahman was asked to translate his Arabic writing into spoken English, and his hearer wrote down what he said. In his elegant Arabic, he wrote, "May God bless Muhammad his Prophet"; in his broken English, he spoke his life story.

But this wasn't the only time Abd al-Rahman wrote one thing and said another. As it turns out, on the scraps of paper he had sold as souvenirs as he toured northern cities, he wrote not the Lord's Prayer, as he claimed, but the "Al-Fatiha" (the Key), the first chapter of the Koran.[48]

Abd al-Rahman's second
"autobiography," 1828.
(Courtesy of the John Trumbull
Papers, Manuscripts and Archives,
Yale University Library.)

Why? Perhaps Abd al-Rahman was not as well educated as he claimed or as his sponsors liked to believe. Perhaps the Koran, or its opening passages, were all he really *could* write. Perhaps he had never been a better scholar, or perhaps he had lost much of the suppleness of literacy during forty long years writing only with a stick in the dirt of a cotton field. Or perhaps the Koran was all Abd al-Rahman *wanted* to write. Perhaps he clung to his Islamic faith tenaciously, even as he collaborated with Christian missionaries like Gallaudet, and remained true to himself in what he wrote.

Unfortunately, it's probably impossible to know. It seems likely, from the evidence, that Abd al-Rahman remained a Muslim, toying with Christianity only to please his sponsors. In any event, from his actions, it is certain that he never considered himself an American. Even after living most of his life in the United States and marrying an American-born woman, Abd al-Rahman felt no loyalty to the Republic (and why should he?). Nor did he plan to remain an inhabitant of the American colony of Liberia; as he made clear immediately after his arrival in Africa, he planned to travel to the interior for a reunion with his brother, who had replaced their father as a powerful local ruler.

If Abd al-Rahman never called himself an American, he never called himself a "negro" either; nor is it clear that he himself used the word *Moor*. In Gurley's version of the "Prince's" "autobiography," Abd al-Rahman

Abd al-Rahman's Arabic "Lord's Prayer," 1828. (Courtesy of the American Philosophical Society.)

distinguishes himself from "Africans" when in telling of his capture, he claims to have shouted to his enemies, "I will not run for an African."[49] Gurley might have employed the term to distinguish Abd al-Rahman, the (not-so-black) Moor from the (black) African, but what Abd al-Rahman meant, if indeed he said what Gurley wrote, is uncertain.

Abd al-Rahman's sense of himself and his motives in acting as he did are even murkier than Sequoyah's. This is a consequence not only of the paucity of sources but also of Abd al-Rahman's own chameleonism. To southern slaveholders he was at first a princely light-skinned Moor, "superior to the generality of Africans," who ought to be returned to his native land. Later he was to these same people a shrewd, deceitful dark-skinned "negro." To northern missionaries he was a model Christian convert, destined to become a persuasive missionary. To free blacks, he was a man of inspiring dignity who might aid the cause of abolition.

Despite his inscrutableness, Abd al-Rahman's story reveals the vulnerability of "a negro who can read and write." And, most of all, it points out just how invested most freed slaves were in assimilation, rather than colonization, in language as in all else. Frederick Douglass might, after all, have adopted a strategy like Sequoyah's—he might have insisted that true freedom for American blacks lay in a kind of linguistic secession and rejected English-language and Roman-alphabet literacy altogether—but instead he insisted that American blacks can be both black and literate in English and, ultimately, American.

That Abd al-Rahman Ibrahima became a political issue, if a very minor one, in the Adams-Jackson campaign of 1828 must have surprised him. He displayed, after all, precious little interest in national politics and little partisanship. He ruthlessly chose his allies for what they could do for him, not for their political views. Perhaps he sensed the shallowness of northerners' sympathy for him, a foreigner, in an age of growing nativist sentiment. "All this stupid ostentation of kindness towards the Prince of Timboo, is nothing but cant—sheer hypocrisy," P. K. Wagner pointed out in the *Louisiana Advertiser*. "It is strange to see the infatuation of the northern aristocracy, in thus loading the negro with adulation and caresses—when the same nabobs have declared that the contact of white Europeans, Irishmen, Dutch, French, &c. was contaminating the morals of the nation."

In an age when the increasingly virulent nativism of the North was to lead to new language schemes, including Samuel Morse's telegraphic code, designed to protect the Republic from a foreign conspiracy to destroy American democracy, Wagner could rightly complain: "If this prince were a white man born in Ireland or in France, even though he had been naturalized in this country, he would meet with nothing but hatred and contumely from these same northern nabobs."[50]

C Wires

COMMUNICA′TION, *n.* . . . . Intercourse by
words, letters or messages . . .
—NOAH WEBSTER,
An American Dictionary, 1828

6

Universal Communication

On September 1, 1858, the people of New York spilled out onto the streets of the city, streets that were at first eerily quiet since nearly all the city's businesses had been closed for the day, in commemoration of the successful laying of the Atlantic cable connecting New York to London by telegraph. The festivities began early. At nine o'clock the bells at Trinity Church rang "Hail Columbia," "God Save the Queen," and "Yankee Doodle," filling the streets with sound. By midmorning thousands of visitors had flocked into Manhattan by train, ferry, and carriage. By one o'clock more than fifteen thousand marchers had formed a procession at the Battery to begin the long, slow parade up Broadway to the Crystal Palace, while onlookers, leaning out of their windows, waved white handkerchiefs. All over the city, businesses and residences posted banners and hung lanterns. At Barnum's Museum, the flags of Britain and the United States hung tied together by telegraph wire. At the Astor House a placard read: "The Atlantic Telegraph transmits the lightning of Heaven, and binds together 60,000,000 human beings speaking the same language."[1]

If New York's Federal Procession in 1788 had celebrated the binding of the nation together by the new Constitution, the events of September 1,

1858, celebrated the reunion of the United States with its mother country. "SEVERED JULY 4, 1776. UNITED AUGUST 12, 1858," read a banner posted at Lafarge House. Throughout the city and the nation, the telegraph was heralded as a tool of "universal communication," and Samuel F. B. Morse, as a champion of peace. In 1855 Morse had predicted, "I trust that one of its effects will be to bind man to his fellow-man in such bonds of amity as to put an end to war."[2] At New York's celebration in 1858 Alderman James Davis declared that the Atlantic cable could not "fail to be the means of promoting peace on earth," and a toast was offered to Morse as "a Cadmus to the lightning of Heaven," who "made it a pen and taught it the syllables of human speech and universal brotherhood." Perhaps the residents of 356 Broadway expressed this sentiment best. On their balcony they carefully placed "rows of upright muskets, with candles stuck in their barrels," and a sign reading: "The Cable with its peaceful tricks/Makes of muskets candlesticks."

More, even, than usher in a new era of peace, the Atlantic cable was expected to destroy national boundaries and national distinctions. At a banquet held the day after New York's procession, a Reverend Dr. Bellows bellowed: "Never before was anything purely human done in the history of the world and the race which stood for One-ness as the successful laying of the Atlantic Cable does! . . . We have hitherto lived in a hemisphere, and we now live on a globe—live not by halves, but as a whole—not as scattered members, but as the connected limbs of one organic body, the great common humanity." And a chronicle of the laying of the cable, published in 1858, declared that the telegraph "binds together by a vital cord all the nations of the earth. It is impossible that old prejudices and hostilities should longer exist, while such an instrument has been created for an exchange of thought between all the nations of the earth."[3]

But New Yorkers' celebrations were premature, in more ways than one. The very day the city held its festivities, the cable failed.[4] Not until 1866 was the Atlantic cable successfully relaid and telegraphic communication between England and America restored. Meanwhile, the promise of world peace went unrealized and the United States plunged into civil war, the first war in which battlefield commands were sent by telegraph.

If the telegraph failed to deliver on its promise of putting an end to war, it did secure the reputation of Samuel Morse as one of the world's most important inventors. In 1871, at a ceremony unveiling a statue of Morse in Central Park, the governor of New York compared Morse's achievement with the invention of the alphabet: "For the second time in the history of the world, the power of language is increased by human agency. Thanks to Samuel F. B. Morse men speak to one another now, though

*Daguerreotype of Samuel Morse,
c. 1844–60.* (Courtesy of the Library of
Congress.)

separated by the width of the earth, with the lightning's speed and as if
standing face to face. If the inventor of the alphabet be deserving of the
highest honors, so is he whose great achievement marks this epoch in the
history of language—the inventor of the Electric Telegraph."[5]

Yet within the story of Morse's invention of "universal communication"
lie some disturbing ironies, not least among them that Morse himself was
no universalist—indeed, he was more of a nationalist and a nativist than
was Noah Webster—and his most intimate personal relationship, his second marriage, was in effect a failure of communication: Morse could not
sign, and his deaf wife could speak only poorly. Moreover, the story of
Morse's invention—of Morse himself—reveals the limits of American
nationalism. Morse's code and telegraph demonstrate once again that the
very wires used to bind Americans together could be just as easily cut.

The American Leonardo

Samuel Finley Breese Morse was born in Charlestown, Massachusetts, in
1791. As a boy he was energetic and restless, with a passion for novelty
that often threatened to distract him from his goals. When he was just ten

years old and a student at Phillips Academy in Andover, his father, Jedidiah, warned him: "Your natural disposition, my dear son, renders it proper for me earnestly to recommend to you to attend to one thing at a time. It is impossible that you can do two things well at the same time, & I would, therefore, never have you attempt it." Morse was keenly aware of his "capricious inclinations." Thanking his parents for their support of his artistic training in London in 1812, Morse assured them that his future biographers would agree "that when my desire for change did cease, it always settled on painting."[6]

Morse was also an impatient man of powerful affections. When he first arrived in London to study painting, he wrote to his parents twice to inform them of his safe arrival and sent the letters on separate ships—just in case. In a third letter, written after he had still had no word from his parents and no reason to believe that they had received either of his earlier letters, he expressed his frustration in a passage that many (including an aging Morse) later found prophetic: "I only wish you now had it to relieve your minds from anxiety, for while I am writing I can imagine Mama, wishing that she could hear of my arrival, and thinking of thousands of accidents which may have befallen me; & *I wish that in an instant I could communicate the information; but 3000 miles are not passed over in an instant,* & we must wait 4 long weeks before we can hear from each other." (Morse had good reason to be especially solicitous of his parents. His mother, Elizabeth, had given birth to eleven children, only three of whom survived infancy, and the possibility of any harm coming to Finley must have terrified her.) And, in 1825, when Morse's beloved first wife, Lucretia, died in New Haven while he was in Washington painting a commissioned portrait of the marquis de Lafayette, the slowness of the mail bringing news of her death meant that he did not reach New Haven until a week after her funeral, to his lifelong regret.[7]

In 1815, when Morse returned to America after studying in Europe, he aspired to found an American national art in much the same spirit as that of Noah Webster laboring to create an American language. Of the founding of an art institution in Philadelphia, Morse wrote, "I wish Americans would unite in the thing . . . let it be . . . national." Writing from London in 1814, he hoped "the arts [would] be so encouraged that American artists might remain at home, and not, as at present, be under the painful necessity of exiling themselves from their country and their friends." But he found himself frustrated again and again. Morse's portrait of Lafayette was one of the high points of his painting career, but for most of the 1820s he found himself reduced to the kind of hackwork he despised, painting the portraits of men like Noah Webster. In 1831 Morse returned to study in Europe and there began what became perhaps his most famous painting, the *Gallery of the Louvre.*

A large canvas containing miniature copies of forty-one masterworks of European art, Morse conceived of the *Louvre* as an encyclopedic teaching tool for philistine Americans, both to introduce them to great works of art and to persuade them of the need for artistic patronage. He included himself in the foreground of the painting, giving an art lesson to a young girl, an emblematic American. Undoubtedly, Morse painted the Louvre in the same spirit in which he asked, "Are not the refining influences of the fine arts needed, doubly needed, in our country? Is there not a tendency in the democracy of our country to low and vulgar pleasures and pursuits?"[8]

In attempting to promote art in America by celebrating masterworks of European painting, Morse typified the new nation's troubled embrace of the Old World. He admired European art; he hoped to cultivate appreciation for art in America by displaying European art. Yet he also hated Europe and all that it stood for. Writing from Paris in 1832, Morse railed against Europeans' hauteur:

> We have no aristocratic grades, no titles of nobility . . . and other gewgaws that please the great babies of Europe, are we therefore to take rank below or above them; I say above them, and I hope that every American who comes abroad will feel that he is bound for his countries [*sic*] sake to take that stand. . . . By what law are we bound to consider ourselves inferior, because we have stamped folly upon the artificial and unjust grades of European systems, upon these antiquated remnants of feudal barbarisms?

Answering the accusation that his national pride was excessive, Morse wrote, "Our disrespect, or what they call National vanity, is a virtue, for it is the maintenance of our sound political and religious principles and these principles we must fearlessly and openly support, or be despised."[9]

Morse's "National vanity" was in greater evidence when he was in Europe than after he returned to the United States in late 1832, when he quickly became disgusted by American philistinism. Morse had conceived of the *Louvre* as a nationalistic project, advancing the cause of art in America, and he had also hoped it would secure his financial future and free him from the vulgar pursuit of portrait painting. Yet perhaps predictably, when the *Louvre* was exhibited in New York, few Americans were willing to pay to see it. Two months after the opening, Morse's brother

Samuel F. B. Morse, Gallery of the Louvre, *1831–33.* (Daniel J. Terra Collection. Courtesy of the Terra Foundation for the Arts, Chicago.)

Richard reported that "the receipts from the *Louvre* are not yet quite sufficient to pay the balance of the rent—$80." The painting had no popular appeal whatsoever; as William Dunlap aptly put it, "it was caviar to the multitude."[10]

Failing exhibit receipts, Morse had hoped to sell the *Louvre* for upwards of twenty-five hundred dollars. In the back left of the painting itself, he had placed his close friend the novelist James Fenimore Cooper, along with his family, whom Morse expected ultimately to purchase the work. In the end Cooper declined, and Morse sold the *Louvre* for a humbling twelve hundred dollars, telling its buyer, "I have lately changed my plans with relation to this picture and to art generally, and consequently I am able to dispose of it at a much less price. I have need of funds to prosecute my new plans." Although he continued to paint sporadically, the *Louvre* was Samuel Finley Breese Morse's swan song to American art. As he confided to Cooper in 1833, "I have been told several times since my return that I was born 100 years too soon for the arts in our country."[11] After the debacle with the *Louvre,* Morse turned his attention more fully to his "new plans."

Those new plans were hatched on his voyage home from Europe in 1832, when Morse, carrying with him the unfinished *Louvre,* casually conversed with other ship's passengers over dinner on the question of electromagnetism. In his sketchbook, Morse drew plans for an electromagnetic telegraph and a coded system of dots and dashes by which it could be used to communicate at a distance.

Morse had long thought of himself as a moonlighting inventor; in 1817 he and his brother Sidney had patented a flexible piston pump for fire engines, and in 1823, the year he painted Noah Webster's portrait, Morse had tried, and failed, to secure a patent for a marble-cutting machine to be used to copy sculptures. Neither of these had brought commercial success. But on that ship's voyage in 1832, Morse came to believe that perfecting the telegraph would bring him the financial support for his art that had so long eluded him.

Trop étendue pour Former une République

In his 1828 dictionary Noah Webster noted that the telegraph had been "invented by the French about the year 1793 or 1794."[12] The age of the modern telegraph did indeed begin during the French Revolution, when, in 1793, the new government's zeal for control of the republic led the National Convention to commission a study of an apparatus designed by the physicist Claude Chappe. Chappe had invented a mechanical or line-of-sight telegraph. A rotating bar with two rotating arms that could pivot from a stationary post was placed on a tower. Different angles of the bar and arms, which could be read through a telescope placed at a tower miles away, communicated different letters of the alphabet.

After studying Chappe's apparatus, the scientist Jacques Lakanal, in his report to the National Convention in July 1793, concluded, "What a brilliant destiny the arts and sciences reserve for a Republic which, by its immense population and the genius of its inhabitants, is called to become the teacher of Europe!" The telegraph, for Lakanal, as for Chappe, was a means of holding the fragile republic together. Answering Montesquieu's prediction that a large republic is doomed, Chappe wrote Lakanal, "The establishment of the telegraph is, in effect, the best response to critics who believe that France is too large to form a republic. The telegraph annihilates distance and in some ways brings together a vast population at a single point."[13] (William Thornton employed this same argument in his proposal for his unified Columbia in 1800, claiming that distance between its capital in Darién, on the Isthmus of Panama, and the outlying parts of North and South America would be irrelevant: "Telegraphs, when perfected, will convey, from the remotest bounds of this vast Empire, any communication to the supreme government in twenty-four hours.")[14]

Convinced by Lakanal's arguments, the National Convention commissioned the building of the first optical telegraph line between Paris and Lille, a distance of about 130 miles. When Napoleon Bonaparte came to power in 1799, he further extended the growing network, which soon reached Strasbourg, Dunkirk, Boulogne, and Milan and played a pivotal role in France's imperial expansion. Keenly aware of the usefulness of Napoleon's network, other European nations soon adopted Chappe's technology, with a host of variations and improvements (all of them optical and mechanical, rather than electrical). Lord George Murray, an English inventor, substituted six wooden shutters for the rotating bar and arms. The shutters, open or closed in various configurations, communicated both numbers and the letters of the alphabet. By the 1830s a combination of Chappe's, Murray's, and other designs dotted western Europe with nearly a thousand telegraph towers, stretching from Amsterdam to Venice.

However wondrous, this network of optical telegraphs had obvious limitations. The enormous machines were extremely expensive to build and required skilled operators. The towers could not be seen in the dark, during a storm, or even on a foggy day. Since the position of the arms and bars, or the shutters, could be seen by anyone within visual range, it was extremely difficult to send secret messages without the use of cumbersome code books, many of which were leaked to the public or, worse, to the enemy.

In both Europe and America, scientists and hack inventors began working on a new kind of telegraph, one that could send invisible messages as an electrical signal along a length of wire. Such telegraphs relied on electromagnetism, the property of an electric current to create a magnetic field, to indicate the presence of a signal at the end of a wire (which would otherwise be undetectable by visual inspection, in just the same way that if you disconnect a lamp fixture from your ceiling, you have no way of knowing if there's a current in the wire—short of shocking yourself by touching it). In many early electromagnetic telegraphs, the magnetic field caused by the presence of the current was detected by the movement of a compass needle.

In Morse's lifetime, a series of innovations in battery technology, the understanding of electricity and magnetism, and the conductivity of wire made an electromagnetic telegraph more and more possible with each passing year. In the late 1820s the American scientist Joseph Henry made a significant improvement when he employed an electromagnet and a large number of small batteries, rather than one large one, to send a signal over a thousand feet of wire. In England, the physicist Charles Wheatstone used Henry's findings to devise an electromagnetic telegraph that sent a signal over even greater lengths of wire and, at each end, recorded and transmitted messages by directing five needles to point to letters on a diamond-shaped grid. (Since Wheatstone's system allowed the possibility of only twenty combinations—5 needles × 4 points of the grid—he, Franklinesque, dispensed with the letters c, j, q, u, x, and z.)

Then, in 1833, Samuel Finley Breese Morse, returning from Europe on board the *Sully,* carrying the unfinished canvas of the *Gallery of the Louvre,* entered a discussion about electromagnetism with the ships' passengers over dinner.

Imminent Dangers

On board the *Sully,* Morse found himself fascinated by the idea of sending messages along an electromagnetic telegraph. "If the presence of electricity can be made visible in any part of the circuit, I can see no reason why intelligence may not be transmitted instantaneously." After arriving in Boston, he almost immediately set about experimenting with his electromagnetic telegraph and the dot-and-dash numerical cipher he had devised aboard ship. In 1834, when Morse sold the *Louvre* for half the price he had hoped for, he wrote to his buyer that he had "lately changed my plans in relation . . . to my art generally." (Morse still pursued painting. The same year he sold the *Louvre,* he hoped to receive the government's commission to paint one of the four panels of William Thornton's Capitol rotunda. Only in 1837, when the four selected artists were announced, and he was not among them, did Morse abandon painting.)[15]

Between 1832 and 1837 Morse earned a living as an art professor at New York University. Meanwhile, he continued his experiments. Much of his time was spent refining his telegraphic apparatus, whose 1837 prototype he built from a canvas-stretching picture frame, a telling metaphor for his move from painting to inventing.

Morse was also occupied with devising a workable code. On the *Sully*, he had conceived of his telegraphic code as a numerical cipher. The dots and dashes were to correspond only to numbers, and each word in the language would be arbitrarily assigned a particular number (for instance, *dog* might be rendered as 4291, or "⁙ ⁚ ⁙———"). To decode a telegraphic message, a user would need to refer to a special dictionary, a list of words "defined" by their corresponding numbers. This dictionary (on which Morse worked tirelessly) would be top secret because in his original vision, the telegraph would be used only by government operatives for secret communiqués. The dictionary, a document of the highest national importance, would be kept under guarded lock and key.

Why a secret code? Morse never said. But at the time he believed there was a clandestine international conspiracy to overthrow the U.S. government, and surely his original plans for the code have something to do with those fears. Following in the xenophobic footsteps of his father, Jedidiah, Morse believed that a plot that was led ultimately by the pope and by which European monarchs were exporting Catholics to the United States to undermine and eventually destroy American democracy, was under way in the 1830s. In a pamphlet titled *Foreign Conspiracy against the Liberties of the United States* (1834), Morse argued that the Austrian Society of St. Leopold was sending Jesuit missionaries to the United States to bring Americans into papal bondage. "We are asleep," Morse warned, "when every freeman should be awake, and look to his arms." In a second tract, *Imminent Dangers to the Free Institutions of the United States through Foreign Immigration* (1835), Morse advocated the passage of a new naturalization law, whereby "no foreigner who comes into the country after the law is passed shall ever be allowed the right of suffrage."[16]

Today, of course, this all sounds like a pretty crackpot conspiracy theory, but in Morse's day it bordered on a legitimate political sentiment. In an age of expanding immigration, particularly of Irish and German Catholics, Morse became a champion of an emerging American nativist movement, and in 1836 he ran for mayor of New York on an anti-immigration platform. He confessed himself astonished when some of his countrymen disagreed with him. "My situation in regard to those who differ from me is somewhat singular," he wrote in 1835. "I have brought against the

Morse's canvas stretcher telegraph, 1837. (Courtesy of the National Museum of American History.)

absolute government of Europe a charge of conspiracy against the liberties of the U.S. I support the charge by facts, and by reasonings from those facts which produce conviction. . . . But those that dispute simply say I don't think there is a conspiracy, yet give no reasons."[17]

Fortunately Morse lost his bid for the mayor's office, but regrettably, he never really retreated from his views about immigration, much to the dismay of many of his friends (including Cooper). Yet he did alter his ideas about the telegraphic code. Later in life, fighting patent disputes, Morse claimed that he had decided to abandon the numerical cipher as early as 1835, throwing away, as he put it, "the big leaves of the numbered dictionary, which cost me a world of labor." Yet the dictionary, "a complete vocabulary of words alphabetically arranged and regularly numbered, beginning with the letter of the Alphabet, so that each word in the language has its Telegraphic number," appeared in Morse's petition for a caveat to the commissioner of patents in 1837.[18]

When Morse finally did abandon his dictionary, in late 1837 or 1838, he turned instead to what he called a conventional alphabet, whereby the dots and dashes would represent not only numbers but letters as well, a refinement that greatly accelerated transmission. As the *Journal of Commerce* reported in 1838, "Professor Morse has recently improved on his mode of marking by which he can dispense altogether with the tele-

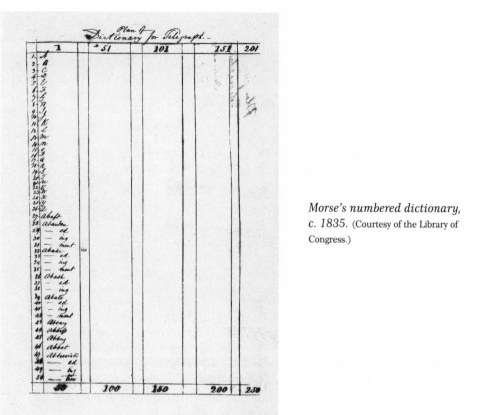

Morse's numbered dictionary, c. 1835. (Courtesy of the Library of Congress.)

graphic dictionary, using letters instead of numbers, and he can transmit ten words per minute, which is more than double the number which can be transmitted by means of the dictionary."[19] No longer to be a secret numerical government cipher, Morse's alphabetic code was to be an open system of communication, easily learned by anyone with the alphabetic key, which was to be made widely available and by which messages could be sent at a much greater speed.

The new code, and the perfected telegraph, were to bring Morse vast wealth and tremendous public acclaim. Riding on the success of his telegraph, he toyed with the idea of returning to his first love, painting, but in 1846 he was again snubbed by the art world when he had another opportunity to paint one of the four panels of the Capitol rotunda since Henry Inman (who had painted Sequoyah and sketched Abd al-Rahman), one of the original four artists, had died. Yet again Morse was passed over. Three years later he wrote to Cooper bitterly, "I could wish that every picture I ever painted was destroyed. I have no wish to be remembered as a painter."[20]

What Hath God Wrought

By 1837 Morse had a working telegraph and an efficient, elegant code. Much as he boasted throughout his life of his "invention" of the telegraph and engaged in endless public debate and litigation to support his claim, it was the code that constituted his major contribution.[21] That code consisted of combinations of dots, dashes, and spaces assigned to each letter of the alphabet, by which telegraph operators could signal any word over a single wire. As the *Richmond* (Virginia) *Inquirer* reported:

> Morse makes an alphabet out of combinations of dots and marks, just as good, when once understood, as if he printed the Roman letter. A dot (.) is his letter E, and represents the same sound; two dots (..) constitute another letter; three another; a dot and a mark (.-) another; and so on through the alphabet. They are learnt as the alphabet is learnt; words are made up with them as the common letters, and a practiced person can read them as he can print.

(Morse had studied quantities of different letter types in a printing shop to determine letter frequency; thus he made *e*, the most common letter in the English language, the simplest in his code.) A poet in the *Chicago Tribune* rhymed in 1847:

> He who created heaven and earth
> Hath kindly unto Morse reveal'd
> What heretofore had been conceal'd.
> A Telegraph he calls its name—
> And with a single vivid flash,
> A dot—a space—a line—a dash—
> Can send around the earth the news,
> Or stop it, just as he may choose.[22]

Morse's alphabetic code, 1837.
(Courtesy of the Library of Congress.)

Morse proceeded to file for an American patent and soon departed for Europe to file for patents there. He acquired the American patent in 1840 and in 1843 convinced Congress to authorize funds to build a test line between Washington and Baltimore. On May 24, 1844, Morse sat at a desk in the sober chamber of the U.S. Supreme Court and prepared to send a message along the newly installed wires connecting Washington and Baltimore. Assembled with him were dozens of onlookers, friends and government officials, many of them deeply skeptical of the project. (During the debate over appropriating thirty thousand dollars to build the forty-mile test line, members of Congress had joked that half the money ought to be set aside for experiments in mesmerism, a science they considered no more plausible than Morse's electromagnetism.)[23]

Morse had asked a young friend, Annie Ellsworth, the daughter of the commissioner of patents, to supply the message he would send, one that he rightly expected would be of tremendous historical importance. Ellsworth chose a passage from the Bible, Numbers 23:23, much to the gratification of the painter turned inventor, the minister's son. Before a hushed crowd, Morse bent over his telegraph machine and carefully keyed the letters *W-H-A-T H-A-T-H G-O-D W-R-O-U-G-H-T*, using his dot-and-dash alphabet. "No words could have been selected more expressive of the disposition of my own mind at that time," he later recalled, "to ascribe all the honor to Him to whom it truly belongs." At the other end of the line, in Baltimore, Morse's colleague Alfred Vail received the message and returned it almost instantly. The age of modern communications had begun.[24]

The telegraph, Morse wrote to Congress two weeks later, "is an engine of power, for good or for evil," which, for the sake of public safety, ought to remain in the hands of the government. Much to his dismay, Congress refused to buy the invention outright, at a cost of one hundred thousand dollars. But the government's loss was the inventor's gain. In 1845 Morse hired Amos Kendall, Andrew Jackson's former postmaster general, as his business agent, and through Kendall's acumen and entrepreneurship in marketing the telegraph to private investors, Morse and Kendall soon became very wealthy men indeed. And the telegraph conquered the continent. By 1860 fifty thousand miles of telegraph wires were stretched across the country, connecting more than fourteen hundred stations, staffed by ten thousand telegraph operators, sending millions of messages in Morse's simple, elegant code.[25]

To many, the size of the country and the speed of the telegraph seemed to be made for each other. With the 1803 Louisiana Purchase (whose 828,000 square miles doubled the size of the country), expansion into the Old Northwest, and the annexation of Mexican territories through the 1848 Treaty of Guadalupe Hidalgo (which added another 522,500 square miles), fears that the nation was too big to be a republic remained alive and well. Morse's invention, like Webster's spelling book, offered a solution: the telegraph annihilated distance. "The greatest revolution of modern times, and indeed of all time, for the amelioration of Society, has been effected by the Magnetic Telegraph," reported the *New York Sun* in 1847. "The transmission of thought by lightning is a triumph of which the ancient world conquerors never dreamed and the annihilation of space by human will is a miracle even in our own age." California might just as well be next door to New York if you could get a message there in just a few minutes. "We are now receiving daily dispatches from Buffalo, Albany, Troy, Boston, Hartford, Philadelphia, Baltimore, Washington, Richmond, Pittsburgh, and Cincinnati," the *Sun* boasted, "to which we shall soon add Charleston, Mobile and New Orleans. Nor will it be long before Louisville, St. Louis, Detroit, Chicago, Milwaukie [sic], Montreal, Quebec, and Halifax are in daily communication with New York." In November 1848 the aptly named *Telegraph* of Poughkeepsie, New York (where Morse made his home), joyfully awaited the first telegraphically transmitted results of a national presidential election: "Before Saturday next, we shall be able to tell how two-thirds of the Union have gone."[26]

To contemporary observers, it seemed that the telegraph could make the country as small as it needed to be to survive as a cohesive nation; it could tie the people together, less like the wispy cobwebs of the Articles of Confederation than like the laces of a tightened corset. As early as 1838 Morse himself had predicted that it would not be long "ere the whole surface of this country would be channelled for those nerves which are to diffuse, with the speed of thought, a knowledge of all that is occurring throughout the land; making, in fact, one neighborhood of the whole country." In 1845 a member of the House Ways and Means Committee declared: "Doubt has been entertained by many patriotic minds how far the rapid, full, and thorough intercommunication of thought and intelligence, so necessary to the people living under a common representative republic, could be expected to take place throughout such immense bounds. That doubt can no longer exist." In 1846 another observer agreed that the telegraph would help glue the sprawling nation together: "The power of the States will be broken up in some degree by this intensity and rapidity of communication, and the Union will be solidified at the expense of the State sovereignties. We shall become more and more one people, thinking more alike, acting more alike, and having one impulse." The telegraph, the *American Telegraph Magazine* reported in the 1850s, "renders us emphatically 'ONE PEOPLE.' "[27] And when telegraph wires finally stretched across the continent in 1861, the first message sent over them embraced the same notion, which by now had become a desperate hope: "May the Union Be Perpetuated."

Civil Wires

In the decades leading up to the Civil War, as Americans were consumed by sectional tensions, the long-standing fear that the Republic could not survive the emergence of factions continued to haunt the nation. In a country so divided by the question of slavery, how could an American character be said to exist? Precious little, it seemed, united the American people.

Fearing the unraveling of the Union, some Americans clung to cherished truths about what bound Americans to one another. "Above all other people we are one," declared Jefferson Davis, future president of the Confederacy, on the eve of the war. "And above all books which have united us in the bond of common language, I place the good old spelling-book of Noah Webster."[28]

But Webster's spelling book, of course, couldn't hold the nation together. (The coming war divided even Webster's family. His only son William's only two sons fought on opposite sides in the war, and both died, leaving Webster with no direct male heirs.) Nor could Morse's telegraph, however valuable to the Republic, save the Union. In the 1850s some pundits even blamed the telegraph's swift transmission of abolitionist rhetoric for the sectional tensions that gave rise to the Civil War. And, as the nation divided, so did the wires. On April 21, 1861, just nine days after Confederate forces fired on Fort Sumter, all telegraph wires connecting Washington to points south were severed. Both sides continued to use the telegraph extensively, but Morse's invention gave the industrialized, and better wired, North an advantage in realizing its war aims, now pursued through the issuance of secretly coded communiqués by telegraph. In February 1862 the federal government finally took control of the telegraph system, as Morse had once hoped it would.[29]

But Morse by then was miserable. An ardent defender of slavery, he had sided with the South. He hated abolitionists (whom he called "conspirators, freedom-shriekers, Bible-spurners, fierce, implacable, headstrong, denunciatory, Constitution and Union haters, noisy, factious"). He despised Lincoln. And he would have been disgusted to learn that the president had drafted the Emancipation Proclamation while sitting at a desk at the Telegraph Office, the place where, other than the White House, Lincoln spent the greatest part of his time.[30]

Morse had dedicated much of his own time in the 1850s to participating actively in a resurgent American nativist movement, led by the new American, or Know-Nothing, party. In 1854 he ran for, and lost, a New York congressional seat and reprinted his *Imminent Dangers* pamphlet. His passion for nativism, however, did little to distract him from his hatred of abolitionism. In 1857 Morse began collecting pamphlets on the subject of slavery, having concluded "that a fearful hallucination, not less absurd than that which beclouded some of the most pious and otherwise intelligent minds of the days of Salem witchcraft, has for a time darkened the moral atmosphere of the North." That hallucination—that slavery was sinful—needed dissipating. "Slavery per se is not a sin," Morse preached. "It is a social condition ordained from the beginning of the world for the wisest purposes, benevolent and disciplinary, by Divine Wisdom."[31]

Ever eager to ferret out a conspiracy, Morse became convinced that abolitionism was a foreign plot. In the 1830s he had argued that the abolitionist movement was a foreign, Catholic conspiracy to ruin the American economy. By the late 1850s he had become convinced that yet another conspiracy now aimed to destroy the Union. "Why are Northerners so blind," he demanded, "as not to recognize the workings of this foreign conspiracy for our destruction, in this fanatical agitation of Abolitionism by British agencies directly in our country?"[32]

Desperate to save the Union, Morse penned a series of essays in 1860 and published them in 1862 as *The Present Attempt to Dissolve the American Union: A British Aristocratic Plot.* Americans, Morse argued, were "the dupes of a long-concocted and skilfully planned intrigue of the British aristocracy," by which the British, by abolishing slavery in all Britain, as well as the British West Indies, deliberately aimed to inspire an American antislavery movement that "would in process of time excite a hostility between the free States and the slave states, would end in a dissolution of the American Union, and the consequent failure of the grand experiment of democratic government; and the ruin of Democracy in America would be the perpetuation of aristocracy in England."[33] So much for the Atlantic cable, which must have seemed, to Morse, just another means by which British aristocrats could import their democracy-destroying views.

Though Morse opposed abolition, he also opposed secession. In the early 1860s, he became president of the proslavery American Society for Promoting National Unity and later of a similar society of so-called Diffusionists. After the attack on Fort Sumter, Morse proposed to serve as "Peacemaker." He determined "to visit personally both sections of the country, the Government at Washington, and the Government of the Confederates at Richmond, to ascertain if there were, by possibility, any means of averting war." Unable to make the journey "from physical inability and age" (he was seventy-one at the time), he sent in his place a representative "who actually visited both Washington and Richmond and conferred with the Presidents and chiefs of each section on the subject." Inasmuch as "his efforts were unsuccessful . . . nothing remained for me," Morse lamented, "but to retire to the quiet of my own study and watch the vicissitudes of the awful storm which I was powerless to avert." In July 1862,

Morse was to write to his old friend and business agent Amos Kendall, "Our country is dead."[34]

Speaking Trumpets

Morse didn't exactly "retire to the quiet" of his study, but he did spend much of the latter half of his life in the domestic sphere. Beginning in the 1850s, the inventor of "universal communication" increasingly sought isolation, and found it, as his conspiracy-fearing politics placed him at odds again and again with prevailing sentiment in the North. Meanwhile, even in his domestic life he created a world of silence.

After the death of his first wife, Lucretia Pickering Walker, in 1825, Morse had lived the life of an itinerant bachelor. In the late 1840s, having secured his long-awaited fame and fortune, Morse turned to his private affairs. In 1847 he purchased a stately house in Poughkeepsie. He then set about looking for a wife, and in the summer of 1848, he found her. Morse had known Sarah Elizabeth Griswold for years before he became reacquainted with her at his son's wedding in June 1848; she was his second cousin, the granddaughter of his uncle. (She was also the first cousin of Morse's son's bride.) At the wedding Morse, who had been enamored of Sarah since she was a teenager, found himself once again "exceedingly struck with her beauty, her artlessness, her amiable deportment." Sarah, then just twenty-six, was less than half Morse's age, fifty-seven. And there was more to her appeal. As Morse explained to his brother Sidney, "her misfortune of not hearing, and her defective speech only excited the more my love & pity for her." Indeed, Sarah's deafness spelled dependence, a quality Morse consciously sought in a wife. As he reminded Sidney, "You used to say, you meant to choose a girl without property but respectably connected & educated, believing that the sentiment of gratitude would add strength and stability to natural affection." By marrying a poor, deaf relative, Morse believed, as he confided to his brother Richard, that he could be "doubly & trebly sure" of "her sincere devoted affection."

He was also confident that her deafness could be conquered. To Richard he wrote that Sarah had "for many years" been "deaf and dumb" but that she had "gradually been recovering both hearing and speech." He told Sidney: "I find no more difficulty in talking with her than with any

Sarah Griswold Morse. (Courtesy of the Harvard College Library.)

other person, and although her articulation is yet defective, I have little doubt that I can with God's help teach her to speak as plain as anyone."[35] In that, it seems, he never succeeded.

Samuel Morse married Sarah Griswold on August 10, 1848, and by all appearances, the two enjoyed a companionable marriage until Morse's death in 1872. Because Morse and his family rarely discussed Sarah Morse's deafness, it's difficult to discover just how deaf she really was and how coherently she spoke. Clearly, she was an avid lip-reader: "the simple movement of the lips seen across the room, without a sound being uttered she understands perfectly," Morse once reported, in a rare revealing moment.[36] Edward Lind Morse, their son, failed even to mention his mother's deafness in his two-volume biography of his father, published in 1914. Yet despite Morse's optimistic pronouncement, there's little evidence that Sarah ever recovered her hearing or speech. Other records demonstrate that her deafness was serious and of a nature not likely to be reversed.

As a girl Sarah had attended the New-York State Institution for the Deaf and Dumb, founded in New York City the same year as Gallaudet's American Asylum. She enrolled in 1833, at the age of twelve (the earliest age at which a student could enroll was ten). The school's records indicate that

Sarah had become deaf at the age of one from a "fall" and that her deafness was "partial," possibly having allowed her to learn some speech in spite of the prelingual onset of her deafness.[37]

Sarah Griswold remained at the New-York Institution for only three years, and the year she left, the school's annual report lamented parents' "frequent practice of withdrawing children from the school before the completion of their regular course of instruction," especially at the end of the third or fourth year. Such early withdrawals were not due to financial hardship; for poor students like Sarah, the state paid all school fees. Instead:

> The opinion is often expressed by the friends of our pupils that two or three years will suffice to give them a respectable, or a sufficient education; which is all they profess to desire. What ideas such persons may have of the amount of education which may properly be called respectable, it would be difficult to determine: but one thing is certain, that the full period of five years, now allotted to the business of instruction in the New-York Institution, is too short to secure, with certainty, even a respectable education to common minds.

Students withdrawn prematurely, the directors regretted, go into the world "with but the very simplest rudiments of language: almost unable to express the most common ideas in words, and totally incapable of deriving pleasure or information from books."[38]

Sarah's parents may have removed her from the school prematurely because they thought that her education was sufficient. They may also have brought her home because they thought that her "partial" hearing was not being cultivated. Students at the New York school were not taught to speak or read lips; instead, they were taught to sign and finger-spell as a means to learn to read and write English. (The school's motto was Vicaria Linguae Manus [The Hand Substitutes for the Tongue], and its icon was a hand making the shape of the letter *A* of the manual alphabet.) "The mode of instruction consists in teaching written language by means of signs," the institution reported the year Sarah was admitted, and articulation had never even been attempted. Beyond basic academic instruction, the only other training the students received was vocational, the boys trained in bookbinding, the girls in sewing and knitting (before her marriage to Morse, Sarah supported herself and her mother by her fine sewing).[39]

By some reckonings, the New-York Institution offered only meager instruction. Laurent Clerc reported in 1827, "I visited their school some years ago. Of systems I saw nothing. Of methods there were hardly any. The signs which they employed were a combination of those used by the Indians, of those they had learned from some of their own pupils, together with what they had gathered from the works of the Abbés de l'Épée and Sicard & those of the English Instructors." What Sarah learned there in three years, and whether she continued her education elsewhere, are difficult to know, yet in later life she could certainly read and write, though probably not with ease. She could also speak, but her speech was "defective," and she was always said to be extremely "shy." During Morse's long sojourns abroad, his wife often declined invitations to state banquets and elegant parties. As Morse's chief biographer put it, "she could hardly enter into conversation in English, much less in French or German."[40]

Morse's wife certainly knew sign language. But as the directors of the New-York Institution admitted, "The signs, which are employed in the instruction of the deaf mute, are of little or no use to him when his education is complete, and when he goes forth into the world."[41] They were probably of little use to Sarah in her relationship with her husband, who, it seems, never learned to sign.

Morse once mentioned sign language in a letter to Sarah. In 1857, while he was in Europe on business related to the laying of the Atlantic cable, he reported to her on French fashion. He was especially amused by "enlarged crinolines," the enormous skirts of fashionable ladies' dresses, which made it difficult even to get near enough to the wearer to carry on an intimate conversation. "Talk no longer of tête-à-têtes; . . . as for conversation, that is out of the question except by speaking trumpets, by signs, and who knows but in this age of telegraphs crinoline may not follow the world's fashion and be a patroness of the Morse system."[42]

That Samuel Morse, inventor of "universal communication," chose a wife whose deafness left her isolated from the hearing world tells us perhaps a good deal about his character and his own deep sense of isolation and alienation. Morse code, devised as a secret cipher at a time when its inventor believed the government had much to fear from foreigners, not only failed to save the Republic, and to isolate it from the rest of the world, but had come to represent the strengthening of global ties. Morse retired, in his final years, to the quiet of his home, where he died in 1872. His long and often bitter life marked the passage of the new nation from the Websterian quest for national independence to a violent struggle for political unity to a wholly new kind of engagement with the wider world made possible, in part, by his telegraph and code.

But Morse's invention also made possible the establishment of the first college for deaf Americans, founded in Washington, D.C., in 1857. Amos Kendall, the business agent who peddled Morse's telegraph, left two acres of land and a great deal of money to what came to be called Gallaudet College, which sits today on Kendall Green.

7

Visible Speech

In July 1864 Alexander Melville Bell exhibited his two teenage sons, Alexander and Melville, before eminent philologists and influential newspaper editors in Edinburgh, Scotland. After welcoming his audience, Bell introduced the boys, then sent them out of the room, "very far beyond the range of earshot." He invited members of the audience to call out words in any of the world's languages. Bell's demanding, skeptical spectators offered some of "the most difficult words" from dozens of languages, including Arabic, Chinese, Sinhalese, Croatian, Danish, Gaelic, Hungarian, Japanese, Polish, Portuguese, Russian, Swedish, and Welsh, as well as random noises, including the "cries of birds and animals." All these Bell transcribed, using his new thirty-four-character alphabet, which, with characteristic flamboyance, he had dubbed Visible Speech, but which, from the audience's perspective, might well have been called Invisible Speech, since Bell, fearing that his alphabet would be stolen, described but did not reveal it. Ushering his sons back into the room, Bell handed them his transcriptions on small scraps of paper, which the boys read aloud and pronounced flawlessly. In every case, the words (and even

Alexander Melville Bell. (Courtesy of
the Library of Congress.)

the bird and animal cries) "were read with the greatest accuracy." P. B.
Reid, professor of Hindustani and Persian at the University of Edinburgh,
tested Aleck and Melly in Hindi, Urdu, and Persian and marveled, "To my
astonishment, the young men sounded them most accurately, and just as
one hears from natives of India," even though, as was made clear, the boys
were entirely ignorant of these languages. It seemed a miracle. "The
search after a universal alphabet has been as eagerly carried on by some as
that of the ancient alchemists after the universal solvent that was to trans-
mute the baser metals into gold," the *Glasgow Herald* rightly reported. "It
would appear, however, that the problem has at last been solved by Mr
A. Melville Bell."[1]

The following month Bell took two of his sons to meet with England's
most famous philologist, Alexander J. Ellis. In London, Ellis tested Aleck,
seventeen, and Ted, at sixteen the youngest boy, with a host of "queer and
purposely-exaggerated pronunciations and mispronunciations, and delicate distinctions," including "Latin pronounced in the Etonian and Italian
fashions, and according to a purposely rather eccentric theoretical fancy;
various provincial and affected English and German utterances . . . [and]
Cockneyisms mixed up with Arabic sounds." Much to Ellis's amazement,
the boys "echoed my very words. Accent, tone, drawl, quantity, all were

reproduced with remarkable fidelity, with an accuracy for which I was totally unprepared." As Ellis reported in the *London Morning Star,* "The problem of a universal alphabet has been for some time recognised as possessing considerable importance linguistically, and even politically, as well as for missionary purposes," yet all existing plans, as well as his own ninety-four-character alphabet for "universal writing" (published in 1856), were at once cumbersome and incomplete. Bell's Visible Speech was neither. "I have made it my business for twenty-one years to study alphabetic systems," Ellis concluded. "I do not know one which could have produced the same results. I do not know one which could have written every sound I used. So far, then, as I am able to judge Mr Bell has solved the problem."[2]

But had he? Had Alexander Melville Bell devised a truly universal alphabet? Does Visible Speech work? To ask the question is to be reminded that all writing systems are technologies: they work or don't work, work badly or work well. But Bell's system, unlike many that had come before it, explicitly took on the trappings of science and technology. Bell called Visible Speech "the Science of Universal Alphabetics" and liked to talk about his "experiments in vocal physiology" and the "mechanical principles of gesture." Noah Webster would never have uttered these words. Webster liked to talk about Cadmus and the Phoenicians, "federal language" and "national character." We might ask whether Webster's reformed orthography "works" or "doesn't work"—does it simplify spelling according to coherent, consistent principles?—but Webster himself worried more about whether his reforms made American spelling distinctive. Webster was a self-professed man of letters; Bell, a self-made man of science.

Because Bell presented Visible Speech as a technology, as an applied science, his system required reproducible results. Hence the repeated experiments, the controlled variables, the boys sent out of the room. Did it work? It seemed to, at least when demonstrated by Bell's gangly adolescent son Aleck. But Aleck, better known by his full name, Alexander Graham Bell, was an unusually gifted student of sound. From his father and grandfather (both elocution professors), Aleck had inherited not only perfect pitch (he was famous for a parlor trick in which he sang a note into a piano so perfectly that the piano played it back for him) but also a passion for the study of voice. As Aleck once warned his father, "People will be apt to say—'It is all very well for your son to produce results, he is, perhaps, exceptionally qualified.' "[3]

Not only was Aleck's participation critical to the success of Melville Bell's early demonstrations, but his role in making speech visible eventually eclipsed his father's. After moving to the United States at the age of twenty-three, Alexander Graham Bell employed the scientific method to invent a technology that took the study of how to record language farther still, almost unrecognizably far, from the world of Noah Webster. "My father invented a symbol," Graham Bell later explained, "and, finally, I invented an apparatus by which the vibrations of speech could be seen, and it turned out to be a telephone."[4]

All Men Are of One Mouth

Alexander Melville Bell wasn't the only man searching for a universal alphabet in the middle decades of the nineteenth century. Following in the footsteps of Sir William Jones, William Thornton, John Pickering, and Constantin Volney, missionaries and philologists in Europe and America had continued collaborating on a universal alphabet in the 1830s and 1840s, and in 1854 the movement gained momentum when a conference of European scholars met in London to discuss the German linguist Max Müller's "Missionary Alphabet." The following year Richard Lepsius, of the University of Berlin, published *Standard Alphabet for Reducing Unwritten Languages and Foreign Graphic Systems to Uniform Orthography in European Letters,* which received the endorsement of both the American Board of Commissioners of Foreign Missions and the English Church Missionary Society. American scholars, too, participated in the search. In 1858 Joseph Henry, the United States' most prominent scientist and founding director of the Smithsonian Institution, discussed "the possibility of establishing a universal alphabet" with members of the Washington Scientific Club and followed developments in Europe with enthusiasm.[5]

Unlike Müller, Lepsius, and most other scholars of universal alphabetics, Alexander Melville Bell was no philologist. Nor was he a missionary. At the time he introduced Visible Speech in 1864, at the age of forty-five, Bell was a professor of elocution whose *Standard Elocutionist,* first published in 1860, was to run to 168 printings in England by 1892 and eventually sold a quarter of a million copies in the United States. (Bell was so well known and widely celebrated that he later served as a source of inspiration for George Bernard Shaw's imperious, fanatical elocution professor, Henry Higgins, in his play *Pygmalion*.)[6]

As Bell saw it, teaching elocution was far better preparation for tackling the problem of a universal alphabet than studying languages. Philologists, he believed, had been "constantly baffled by minute diversities" of speech in the world's languages, with the result that all their efforts to devise a universal alphabet had been flawed. Bell ignored language altogether. "The principle on which I proceeded was, to consider sounds by themselves— not as element of languages at all, but simply as *sounds*."

Bell began his work in 1849 "by mapping out the mouth—as it were, by lines of latitude and longitude," assiduously documenting all the sounds the human voice is capable of uttering. By the early 1860s he had settled on thirty-four sounds, a much smaller number than any philologist had considered possible. Bell's characters were not only small in number but also, as he put it, "self-interpreting." Philologists, "bound by a sort of scholastic red-tape," had confined themselves to refining and elaborating the Roman alphabet, but Bell's thirty-four characters bore no relation to the Roman or any other alphabet or known writing system. Instead, he designed altogether new characters, characters that represented the exact position of the organs of speech—the shape of the mouth, tongue, and palate—necessary to make the corresponding sound.

To get a sense of how Bell's system works, consider the consonants, as they appear in several simple words on the first page of his *Visible Speech Reader for the Nursery and Primary School*, a children's primer that Bell advertised as "requiring no preparatory knowledge of Visible Speech on the part of the Teacher." All of Bell's consonants are variations on a curve, open at one side. Upright, it looks much like a C, and signals the sound of *ch* in the German *ach*, emitted by breath through an open mouth with a lowered, forward tongue. Turned on its side, or upside down, the C-curve signals different sounds, while lines that cut through it, or close it, represent closings of the lips and movements of the uvula and tongue, as in the first character in Bell's rendering of *boy, girl,* and *dog*.

Spelling reforms like Webster's and Franklin's might claim to make speech visible, by ensuring that words are spelled exactly as they are spoken. Bell's work took this claim one step further: his symbols were not abstract characters, like A, B, and C, whose sound values need to be learned. (Indeed, Bell's system did away with the need for "spelling" altogether.) To read Visible Speech, Bell asserted, required only to look at it.

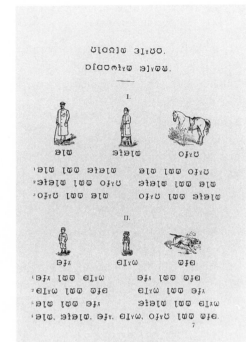

Once he had perfected his system, Bell presented it to the British government. In a letter sent to every member of the queen's cabinet, Bell offered to demonstrate Visible Speech and urged the formation of a Committee of Examiners to investigate it. For the cabinet members, Bell enumerated two "International Results" of his invention (1. "All languages will everywhere be equally legible"; 2. "Telegraphic despatches will be transmissible through any country without translation") and two "Scientific and Other Results" (1. "Philologists will be enabled to compare dialect with dialect, and language with language"; 2. "A Universal Language will be rendered practicable").

Here, as elsewhere, Bell emphasized Visible Speech's scientific disinterestedness and "universal" or international usefulness. He asserted that by ignoring language in favor of studying disembodied sounds, he had ignored race. "All men are of one mouth," he observed; "black men, red men, white men, have the same tongue, lips, palate."

Yet for all its claims to disinterestedness, Bell's system was no less political than any other: he promoted Visible Speech as a technology that would serve the interests of the British Empire. In his letter to the queen's cabinet, Bell boasted that Visible Speech was "calculated to confer impor-

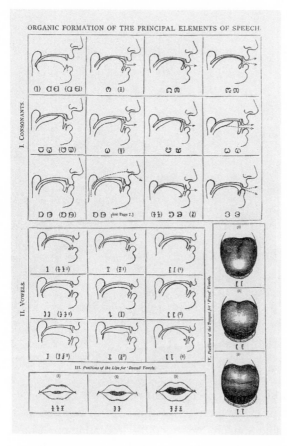

Alexander Melville Bell's Visible Speech. (Courtesy of the Harvard College Library.)

tant benefits on mankind, and, in particular, on the British Nation and Colonies."

Those benefits included improved communication by telegraph. Even before Bell began his public demonstrations in 1864, he had formed "a code of telegraphic signals to represent his characters," whose purpose was soon made clear. Telegraphing in coded Visible Speech, the *Glasgow Herald* reported, "will enable an ordinary English clerk in a telegraph office to transmit messages in Russian, Hindustani, or Chinese, with the same facility with which he would transmit a message in his native tongue." According to the *London Morning Star,* "a telegraph clerk could take down the utterances of a Chinese from his own lips, and, though he knew nothing of the language, could transmit them to be again reproduced in California, or Australia, or London, from the sound symbols, exactly as the sender of the message first uttered them." Visible Speech, that is, would help hold the British Empire together.

In his letter to the queen's cabinet, Bell took great pains to list Visible Speech's anticipated "National Results": within Great Britain, it would reduce or even eradicate illiteracy, homogenize pronunciation, and facilitate the learning of foreign languages. But the "Colonial Results" were more profound still:

I. The language of any Nation or Tribe will be written in characters which all men may read.

II. Those to whom any language is vernacular, will, in a few days, learn to read such language from the Physiological Symbols; and, when this power is acquired, English, or any other words, will be legible without further or special instruction.

III. The national language of Great Britain may thus be speedily diffused over the most remote of her dependencies.

IV. Students for all departments of the National Service—Civil or Military—will be readily trained to *speak* the native languages of India, &c., with vernacular correctness, before leaving the shores of Great Britain.[7]

Melville Bell may have understood that "all men are of one mouth," but he was by no means opposed to imperialism. Instead, he promoted Visible Speech as a tool of empire, one that would allow British bureaucrats and soldiers to function efficiently in faraway lands and ensure the diffusion of the English language around the globe. (Recall that Bell's public demonstrations all involved reading words in the languages of Britain's colonies, from Gaelic to Hindi.) In this sense, Bell's system was exactly the inverse of Noah Webster's: Webster wanted to liberate the United States from its status as a language colony of Britain; Bell wanted to help Britain colonize all the world's languages.

Alas, Bell met with little success. Having failed to convince the British government to purchase his invention, Bell finally published his characters in 1867, with the intention of convincing the public to adopt his system. The following year, in *English Visible Speech for the Million*, he urged its use among all ranks of society, especially among the illiterate. In years to come, he continued to publish Visible Speech charts and primers, devised both a long- and a shorthand version, and, for the rest of his life, promoted his system in public lectures and demonstrations.[8]

And still, Visible Speech failed to achieve popular or even scholarly adoption. Perhaps Bell's closest brush with success came when James Murray, a former student of his and a close friend of Aleck's (the younger Bell served as best man at Murray's wedding), considered using Visible Speech as the phonetic guide in what became the *Oxford English Dictionary.* (In the end, Murray instead chose the Roman alphabet–based characters of what is now called the International Phonetic Alphabet.)[9]

Why did Bell's Visible Speech fail? Didn't it work? Hadn't the finest philologists found it marvelous? Not all of them. In a scathing essay in the *North American Review* in 1868, America's preeminent philologist, William Dwight Whitney, attempted to demonstrate that Bell had not, after all, devised a perfect, universal alphabet: "We are not disposed to concede to Mr. Bell's alphabet any special merit; indeed, we do not see that he has notably advanced in a single particular or scientific comprehension of the processes of utterance." According to Whitney, Bell's system included symbols for sounds a human voice cannot make and lacked symbols for sounds it can. Visible Speech, Whitney remarked, "does violence to nature, both by introducing symbols for unreal acts, and by omitting to symbolize others having a real existence and importance." Whitney complained that no one who had not been taught in person by Bell himself could read Visible Speech. The symbols did not immediately and transparently communicate anything at all; they could communicate only what Bell personally might instruct a student to pronounce. Merely reading his books, even his children's primers, couldn't teach anyone anything. "Mr. Bell places before our eyes . . . a scratch on paper which directs us to approximate the back and front of the tongue together toward the palate to a medium degree, to open the organs behind the configurative aperture, and to apply a rounding effect? Now who in the world . . . is going to give him the sound he expects?"

Whitney faulted Bell most of all for "exaggerating beyond measure the usefulness of his invention" and attacked his "unbounded expectations" for the popular adoption of Visible Speech. "That the new alphabet is going to help all the classes for whom Mr. Bell destines it we do not venture to hope." Whitney suggested instead that Visible Speech was of interest—and then merely as a curiosity—only to phoneticians. "Mr. Bell," Whitney concluded, "will have to learn to be content with addressing chiefly those interested in phonetic science, instead of the great public."[10]

To reach that great public, Bell eventually came to rely on his middle son, Aleck.

Mama!

Alexander Graham Bell was born in Edinburgh in 1847. Even as a young boy he was interested in speech and sound, an interest his father energetically promoted. In the summer of 1862 the elder Bell challenged Aleck and his brother Melly to build a speaking machine, a mechanical device that could make the sounds of the human voice. Together the boys built a gruesome working model out of a skull, wood, and rubber, which so convincingly cried "Mama!" that it worried neighbors. Aleck also managed to teach the family's Skye terrier to "speak" by manipulating its jaw and muzzle to utter "ga-ga" and "ma-ma." "By practice this was made to resemble, in a ludicrous degree, the word 'grandmamma' (pronounced ga-ma-ma)," Bell later recalled, and "The dog became quite fond of his articulation lessons."[11]

Aleck's interest in speech and sound had another source as well. His mother, Eliza Grace Symonds Bell, had been deafened as a young girl. She retained some hearing; she was severely rather than profoundly deaf, and she could read, write, and speak and even play the piano, having learned to listen to the instrument "by resting a piece of solid stick on the sounding board and holding it there with her teeth." Yet Aleck's mother was not unaffected by her deafness; she could not lip-read and could not follow conversation without using a cumbersome ear trumpet. She also often relied on her young son Aleck as an interpreter. She taught him the British two-hand manual alphabet, and he learned to communicate with her, without the ear trumpet, by pressing his lips to her forehead as he spoke.[12]

Passionately interested in deafness, it was Aleck who first realized that Visible Speech might prove to be of use in teaching the deaf to speak. After all, it was designed to communicate how sounds can be produced merely by looking at symbols; using Visible Speech, neither hearing nor knowledge of the language is necessary for pronunciation. Although the elder Bell never pursued this application of his work, Aleck was keen to undertake it. In 1868, when a former student asked Melville Bell to employ Visible Speech in teaching students at a school for deaf children in London, he sent Aleck in his stead.[13]

Meanwhile, the elder Bell continued demonstrating and lecturing on Visible Speech in Scotland, England, Canada, and the United States. And,

after both of Aleck's brothers died of tuberculosis, his parents determined to immigrate to the more healthful environment of Canada and to bring their only surviving son with them. In 1870 they settled in Ontario. The following year, when a school for the deaf in Boston asked the inventor of Visible Speech if he would agree to teach at her school, he again sent Aleck.

By 1871 Alexander Graham Bell, now twenty-four, had become deeply committed to the education of the deaf. In Boston, as in London, when he used Visible Speech to train partially deaf students in articulation, he achieved impressive results. Flushed with enthusiasm at his early suc-cesses, Bell became convinced that training in Visible Speech would allow deaf students, even the congenitally and profoundly deaf, both to speak and to lip-read. By December 1871 he was conducting his own exhibitions of Visible Speech in Boston—with deaf students. In a public examination modeled after his father's early exhibitions in Edinburgh and London, Bell presented a congenitally deaf girl, Theresa Dudley, before "all the influential Educationalists of Boston," reading Visible Speech symbols to pronounce words "in German, French and Zulu," including even Zulu clicks. Bell, like his father before him, then "invited the audience to dic-tate words in *any language*," and "Theresa Dudley did not fail in a solitary instance." She could pronounce the words perfectly, even though she could not possibly hear them.[14]

Aleck's father was gratified that his son had taken up the cause of Visi-ble Speech, and urged only that he devote more of his time to promoting

Alexander Graham Bell, 1875.
(Courtesy of the Library of Congress.)

it among both the deaf and the hearing. In the 1870s the elder Bell, wounded by the dismissal of his work by linguists like William Dwight Whitney, increasingly relied on his son to continue his life's work, instructing Aleck to lecture on Visible Speech, distribute Visible Speech tracts, and publish a Visible Speech journal (the *Visible Speech Pioneer*). All these he dutifully did, but not without considerable resentment. "You have never assisted me to the extent of *one cent* in advancing your system here," Aleck wrote bitterly from Boston. " 'My system,' " Melville retorted, "has been your living."[15]

Meanwhile, and no doubt partly in the pursuit of a better living, Alexander Graham Bell found himself increasingly drawn to the study of telegraphy.

A Dead Man's Ear

The younger Bell seems at first an unlikely telegraph tinkerer. He had little expertise in electricity. "My inexperience in such matters is a great drawback," he admitted. But he took inspiration from the telegraph's inventor. "Morse conquered his electrical difficulties," Bell noted, "although he was only a painter."[16] However inexperienced in electricity, Bell considered himself well qualified to advance telegraph technology because of his extensive knowledge of speech and sound. Indeed, he sought to apply that knowledge to a very particular end. By experimenting with the telegraph, Bell hoped to develop a device that might be of use to his deaf students; he hoped to make speech visible in wholly new ways.

In the spring of 1874 Bell designed a phonautograph. He attached a human cadaver's ear (provided by a Boston ear specialist) to a stalk of hay. He then used a speaking tube to speak into the ear, which vibrated its bones, which in turn vibrated the tip of the haystalk, which traced the vibrations onto smoked glass passing below it. With the phonautograph ("a machine that writes one's speech"), Bell had invented a mechanical form of Visible Speech; the phonautograph's tracings served as a set of characters that exactly recorded sound. "In any future publication concerning Visible Speech," Bell promised his father, "pictures of the vibrations due to each sound could be given, and thus the sounds be identified through all eternity." Bell was most excited about the phonautograph's use in teaching pronunciation to deaf students. "If we can find the definite shape due to each sound—what an assistance in teaching the deaf & dumb!!"

Since the deaf cannot hear sound, articulation instructors had long employed techniques designed to help them to see or feel sound, like holding mirrors before their mouths (to show the breath exhaled when making sounds like *puh*) or placing hands on their throats (to feel the vibrato of sounds like *grr*). Now they might use Bell's phonautograph to see sound. When Bell said, "How do you do?" into the speaking tube, it resulted in a very specific tracing on the smoked glass, after which his deaf student could try to say, "How do you do?" into the speaking tube, and although she could not hear whether she had echoed the sound, she could see if she had duplicated the tracing.[17]

The phonautograph makes speech visible by transmitting it along a haystalk and writing it onto smoked glass. It made Bell wonder if he could transmit speech along a wire to make speech audible over great distances. In the summer of 1874 the insights Bell had gained from the phonautograph and, more, his experiments in multiple or harmonic telegraphy (sending multiple signals along a single wire) led him to conceive of a telephone, an apparatus by which the human voice could be transmitted along telegraph wires. As Bell recalled in later life, "I arrived at the conclusion that if I could make iron vibrate on a dead man's ear, I could make an instrument more delicate which would cause these vibrations to be heard and understood." The telephone, in part, emerged out of Bell's work with Visible Speech and the deaf. As he put it, "the telephone grew

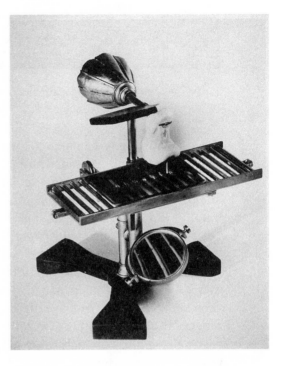

Alexander Graham Bell's phonauto-graph. (Courtesy of the National Geographic Society Image Collection.)

from my experiment to teach the deaf how to understand and to talk so that they could be understood."[18]

Telegraphy and Visible Speech Together

On Friday, March 10, 1876, Alexander Graham Bell communicated by telephone with his assistant, Thomas Watson. Later that day, he wrote to his father to tell him of his "great success": "Articulate speech was transmitted intelligibly this afternoon. I have constructed a new apparatus operated by the human voice. I was in one room at the Transmitting Instrument and Mr. Watson at the Receiving Instrument in another room—out of ear-shot. I called out into the Transmitting Instrument, 'Mr. Watson—come here—I want to see you'—and he came! This is a great day with me," Bell announced, and added, displaying a fine sense of prophecy, "I feel that I have at last struck the solution of a great problem—and the

Tracings from the phonautograph. (Courtesy of the Library of Congress.)

day is coming when telegraph wires will be laid on to houses just like water or gas—and friends converse with each other without leaving home."

And then, in the closing paragraph of the letter, Bell turned to more mundane matters, confirming an arrangement by which his father was to travel to Boston to award the diplomas at the graduation ceremony of Bell's deaf students "upon the last of April . . . as that is the anniversary of the Introduction of Visible Speech into America."[19]

For Bell, Visible Speech, teaching deaf students, and the telephone were inextricably linked, although they often competed for his attention. Even the money that made his experiments possible came from his work with the deaf. After his initial experiments with the phonautograph, the telephone, and the multiple telegraph, Bell's inventions were funded by Gardiner Greene Hubbard, a man he first met in 1872 at the Clarke School for the deaf in Northampton, Massachusetts, where Bell was a visiting instructor. Hubbard, a funder and promoter of improvements in transportation and telegraphy, served as the school's president and had backed its founding in 1867 by exhibiting his deaf ten-year-old daughter Mabel before a committee of Massachusetts legislators.

Born in 1857, Mabel Hubbard had lost all her hearing at the age of five, during a bout of scarlet fever. Her parents, who refused to send her to the American Asylum in Hartford because they did not want her to learn sign language, hired tutors to work with her to retain her speech, and had achieved quite dramatic success. Partly on the basis of Mabel's convincing performance, the legislature issued a charter for the Clarke School, which was to become the American Asylum's chief rival.

In 1873, while Bell served as professor of vocal physiology and elocution at the newly founded Boston University, he accepted Hubbard's daughter as a private pupil. As Bell's student Mabel continued to improve her speech. Her father, impressed with Bell's skills as a teacher, soon became interested in his telegraphic inventions. In February 1875, Hubbard began providing financial backing for Bell's experiments. Five months later Bell confessed his love to Mabel (then seventeen) and, after a frenetic, troubled courtship, became engaged to her in November.[20]

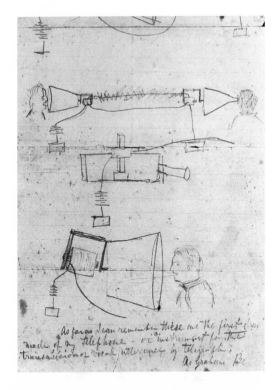

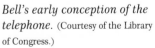

Bell's early conception of the telephone. (Courtesy of the Library of Congress.)

Bell's partnership with Hubbard and his engagement to Mabel put considerable pressure on his work. His own father wished him to spend his time promoting Visible Speech; Mabel and her father wanted him to abandon it. Even as Bell attempted to tutor Mabel in Visible Speech (suggesting, "A more distinct articulation will open the door of many a new friend for you in the future—and bring you closer into communion with all who love you"), both Mabel and Gardiner Hubbard urged him to put aside Visible Speech as an unprofitable distraction from his promising inventions in telegraphy.[21]

But Bell was genuinely committed to his father's invention, and not only out of filial obligation. "I confess that there are many things about 'Visible Speech' that I regret," he admitted to Hubbard in November 1875, "and that I would change were I free to do so—among other things the *name itself* which is distasteful to me—but . . . Whatever the defects of the system may be—I believed in the great practical uses pointed out by my father—and it will be ever one of the main objects of my life—to bring about—by publications and by private teaching—the stupendous reforms aimed at by him." Indeed, it was Bell's plan to use proceeds from the telephone to promote his father's system. "Should I be able to make any

Mabel Hubbard Bell. (Courtesy of the Library of Congress.)

money out of the idea," he wrote to Melville in 1874, "we shall have Visible Speech put before the World."[22]

Pulled in two directions—his electrical experiments in telegraphy and telephony, on the one hand, and his work with Visible Speech and the deaf, on the other—Bell suffered extraordinary stress. He endured migraines, insomnia, and a general malaise that alarmed nearly everyone around him. Matters only worsened after his successful experiment with the telephone in March 1876. Three months later, at Mabel's urging, Bell traveled to Philadelphia to attend the Centennial Exhibition. There the divided Bell displayed two separate exhibits, one on Visible Speech and one on the telephone. His demonstration of the telephone made an extraordinary splash (according to the Centennial Commission's report, "This telephone . . . was considered by the Judges the greatest marvel hitherto achieved by the telegraph"). His Visible Speech exhibit won acclaim as well. "I find that I am to be the recipient of *two* Centennial medals," Bell wrote to Mabel, "one for Visible Speech and the other for the Telephone."[23]

Bell might take pride in his twin successes, but he found little comfort there. Even while in Philadelphia he complained to Mabel, "If I don't make a change and very soon—Telegraphy and Visible Speech together will be the end of me—and then we shall never be married at all." Much to Bell's dismay, however, his fiancée echoed her father's sentiments, and promoted his interests, by continuing to be unenthusiastic about Visible Speech. "What I think of it now," she wrote Bell in July 1876, "is that it will be of the greatest value to learners, deaf or hearing. But I think it will be a very long time before it will come into general use. There may be money in it, but you are not the one to get that money, because you love your work and cannot bear to ask pay for that labor of love. I think of the two you are more likely to make something out of telegraph and if you do you will be the better able to carry out your work."[24]

In July 1876, as Mabel urged Aleck, yet again, to abandon Visible Speech, he tested his telephone apparatus using telegraph wires stretched between Boston and Rye Beach, New Hampshire. The experiment was a great success. And, as Bell told his parents, his deaf fiancée, who would never be able to use a telephone receiver, was the first to send a message: "Mabel's voice has been the first human voice to traverse a real telegraph wire."[25]

Aleck and Mabel married in July 1877, two days after Bell and Gardiner Hubbard, along with Thomas Watson and another investor, had formed the Bell Telephone Company. Yet neither the growing financial success of the telephone nor his marriage to Mabel lessened Bell's commitment to Visible Speech and the education of the deaf. Indeed, as time passed, he became only more interested in the deaf and less interested in the telephone. In 1876 he had written Mabel, "Of one thing I become more sure every day—that my interest in the deaf is to be a lifelong thing with me. . . . I shall never leave this work . . . —your husband will always be known as a 'teacher of deaf-mutes.' " Two years later he had not changed his mind. "Of one thing I am quite determined," he told Mabel, "and that is to waste no more time and money upon the Telephone."[26]

Strictly by Mouth

He kept his word. In the 1880s, withdrawing from active participation in the business of the telephone company, Bell turned his attention to new inventions and "to the object that is nearest my heart": the education of the deaf, which, for him, meant teaching the deaf to speak.[27]

When Bell introduced his telephone, no one had tried to claim that this mere piece of technology could heal the sectional wounds that still plagued the nation in the aftermath of the Civil War. Bell himself, however, was committed to eradicating one kind of nation within the nation, the community of deaf signers. Strongly influenced by Darwin and late-nineteenth-century ideas of racial science, Bell became convinced that deaf Americans who communicated exclusively by sign language risked evolving into a separate race, a development he was determined to halt. For Bell, the secrecy of sign language—the fact that hearing Americans couldn't understand it—undermined American unity. For Bell, unlike all those who had come before him, distinct languages within the United States posed a wholly new kind of risk, one that was biological and heritable.

Early in his career Bell had opposed teaching the deaf to speak at the expense of teaching them to sign. He favored teaching finger spelling as well as sign language as complements to training in articulation and lipreading.[28] During his visit to the Clarke School in 1872, Bell had learned that active suppression of sign language and the manual alphabet had painful consequences for deaf children. He confided to his parents: "It makes my very heart ache to see the difficulties the little children have to contend with on account of the prejudices of their teachers. You know that here all communication is strictly by mouth—even a finger alphabet being excluded. You must know the theoretical difficulties of Lip-reading—and just fancy the little children who have no idea of speech—being dependent on Lip-reading for almost every idea that enters their heads."[29]

The same year Bell visited the American Asylum, where he became a competent signer and came to admire the language's grace, beauty, and expressiveness; invited to speak at the school's commencement, he delivered his address in sign. Yet, at Hartford, Bell became convinced that instruction exclusively in sign language was just as harmful as exclusive oral education. In a letter from Hartford to his parents he told of the death of one of the students. "Nothing can show better how the too great use of signs tend to isolate deaf-mutes and constitute a class apart from hearing people than this boy's case," he wrote. "When he was dying, he did not *want to go home*. His friends, he said, could not *understand* him and he was happier in the Asylum."[30]

In 1873, when Bell began to teach a congenitally deaf six-year-old boy named George Sanders, he employed manual communication only as a first step toward teaching articulation. With "little Georgie," Bell employed a "glove alphabet": he carefully wrote the letters of the alphabet on the

A glove used by Alexander Graham Bell to teach his own variety of finger spelling. (Courtesy of the Library of Congress.)

fingertips, knuckles, and palm of a white glove. "This glove I presented to him one morning as a new plaything," Bell later recalled.

> He put it on his left hand, and then went to the cardrack, as usual, and presented me with the word for some object he desired; we shall suppose the word "doll." I then covered up the word with the exception of the first letter, "d," and directed his attention to the glove. After a little searching he discovered the corresponding letter upon the glove. I then showed him the letter "o" on the card, and he soon found it on the glove: and so with the other letters.

George adored the glove. "For a long time he was very proud of his glove, and was delighted to find that he could communicate with his parents and friends, and they with him, by simply pointing at the letters on his hand." Soon Bell could communicate with his pupil without the glove, by simply touching parts of his ungloved hand. "He did not require to look," Bell reported. "He could *feel* where he was touched. . . . As I had five fingers, I could touch five letters simultaneously, if I so desired, and a little practice enabled me to play upon his hand as one would play upon the keys of a piano, and quite as rapidly." Bell tapped on George's fingers everywhere they went, happily explaining the world to him, as on the day he "took him to Barnum's museum and talked to him all the time the lions were being fed."

But, even as he employed the glove alphabet with young George, Bell attempted to wean him of other kinds of manual communication, pretending to have "difficulty in understanding his gestures": "My pretended difficulty in understanding his signs increased from day to day, so as to force him more and more to attempt to express his thoughts by English words." For Bell, the goal of teaching little George Sanders was to teach him to talk.[31]

As the years passed and especially in the decade following his invention of the telephone, Bell came more and more to oppose instruction exclusively by signs. In 1872 he had insisted that "Visible Speech takes *no part* in the contest between articulation, on the one hand, and signs and manual alphabets on the other."[32] But by the 1880s he was actively promoting Visible Speech and articulation instruction and advocating the suppression of sign language.

In the mid-1880s Bell undertook an extensive survey of methods used to teach the deaf in American schools and was alarmed, though perhaps not surprised, to learn that Visible Speech was little employed. Of the institutions responding to his queries, eighteen had never used Visible Speech, eighteen had once used it but did so no longer, and eighteen were still using it. More alarming still was the lack, in many schools, of any method of speech instruction at all. "The great object of the education of the deaf," he insisted, "is to enable them to communicate readily and easily with hearing persons, or rather to render intercommunication between the deaf and the hearing easy and certain. That is what is meant by 'restoring the deaf to society.' "[33]

Bell's investigation of the hereditary nature of deafness documented an important trend, the increasing likelihood, over the course of the nineteenth century, of deaf Americans marrying one another. "*Of the deaf mutes who marry at the present time,*" he reported, "*not less than 80 per cent. marry deaf-mutes, while of those who married during the early half of the present century the proportion who married deaf-mutes was much smaller.*" Bell was appalled. "We do not find epileptics marrying epileptics, or consumptives knowingly marrying consumptives," but the deaf did tend to marry each other. "In this country *deaf-mutes marry deaf-mutes,*" he wrote, and "If the laws of heredity that are known to hold in the case of animals also apply to man, the intermarriage of congenital deaf-mutes through a number of successive generations should result in the formation of a deaf variety of the human race."[34]

This shocking trend of deaf intermarriage was due, Bell determined, to easily identifiable, and preventable, forces. "The causes that operate to produce attachments between Deaf Mutes of opposite sex are numerous," he asserted in 1884, but "two causes take the lead. They are first: Institution life and secondly: the use of a special language."[35]

Bell had been an early convert to Darwinism, writing to his father in 1873, "I cannot understand the prejudice with which many people view an honest and hard-working investigator like Darwin." Indeed, he was so taken with Darwin that upon the birth of their daughter in 1878, Mabel wrote to Bell's mother, "Alec's next choice of a name for baby is Darwinia."[36]

To prevent the formation of a "deaf variety of the human race" that Darwinianism predicted, Bell decided to campaign for the eradication of residential schools for deaf children and for the suppression of sign language. In this campaign he encountered powerful opponents, most prominently Edward Miner Gallaudet, president of Gallaudet College. The younger Gallaudet, following his father, argued that sign language was natural. Bell disagreed. "The proposition that the sign language is the only language that is natural to congenitally deaf children is like the proposition that the English language is the only language that is natural to hearing children. It is natural only in the same sense that English is natural to an American child. It is the language of the people by whom he is surrounded."[37]

The proper solution, Bell believed, was to surround a deaf child with the language of his countrymen. To place such a child in a residential signing school was to deprive him of his "native tongue" and, in effect, to deny him citizenship. "The deaf-mutes *think* in the gesture language, and English is apt to remain a foreign tongue," Bell observed. Such people are more like foreigners than native-born Americans. "They often write in broken English as a foreigner would speak." They are "cut off from our literature" and from "the political speeches of the day."[38]

Like Thomas Hopkins Gallaudet, Bell understood that sign language is a "foreign language"—foreign, that is, to hearers. Gallaudet had made that point in support of his more general contention that uneducated deaf Americans were "heathens" in need of conversion, just like Cherokee Indians or the natives of the Sandwich Islands. But for Alexander Graham Bell, the foreignness of sign language meant that it ought to be extinguished, just as the languages of immigrants to the United States ought to be abandoned: because foreign languages—foreign peoples—threaten the health of the Republic. As Bell wrote in 1913, "I believe that, in an English speaking country like the United States, the English language, *and the English language alone,* should be used as the means of communication and instruction—at least in schools supported at public expense."[39]

Beyond fearing the genetic formation of a "deaf variety of the human race," Bell also feared the political formation of a deaf commonwealth, like that proposed by the eccentric John J. Flournoy in the 1850s, an episode with which Bell was well acquainted: Flournoy's scheme, "though quite impracticable, brought forward the fact that a number of schemes of somewhat similar character were in the minds of deaf-mutes in different parts of the country," he wrote in 1883. "Since then the subject has not been publicly discussed, to my knowledge; but such a scheme is still favored by individual deaf-mutes, and may therefore be revived in organized shape at any time."[40]

In the 1880s the specter of linguistic separatism still haunted the Republic. Or at least it haunted Alexander Graham Bell. For the rest of his life, he was to spearhead an extraordinarily successful campaign to promote articulation instruction in the United States, a campaign that, tragically, and despite Bell's passionate and genuine commitment to improving the lives of the deaf, dragged deaf Americans into the Dark Ages. Hands tied behind their backs, hundreds of thousands of congenitally and profoundly deaf American children received an exclusively oral education, in which they were expected to learn to lip-read and to articulate speech, even at the cost of denying many of them any language at all.

A Truly American Race

One story about Alexander Melville Bell and his son goes like this. In later years father and son were riding together when Aleck said,

> "Father, the discovery of visible speech was far more important than the discovery of the telephone."
> The old gentleman quietly took his cigar from his mouth and said:
> "Well, Alex, there was not so much money in it."[41]

In moving from Visible Speech to the telephone, Alexander Graham Bell grew rich. He supported Mabel more luxuriously than even Gardiner

Hubbard had, cared for his own father in his old age, and built a mansion on Cape Breton. He founded the National Geographic Society and became a world traveler. And he indulged his interest in heredity, an interest that did not end with the study of the deaf. In the 1880s Bell briefly attempted to breed deaf blue-eyed white cats, and for much of the rest of his life, he brought mutant sheep from all over Nova Scotia in an attempt to breed a multinippled flock.

Meanwhile, Bell became committed to the principles of selective breeding among humans as well, joining the American Breeders Association (later the American Genetic Association) and lending prestige to the growing eugenics movement. Himself a naturalized American citizen, Bell had become alarmed by the tainting of American stock with non-English-speaking immigrants. Eventually the same ideas that led him to discourage deaf men and women from marrying each other led him to become a nativist and a eugenicist. In "Is Race Suicide Possible?," published in 1920, Bell warned, "The birthrate of America is declining; the spirit of avoiding maternity is on the increase; and the immigrant races are increasing at a much greater rate than our own. The only hope for a truly American race lies in the restriction of immigration."[42]

Bell's commitment to eugenics and nativism was vague and half-hearted; as with his opposition to deaf intermarriage, he couldn't bring himself to support legislation to enforce his views. But in this, the final character in a book about language, race, and nation, Bell's turn to nativism seems fitting, even predictable. Bell's father's work embodied the spirit of William Thornton and the philosophical, and later scientific, quest for a universal alphabet. And Melville Bell's plans for using characters to strengthen the British Empire reflect (or, rather, invert) Noah Webster's plans to declare orthographic independence from England. But in his son's hands, Melville Bell's Visible Speech was transformed from a quixotic search for universal communication to a campaign, newly buttressed by evolutionary science, for language uniformity.

Epilogue

Men of Progress

IN'NOVATE, *v.i.* To introduce novelties. . . . It is often dangerous to *innovate*
on the customs of a nation.
—NOAH WEBSTER,
An American Dictionary, 1828

In 1857 Christian Schussele was commissioned to paint *Men of Progress,* a who's who of nineteenth-century inventors. Over the next five years Schussele, a professor at the Pennsylvania Academy of Fine Arts, visited nineteen American innovators; in their parlors, he took their likenesses. Back at his studio in Philadelphia, Schussele sketched his characters onto a four-by-six-foot canvas, posing them as if they had just gathered for a stimulating evening in a well-appointed sitting room at a posh gentlemen's club. At the room's center Schussele placed Samuel Morse, now not the painter but his subject.

Morse and his telegraph dominate Schussele's *Men of Progress.* An aging, dignified, bespectacled Morse reclines in a handsome wood-framed

Christian Schussele, Men of Progress, *1862.* (Courtesy of the National Portrait Gallery.)

leather chair, basking in the attention of his companions. His hand rests
on a draped table behind him. On the table, at the painting's exact center point, and immediately below the room's prominent pillar, sits the
telegraph.

The eighteen other men crowded into Schussele's *Men of Progress* like
gate-crashers at Leonardo da Vinci's *Last Supper* are a curious lot. Many
of them—Charles Goodyear, Samuel Colt, Elias Howe—were prominent
in their day and remain well known today, but others, including coal stove
inventor Jordan Mott, who sits at Morse's table, are rather obscure. (Mott
is the sitting figure wearing glasses, staring directly at Morse.)

This is hardly surprising: it was Mott who had commissioned Schussele
to undertake the work and had provided the artist with a list of those to be
included. No doubt Mott wished both to celebrate the century's most
important living inventors and to count himself among them. Who those
important inventors were he left to his own appraisal. Predictably, he
favored friends over men unknown to him. Widely celebrated inventors
like Morse and Goodyear were obvious choices, but Mott also used the
painting to express his respect for James Bogardus, an inventor of engraving machines, and Joseph Saxton, who devised gauges, hydrometers, and
minting presses.

If Mott's crew is motley, it is also artificial. These nineteen inventors never sat together in the same room. (Indeed, Goodyear, who sits opposite Morse, resting his elbow on the table, had been dead for two years by the time Schussele completed the painting.) Instead of assembling and posing his subjects together, an impossible and, at any rate, unnecessary task, Schussele simply collected their likenesses—their faces—and copied them onto a single large canvas (this perhaps explains why *Men of Progress* is populated by finely rendered heads swimming in a blurry black tuxedo sea).[1] The sense of fraternity and common cause expressed in the painting, in which these sober, well-heeled men gather together under the watchful eye of Benjamin Franklin, is entirely illusory.

Nonetheless, the list of names Jordan Mott handed over to Christian Schussele was by no means wholly idiosyncratic. The nineteen men in Schussele's painting actually share a good deal more than Jordan Mott's esteem: nearly all contributed to American industrialization. Cyrus McCormick invented the reaping machine; Peter Cooper, the steam locomotive; Erastus Bigelow, the power carpet loom; Richard Hoe, the rotary printing press; Howe, the sewing machine.[2] *Men of Progress* presents a very particular vision of progress, one that, just as it celebrates Morse as an inventor rather than as a painter, idolizes Franklin as a scientist rather than as a philosopher, writer, or politician. The "progress" in *Men of Progress* isn't about art or literature or government or religion; it's about technology and commerce. Mott's "progress" is the progress of factories, railroads, and telegraph wires.

A Is for American is a bit like *Men of Progress,* a collection of portraits of men who never met (except for Morse and Webster, who once sat together in Webster's parlor and stared at each other for a good long while). I've gathered their likenesses together in the pages of this book much as Schussele painted his nineteen characters on his broad canvas. Why bring them together?

Noah Webster hoped to strengthen the American nation by codifying American spelling. Inspired by the Enlightenment, William Thornton dreamed of a universal alphabet for all the world's peoples. Hoping to hold his people together, Sequoyah devised a syllabary for the Cherokee language. Thomas Hopkins Gallaudet brought French sign language to the deaf in America and believed it to be humankind's natural, universal language. Abd al-Rahman employed his Arabic literacy to insist that he did *not* belong to the American nation. The universal communication of Samuel Morse's telegraphic code promised to usher in a new age of peace and harmony. And Alexander Graham Bell's telephone grew out of his father's Visible Speech, which Bell used to teach the deaf to speak, hoping to prevent the formation of a "deaf variety of the human race."

Like Mott's inventors, these seven men actually share a great deal. There are small likenesses. Three had deaf wives: Gallaudet and Bell married former students while Morse sought a wife of whose dependence and gratitude he could be certain. All made pilgrimages: Webster, late in life, traveled to Europe to trace the origins of words; Thornton sailed to Tortola to reckon with slavery; Sequoyah walked to Mexico in search of a lost band of Cherokees; Gallaudet trekked across Europe to find out how to teach the deaf; Abd al-Rahman found his way back to Africa; Morse went to London and Paris to learn his art; Bell emigrated from Scotland to the United States.

But the larger likenesses, of course, matter more. Webster, Thornton, Sequoyah, Gallaudet, Abd al-Rahman, Morse, and Bell all struggled with the way alphabets, syllabaries, signs, and codes can be used to build national ties or to break them down. Each of their stories, and the letters and other characters with which they communicated, trace the tension in the United States between nationalism, often fueled by nativist prejudices, and universalism, inspired by both evangelism and the Enlightenment.

From Webster's reformed spelling to Bell's Visible Speech, all the schemes in *A Is for American* bear on this tension. "All men are of one mouth," Alexander Melville Bell observed. But how they write down what they have to say matters a great deal. It can tie them to the nation, or it can remind them of their universal humanity.

Told together in these pages, the stories of Webster, Thornton, Sequoyah, Gallaudet, Abd al-Rahman, Morse, and Bell also illuminate a curious paradox: American nationalism has universalist origins. The United States was founded on what the Enlightenment claimed to be "self-evident truths" and "natural laws." Yet the founders employed these "universal" truths and rights to declare independence as a nation. How can a nation be established on universal principles? If "all men are created equal," how can Americans claim to be any different from anyone else? Such a nation must always be in danger of losing its nationness, of becoming part of something bigger than itself (as William Thornton hoped it might when he proposed his constitution for a united Western Hemisphere).

In the century following the nation's founding, Americans from Jedidiah to Samuel Morse answered this challenge with passionate, persistent nativism. All men are created equal, but only if they're born here and if they speak the language. Desperate to hold the nation together by strengthening its borders, Webster, Morse, and Bell all advocated restrictions on immigration. They sought to remedy the frailty of American nationalism with bracing legislation. Meanwhile, the American people's long-standing passion for evangelical Christianity, which seems at first so opposed to the principles of the Enlightenment, came with its own universalist implications. Millennialist campaigns to bring the "universal truth" of the Gospel to the world's "heathens" tended to further fray the nation's edges, as Sequoyah, Gallaudet, and Abd al-Rahman discovered, to their peril or profit.

The seven men of *A Is for American* all wrestled with the tension between nationalism and universalism by experimenting with letters and other characters, but Morse and Bell experimented with machines too, and that explains why we remember them so well today. In Jordan Mott's day, the celebration of progress as technological innovation in the service of economic development was prominent, although not without its critics.[3] Today a related notion of progress prevails, as revealed in *People of Progress,* a 1999 sequel to Schussele's painting. In *People of Progress,* the artist Edward Sorel offers caricatures of the century's most famous innovators, as determined by the editors of the magazines *American Heritage* and *American Heritage of Invention & Technology,* along with "several outside experts." Among the people of progress: Henry Ford, the Wright brothers, Bill Gates, Robert Goddard, and the inventors of television, radio, the Internet, lasers, air conditioning, and integrated circuits. (Thomas Edison occupies Franklin's place.) With the exception of the scientists Jonas Salk, Albert Einstein, and James Watson, and the environmental writer Rachel Carson, nearly all of Sorel's subjects are inventors of transportation, communications, or computer technologies, or entrepreneurs peddling them. Sorel's "progress" is the progress of televisions, microchips, and stock options.

Might the twentieth century's American "people of progress" have included Martin Luther King, Frank Lloyd Wright, Margaret Sanger, Franklin Roosevelt, or Louis Armstrong? *American Heritage*'s editors admitted that they had employed Mott's own "battered" notion of progress in selecting the "people of progress." But they defended their decision by observing that "the role of technological pathbreakers in society has only magnified over a century and a half."[4]

It had magnified during Noah Webster's lifetime as well, which is a good part of why Samuel Morse abandoned painting for inventing and why Morse code became more important than Websterian spelling. The

Edward Sorel, People of Progress, *1999.* (Courtesy of The Cooper Union.)

turn to technology as the most important kind of progress also helps explain why the QWERTY keyboard has a far greater impact on many of us than most of the schemes examined in this book. Beginning with Morse, proposals to reform spelling or universalize the alphabet were gradually replaced by machines to speed communication. (Shorthand systems, many of which were pioneered in the first half of the nineteenth century, were a kind of intermediary.) That the two competed, briefly, is well illustrated by Alexander Graham Bell's dividing his time between Visible Speech and the telephone, but there's no question which won out.

Meanwhile, the idea that languages define nations, a ruling political idea of Noah Webster's time, remains a prevailing, if controversial, political idea of *our* times. In the face of the transnational European union and the globalization of English, the French have tried to preserve their Frenchness by keeping Americanisms from *weekend* to *CD-ROM* out of their lexicon, while other Europeans see English "as a language that might, in the end, bind the continent together."[5] Elsewhere, sprawling postcolonial nations like India and Congo have undertaken massive programs to forge a national identity by establishing a common tongue. In the United States Americans continue to fear ethnic and racial dialects like Spanglish and Ebonics, just as Americans in Webster's day disapproved of any dictionary that might include such un-English words as *possum* and *banjo.* In the wake of Islamic terrorism, Americans have come to view Arabic writing as somehow itself sinister. Language, for many people around the globe, is still politics by other means.

But ideas about letters and other characters are now often mediated, if not dictated by, computer technology. In the last decade, e-mail has spawned an "e-style" orthography, one that combines phonetic spelling, inventive punctuation, absent capitalization, and abundant abbreviation (as in "btw, i'll cu @ mark's fri tho not w/ Geo :)," which translates loosely as "By the way, I'm looking forward to seeing you at Mark's on Friday, although George won't be there").[6] And perhaps the era's most popular new script, the Graffiti® alphabet, aspires to be neither perfect nor universal, but instead "global" and, most of all, profitable.[7]

The Graffiti alphabet was designed by Jeff Hawkins, the inventor of the phenomenally popular computer known as a Palm™ handheld. Hawkins was frustrated with computers' inability to read handwriting, which had posed a long-standing obstacle to keyboardless computers. Instead of training computers to read how people write, as most other designers had done, Hawkins "got the idea to turn it around and get people [to] learn how to write in a way that computers can read."[8]

Nearly all the characters of the Graffiti alphabet require only a single stroke to write. A stroke begins when the stylus touches the computer screen (signaled by the character's "heavy dot," a spray paint–like blob) and ends when the stylus is raised. Single-stroke alphabets, like a predecessor of Graffiti called Unistrokes, eliminate a great deal of the variability of handwriting caused by letters running into one another and are much easier for computers to recognize. (Unistrokes made little effort to mimic the shape of letters in the Roman alphabet, but the Graffiti alphabet does, making it easier for people to learn.) And, because the computer reads each letter as it is written, it is possible to write characters on top of one another on the computer screen, rather than in a line from left to right.[9] But to what end?

The Graffiti alphabet is not a scheme, like Webster's, put forward to bind the nation. Nor is it a philosophical undertaking, like Thornton's planned universal alphabet. Nor did Hawkins attempt to sell it to the government, as did Morse with his code and telegraph and Melville Bell with Visible Speech (although Hawkins has made a pile of money and, if such claims are to be believed, has "created over $50 billion in wealth"). Graffiti is a trademarked alphabet. It was designed as "a commercial product of the Palm Computing Division of USRobotics" (although, in the spirit of the age, USRobotics was subsequently bought by 3COM). Its purpose is neither to help form "national ties" nor to make "all the world more nearly allied." Hawkins has no plans to use the Graffiti script to globalize the Roman alphabet. In fact, users can download "National Graffiti" from the

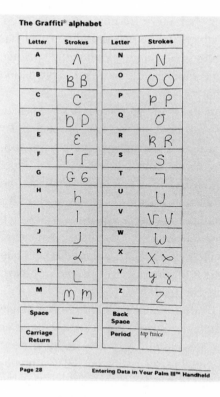

The Graffiti® alphabet

Letter	Strokes	Letter	Strokes
A	Λ	N	N
B	B B	O	O O
C	C	P	P P
D	D P	Q	Q
E	Ɛ	R	R R
F	Γ Γ	S	S
G	G 6	T	⌐
H	h	U	U
I	I	V	V V
J	J	W	W
K	⪦	X	X ⋉
L	L	Y	Y γ
M	m m	Z	Z
Space	—	Back Space	—
Carriage Return	/	Period	*tap twice*

Page 28   Entering Data in Your Palm III™ Handheld

Graffiti alphabet. (Courtesy of Palm, Inc.)

Web (to replace their default Roman alphabet with Russian, Greek, or Ukrainian characters).[10] The purpose of the Graffiti alphabet is not to make spelling simpler, to eradicate dialect, to make Christian converts, to teach the deaf, to build national ties, or to break them down, but to help us communicate better and faster with tiny beeping computers we hold in the palms of our hands.

All this is not to say that the Graffiti alphabet is apolitical. Far from it. Hawkins's innovation was to turn conventional wisdom on its head, to abandon trying to teach computers to read people's handwriting and instead to convince them to "learn how to write in a way that computers can read." His was an innovation of the "digital age," in which communicating with computers is as important as, if not more important than, communicating with people. Graffiti, and the other computer-friendly alphabets that will inevitably replace it, are designed to help speed "the flow of information" along what Bill Gates, in a book with the e-style title *Business @ the Speed of Thought,* calls the digital nervous system: "It's like the human nervous system. The biological nervous system triggers your reflexes so that you can react quickly to danger or need. . . . Companies need to have that same kind of nervous system—the ability to run smoothly and efficiently, to respond quickly to emergencies and opportunities, to quickly get valuable information to the people in the company who need it, the ability to quickly make decisions and interact with customers."

The buzzword of Hawkins's and Gates's world is not *progress* but *innovation,* a term that had decidedly negative connotations in Noah Webster's day, when it usually referred to politics and Federalists frequently complained that the French Revolution perfectly illustrated its perils. In 1794 a friend informed Webster that "the duty of an American Citizen is . . . to . . . reject all novelties and innovations."[11] This notion of innovation as a kind of radical departure from tradition did not die slowly. As late as 1828 Webster could editorialize in his dictionary definition for *innovate:* "It is often dangerous to *innovate on* the customs of a nation."

Today *innovation* carries little connotation of danger. Instead, innovations like the Graffiti alphabet are said to "create wealth." Gates and other digital impresarios claim that this kind of innovation-driven wealth is a global equalizer, a force tending toward universal prosperity. "The Web lifestyle will increasingly equalize opportunities for skilled people around the world," Gates asserts, and will be a harbinger of democracy. Leapfrogging over James Madison, Gates embraces Montesquieu's preference for small republics: "Leadership examples around the world make it clear that much of the innovation is happening in smaller governments— smaller nations and municipalities, counties and provinces, and the state levels of larger nations. Smaller governments, being less fragmented and less complex, can experiment and deploy solutions on a smaller scale."

In this half-real, half-imagined digital world, where innovation thrives in small countries because they are free from faction, there are no citizens, only customers, and no nations, only "small governments" and very large transnational businesses held together by "digital nervous systems." The Graffiti alphabet, with its spray paint blobs and letters written on top of one another on palm-size computers, is the alphabet of the age.

More than a century and a half ago, Samuel Morse, tinkering with his telegraph, quite literally anticipated Bill Gates's "digital nervous system" operating "@ the speed of thought" when he predicted that it would not be long "ere the whole surface of this country would be channelled for those nerves which are to diffuse, with the speed of thought, a knowledge of all that is occurring throughout the land; making, in fact, one neighborhood of the whole country." Morse hoped his speed-of-thought nervous system would unify the nation and "bind man to his fellow-man in such bonds of amity as to put an end to war." Gates wants to make everyone rich. *Busi-*

ness @ the Speed of Thought "was written to inspire you to demand—and get—more from technology, enabling you and your company to respond faster to your customers, adapt to changing business demands, and prosper in the digital economy."[12]

Bill Gates may wish to make "all the world more nearly allied," as William Thornton did, but his globalism is a far cry from the universalism of Thomas Jefferson's "all men are created equal" or Thomas Hopkins Gallaudet's "fellow-men . . . bone of your bone and flesh of your flesh" or even Alexander Melville Bell's "all men are of one mouth." Still, Gates's and Graffiti's globalism has roots in evangelical and Enlightenment universalism as much as in Morse's and Bell's innovations. And it hints at how, in the transformation from a "republic of letters" to a "digital economy," we've replaced characters with numbers.

Abbreviations

MANUSCRIPT COLLECTIONS

AGBP	Alexander Graham Bell Papers, Library of Congress
GP	Gallaudet Papers, Library of Congress
LCP	Laurent Clerc Papers, Yale University
NWP	Noah Webster Papers, New York Public Library
SMP	Samuel Morse Papers, Library of Congress
WTP	William Thornton Papers, Library of Congress

PRINTED MATTER

AADD	*American Annals of the Deaf and Dumb*
AMAA	Allan D. Austin, ed. *African Muslims in Antebellum America: A Sourcebook.* New York: Garland, 1984.
ANW	Richard M. Rollins, ed. *The Autobiographies of Noah Webster from the Letters and Essays, Memoir, and Diary.* Columbia: University of South Carolina Press, 1989.
BWNW	Emily Ellsworth Ford Skeel, compiler; Edwin H. Carpenter, Jr., ed. *A Bibliography of the Writings of Noah Webster.* New York: New York Public Library, 1958.
LJP	Mary Orne Pickering. *Life of John Pickering.* Boston, 1887.
LNW	Harry Warfel, ed. *Letters of Noah Webster.* New York: Library Publishers, 1953.
NLNW	Emily Ellsworth Fowler Ford, compiler; Emily Ellsworth Ford Skeel, ed. *Notes on the Life of Noah Webster.* New York: Burt Franklin, 1971. 2 volumes.
PBF	William B. Willcox, ed. *Papers of Benjamin Franklin.* New Haven, Conn.: Yale University Press, 1972.

PWT	C. M. Harris, ed. *Papers of William Thornton,* Volume 1, *1781–1802.* Charlottesville: University Press of Virginia, 1995.
SMLJ	Edward Lind Morse, ed. *Samuel F. B. Morse, His Letters and Journals.* Boston: Houghton Mifflin, 1914. 2 volumes.

PEOPLE

AGB	Alexander Graham Bell
AMB	Alexander Melville Bell
AR	Abd al-Rahman Ibrahima
BF	Benjamin Franklin
CV	Constantin Volney
GW	George Washington
JP	John Pickering
NW	Noah Webster
SM	Samuel Morse
TJ	Thomas Jefferson
THG	Thomas Hopkins Gallaudet
WT	William Thornton

Notes

PROLOGUE: A LIKENESS

1. NW, *Dissertations on the English Language* (Boston, 1789), 179.
2. Jeremy Belknap to Ebenezer Hazard, September 14, 1790, *NLNW*, 1:297. NW to Timothy Pickering, May 25, 1786, *LNW*, 52. "Essay on American Language and Literature," *North American Review* 1 (September 1815): 309.
3. Thomas Dawes to NW, August 14, 1806, *NLNW*, 2:9. Emphasis in original. On sales, see Harry R. Warfel, *Noah Webster: Schoolmaster to America* (New York: Macmillan, 1936), 71; Horace E. Scudder, *Noah Webster* (Boston: Houghton Mifflin, 1881), 71; and E. Jennifer Monaghan, *A Common Heritage: Noah Webster's Blue-Back Speller* (Hamden, Conn.: Archon Books, 1983), 11–12, 31, 51–54, 57, 71–72.
4. *Connecticut Journal,* June 4, 1800. *Boston Palladium,* October 2 and November 6, 1801. *Gazette of the United States,* June 12, 1800.
5. Quoted in Warfel, *Noah Webster,* 68. A miniature of Webster had been made in 1788 (William Verstille, *Noah Webster,* 1788, Litchfield Historical Society, Litchfield, Connecticut) and a pastel portrait not long after (James Sharples, *Noah Webster,* c. 1793–1801, Metropolitan Museum of Art), but both were now outdated.
6. Samuel F. Jarvis to SM, January 29, 1816, SMP, box 4.
7. *Diary of William Dunlap (1766–1839),* New-York Historical Society Collections (New York: Benjamin Bloom, 1930), 1:21–22.
8. Rebecca, on seeing another of Morse's portraits, wrote to her husband, "I wish you could see the portrait of Dr Smith just completed—if possible, it exceeds yours, as Dr Smith's features & attitude are more strongly mark d than yours—the likeness appears more striking." But Rebecca's effusive praise of Morse's portrait of Dr. Smith ("I certainly never saw anything more perfect") only little diminishes her admiration for his portrait of her husband. Rebecca Webster to NW and William Webster, February 10, 1825, *NLNW,* 2:282. Rebecca Webster to NW, March 10, 1825, *NLNW,* 2:285. *NLNW,* 2:198.

9. SM, *Imminent Dangers to the Free Institutions of the United States through Foreign Immigration* (New York, 1835), 28.

10. *SMLJ*, 2:61–68.

11. Quoted in Daniel J. Czitrom, *Media and the American Mind: From Morse to McLuhan* (Chapel Hill: University of North Carolina Press, 1982), 11–12, and in Annteresa Lubrano, *The Telegraph: How Technology Innovation Caused Social Change* (New York: Garland, 1997), 152. J. Cutler Andrews, "The Southern Telegraph Company, 1861–65: A Chapter in the History of Wartime Communication," *Journal of Southern History* 30 (1964): 319. SM to Norvin Green, July 1855, in *SMLJ*, 2:345.

12. NW to Joseph Priestley, January 20, 1800, *LNW*, 214–15.

1. AN AMERICAN LANGUAGE

1. Webster wrote the official description of the procession, which appeared in the *New York Packet,* August 5, 1788, pp. 3a and b. He also noted the procession in his diary, *ANW,* 257, and placed the announcement of the society's formation in *American Magazine* (April 1788), 347. On the procession, see Sarah H. J. Simpson, "The Federal Procession in the City of New York," *New-York Historical Society Quarterly Bulletin* 9 (July 1925): 39–57.

2. *New York Packet,* August 5, 1788, pp. 3a and b. On the New York Philological Society, see Allen Walker Read, "The Philological Society of New York, 1788," *American Speech* 9 (1934): 131–36.

3. Isidore translated and quoted by Hans Aarsleff in *From Locke to Saussure: Essays on the Study of Language and Intellectual History* (Minneapolis: University of Minnesota Press, 1982), 99, n. 39. On nations as "imagined communities," see Benedict Anderson, *Imagined Communities: Reflections on the Origin and Spread of Nationalism* (London: Verso, 1983). Suzanne Romaine, *Language in Society: An Introduction to Sociolinguistics* (Oxford: Oxford University Press, 1994), 33–34.

4. Paul de Bourgoing, *Les Guerres d'idiome et de nationalité* (Paris, 1849), quoted in Frances Bowen, "Article X," *North American Review* 70 (1850): 478.

5. Anderson, *Imagined Communities,* 47–48.

6. Sylvius, *American Museum* 2 (August 1787): 118. NW, *Dissertations on the English Language* (Boston, 1789), 179.

7. NW, *Sketches of American Policy* (Hartford, Conn.: Hudson and Goodwin, 1785), 30–48. Biographies of Webster include: Chauncey A. Goodrich, "Life and Writings of Noah Webster . . . ," *American Magazine* (1848): 5–32; [William Chauncey Fowler], "Memoir," in *A Dictionary of the English Language,* rev. ed. (New York: Huntington and Savage, 1845); Horace E. Scudder, *Noah Webster* (Boston: Houghton Mifflin, 1881); John S. Morgan, *Noah Webster* (New York: Mason Charter, 1975); Richard Rollins, *The Long Journey of Noah Webster* (Philadelphia: University of Pennsylvania Press, 1980); Richard Moss, *Noah Webster* (Boston: Twayne Publishers, 1984); and a fascinating essay on Webster in Joseph Ellis, *After the Revolution: Profiles in Early American Culture* (New York: Norton, 1979). One of Webster's earliest biographers once wrote that Webster "liked to think he had a hand in pretty much every important measure in the political and literary history of the country" (Scudder, *Noah Webster,* 6). His claim about the Constitution first appeared in NW, "To the Public" in the *New York Herald* in 1796 (*Herald,* New York, July 20, 1796; reprinted in *LNW,* 139). See also NW

to James Kent, October 20, 1804, *ANW,* 90–93; *ANW,* 142; NW to Jedidiah Morse, May 15, 1797, *LNW,* 148; NW to James Madison, August 20, 1804; and James Madison to NW, October 12, 1804, in NW, *A Collection of Papers on Political, Literary, and Moral Subjects* (New York, 1843), 168–70.

8. GW to Benjamin Harrison, January 18, 1784, George Washington Papers, Library of Congress.

9. NW, *Sketches,* 32, 31, 33.

10. Pelatiah Webster, *A Dissertation on the Political Union and Constitution of the Thirteen United States of North America* (1784).

11. NW, *Sketches,* 30, 44–48.

12. NW, *Grammatical Institute of the English Language,* Part I (Hartford, Conn., 1783), 14. Timothy Pickering to Mrs. Pickering, October 31, 1783, *NLNW,* 1:96–97.

13. Marquis de Chastellux, *Voyages . . . dans l'Amérique* (1787; Paris, 1791, 2d ed.), 2:203. E. H. Barker to NW, June 27, 1831, *NLNW,* 308. Herbert Croft, *A Letter from Germany to the Princess Royal of England; on the English and German Languages* (Hamburg, 1797), 8n. Dennis E. Baron, *Grammar and Good Taste: Reforming the American Language* (New Haven, Conn.: Yale University Press, 1982), 12–13. *Quarterly Review* [London] 10 (1814): 528. Charles Jared Ingersoll, *Remarks on the Review of Inchiquin's Letters* (Boston, 1815), 138–39, emphasis in original.

14. NW, *Dissertations,* 22–23.

15. NW, *Grammatical Institute,* 5–7; NW, *Dissertations,* 19–20.

16. Peter Rickard, *A History of the French Language* (London: Hutchinson University Library, 1974), 98, 108.

17. NW, *Grammatical Institute,* 6.

18. *ANW,* 246. Catherine Drinker Bowen, *Miracle at Philadelphia: The Story of the Constitutional Convention, May to September 1787* (Boston: Little, Brown, 1966), 255.

19. *ANW,* 246–47, 148–49.

20. Jonathan Elliot, *The Debates in the Several State Conventions on the Adoption of the Federal Constitution as Recommended by the General Convention at Philadelphia in 1787* (Philadelphia, 1863), 2:301. Gordon S. Wood, *The Creation of the American Republic, 1776–1787* (Chapel Hill: University of North Carolina Press, 1969), 469.

21. James Madison, Alexander Hamilton, and John Jay, *The Federalist Papers,* ed. Isaac Kramnick (New York: Penguin, 1987), 123–24, 126–27. For the best discussion of this period, see Wood, *The Creation of the American Republic,* especially 499–506.

22. Madison et al., *Federalist Papers,* 91. Emphasis mine.

23. Thomas Paine, "The Rights of Man [1790]," in *The Complete Writings of Thomas Paine,* ed. Philip S. Foner (New York: Citadel Press, 1969), 1:360. Emphasis mine.

24. Don Dodd, *Historical Statistics of the States of the United States: Two Centuries of the Census, 1790–1990* (Westport, Conn.: Greenwood Press, 1993). Marc Shell, "Babel in America; or, the Politics of Language Diversity in the United States," *Critical Inquiry* 20 (Autumn 1993): 105. James Schouler, *Americans of 1776* (New York, 1906), 308. Colin Calloway, *The American Revolution in Indian Country: Crisis and Diversity in Native American Communities* (Cambridge, England: Cambridge University Press, 1995), 3.

25. Peter Kolchin, *American Slavery, 1619–1877* (New York: Hill & Wang, 1993), 241–42. Hugh Jones, *The Present State of Virginia* (London, 1724; rep. 1865), 43.

26. The 1990 census can be found at www.census.gov.

27. Allen Walker Read, "Bilingualism in the Middle Colonies, 1725–1775," *American Speech* 12 (1937): 93–99.

28. Benjamin Franklin, "Observations concerning the Increase of Mankind and the Peopling of Countries," in *The Complete Works of Benjamin Franklin,* ed. John Bigelow (New York, 1887), 2:233–34. "Mixed Languages and Dialects," *Niles' Weekly Register,* June 30, 1821.

29. Shirley Brice Heath, "Why No Official Tongue," *Language Loyalties: A Source Book on the Official English Controversy,* ed. James Crawford (Chicago: University of Chicago Press, 1992), 23. German editions of the Constitution: *De Constitutie, Eenpariglyk* (Albany, N.Y., 1788); *Die Constitution* (Albany, N.Y., 1788); *Verfahren der Vereinigten Convention* (Frederick Town, Pa., 1787); *Verfahren der Vereinigten Convention* (Germantown, Pa., 1787?). Richard Sill to NW, April 7, 1786, *NLNW,* 1:113.

30. NW, *Dissertations,* 21. Emphasis in original.

31. This and all subsequent details and quotations about Webster's tour come from his diary entries for May 2, 1785–July 1, 1786 (*ANW,* 211–29). Webster's lecture series was clearly aimed as a means to sell his books (see NW to Hudson and Goodwin, April 3, 1786, NWP, box 1).

32. Franklin had actually given Webster "permission to use a Room in the University for lecturing" (*ANW,* 224). Franklin's *Scheme* is reprinted in Albert Henry Smith, *The Writings of Benjamin Franklin* (New York: Macmillan, 1906), 5:169–77, and is hereafter cited as Franklin, *Scheme.* Franklin had published his scheme in his *Political, Miscellaneous, and Philosophical Pieces* in London in 1779. That Franklin showed a copy to NW is reported in Timothy Pickering to John Gardner, July 4, 1786, *NLNW,* 1:104.

33. Webster further believed that writing *favour* as *favor* was inaccurate. "Thus they write the words *favour, honour,* &C. without *u.* But it happens unluckily that, in these words, they have dropped the wrong letter—they have omitted the letter that is sounded and retained one that is silent" (NW, *Grammatical Institute,* I:11–12).

34. NW to BF, May 24, 1786, *LNW,* 49–50. In March, Webster wrote to Washington, "Dr Franklin has extended my views to a very simple plan of reducing the language to perfect regularity" (NW to GW, March 31, 1786, *NLNW,* 1:110). Webster found Franklin persuasive elsewhere as well. When he published his *Dissertations* in 1789, he dedicated them to Franklin, praising his eloquence: "His pen follows his thoughts, and consequently leads the reader, without study, into the same train of thinking" (NW, *Dissertations,* dedication).

35. NW to BF, May 24, 1786. Unfortunately, the "rough draft" of a new alphabet Webster submitted to Franklin "for adoption, amendment, or rejection" in May 1786 has not survived. Nor have any copies. Webster complained that putting a new alphabet down on paper was painstaking labor, "particularly for me, who am no penman and cannot form the characters exactly as I wish." He sent one copy to Ramsay and no doubt kept one for himself, but both have disappeared, and perhaps to spare himself a tiresome task, he apparently made no more (Timothy Pickering to John Gardner, July 4, 1786). When Webster wrote to Timothy Pickering about the plan, he failed to enclose a copy, urging him instead to visit Franklin to examine his. All that survives is the essay Webster eventually published in 1789, as an appendix to his *Dissertations on the English Language.* Very probably the 1789 essay differs considerably from the rough draft Webster submitted to Franklin in 1786 and from the lecture he delivered in 1787.

36. NW to Timothy Pickering, May 24, 1786, *LNW,* 51–52. Franklin, in his *Scheme,* boasted that his new alphabet had "no letter that is not sounded; and . . . that there be no distinct sounds in the language *without letters* to express them" (BF, *Scheme,* 173; emphasis in original). Webster's "Essay" lamented that in English, "the same letters [are] often representing different sounds, and the same sounds often expressed by different letters" (NW, *Dissertations,* 391).

37. George Bernard Shaw, *On Language* (New York: Philosophical Library, 1963), xvii.

38. On the state of English linguistic inquiry in the eighteenth century, see Hans Aarsleff, *The Study of Language in England, 1780–1860* (Princeton, N.J.: Princeton University Press, 1967). Webster cited several earlier proposals in a footnote to his *Dissertations* (394): Sir Thomas Smith's *De recta et emendata linguae anglicae scriiptone* (1568), Alexander Gill's *Logonomia anglica* (London, 1621), Charles Butler's *English Grammar* (Oxford, 1633), and James Elphinston's *Inglish Speech and Spellin* (London, 1787). Webster borrowed several of these books from Franklin, as well as John Horne Tooke's 1786 *Diversions of Purley* (which members of the New York Philological Society carried as a prop in the Federal Procession in 1788). While Webster was in Philadelphia, Franklin gave him "free access to his library" (*ANW,* 37; see also Julie Tetel Andresen, *Linguistics in America, 1769–1924: A Critical History* [New York: Routledge, 1990], 26).

39. BF to Mary Stevenson, July 20, 1768, *PBF,* 15:178.

40. Following in the tradition of BF, the American spelling reformer Thomas Embree declared in 1813 that an English speaker must "trust to his memory, like the Chinese, whose alphabet contains thousands of characters." Embree believed that the Roman alphabet required 273 combinations of letters to make all the "sounds" in the English language; he suggested an alphabet that could do it in 13 (Thomas Embree, *Orthography Corrected* [Philadelphia, 1813], 17, iv). Joseph Neef, in his 1808 American spelling reform proposal, writing in the voice of a fictional Cadmus, attacked Webster's modest spelling reform as he chided an American schoolmaster, "You pity the Chinese, you laugh at the truly laughable absurdity of their writing system. But first look at your own writing system. Is not the knowledge of which I am speaking, an exclusive appendage among your literati, as well as in China; nay, even your learned people do not themselves agree about the matter; since they gravely but very ridiculously dispute, whether honour, favour, liar, should not rather be spelled honor, favor, lyar; and so forth" (Neef, *Sketch of a Plan and Method of Education* [Philadelphia, 1808], 34). For nationalist reformers like Ewing, the Chinese language, paradoxically, had its virtues too. Even as Franklin and others loathed and disdained the Chinese language as cumbersome, chaotic, and ultimately meaningless, many Americans nonetheless admired the fixity and closed nature of the Chinese written language. By refusing to change their script, the Chinese had managed to conserve the language itself, to halt the creep of local dialects and to block foreign imports. A writer in *Parterre* said in 1816: "The Chinese adopt no customs or improvements from other nations: and their language contains no words derived from a foreign source. Hence their dialect is unadulterated; but who would weight so frivolous an advantage against their ignorance so gross, so long continued, and so deeply rooted? Yet their example may so far supply us with a motive for imitation as to keep our language from being deformed by the affected use of foreign terms in their primitive state and attire" ("On Language," *Parterre,* December 28, 1816).

41. BF, *Scheme,* 170–73.

42. NW, *Dissertations*, 394–96. Webster's reformed spelling looks very much like that of James Elphinston, whose 1787 treatise *Inglish Speech and Spellin* (a copy of which Webster borrowed from Franklin) attempted to fix "Inglish Speech in Inglish Orthoggraphy to secure dhe unfading luster ov Truith" (Elphinston, *Inglish Speech*). On NW's borrowing Elphinston from BF, see NW to BF, undated, *NLNW*, 2:454.

43. BF to NW, June 18, 1786, *NLNW*, 2:457. Webster wrote, "He thinks himself too old to pursue the plan; but has honored me with the offer of the manuscript and types, and expressed a strong desire that I should undertake the task" (*Dissertations*, 407). Franklin's "dictionary" may have really only been a short word list (see editor's note in *PBF*, 15:173–74). Webster's plan would not require Franklin's special types, since Webster preferred placing accent marks over existing letters to the invention of new letters. "If any objection can be made to his scheme," Webster wrote of Franklin's proposal, "it is the substitution of *new* characters, for *th, sh, ng,* &c." For these, Webster proposed instead "a small stroke, connecting the letters . . . as these combinations would thus become single letters, with precise definite sounds and suitable names" (NW, *Dissertations*, 406).

44. Although Franklin's spelling scheme was not nationalistic, Christopher Looby argues persuasively that it did have a political purpose: "the occultation of class" ("Phonetics and Politics: Franklin's Alphabet as a Political Design," *Eighteenth-Century Studies* 18 [1984]: 1–34).

45. NW to Timothy Pickering, May 25, 1786, *LNW*, 52.

46. NW, *Dissertations*, 397–98; emphasis mine in the first quote, NW's in the second. In his "Essay," Webster supplied a list of advantages nearly identical to the one he had sent Pickering three years before, adding only that his reform would also greatly reduce the price of books since it "would diminish the number of letters about one sixteenth or eighteenth." Webster wasn't the only American to propose a new national alphabet. In 1791 Joseph Chambers published "An Attempt to Form a Complete System of Letters," whose success was assured, he believed, because "The united states have exhibited to the world a singular felicity, in shaking off the shackles of antiquated prejudices" (J[oseph] G. C[hambers], "Elements of Orthography; or an Attempt to Form a Complete System of Letters," *Universal Asylum and Columbian Magazine* [August 1791]: 114). When Chambers published his proposal in book form in 1812, he dedicated it "To the Most Excellent President; and Honorable Congress of the United States; And to the Worthy Governors, and Legislators of the States; Together with all other Eminent and Patriotic Citizens," hoping that his system would be considered "an experiment worthy of, and especially adapted to the characteristic liberality of sentiment, and enterprizing genius of United America" ([Joseph G. Chambers], *Elements of Orthography* [Zanesville, Ohio, 1812]). In 1798 James Ewing proposed a patriotically named Columbian Alphabet of thirty-three characters and, nine years later, Abner Kneeland expressed confidence that Americans would abandon their twenty-six-letter alphabet in favor of his set of thirty-five characters because "The United States have changed from a *Monarchical government* to a *republican;* from *dependence* to *independence.* And why not change in other respects?" (James Ewing, *The Columbian Alphabet* [Trenton, N.J.: Matthias Day, 1798]; Abner Kneeland, *A Brief Sketch of a New System of Orthography* [Walpole, N.H., 1807]; Joseph Neef, *Sketch of Plan and Method of Education* [Philadelphia, 1808], 35). The same year William Pelham suggested borrowing the French system of accenting vowels and, in his proposal, supplied the entire accented

text of Samuel Johnson's *Rasselas* as a demonstration (William Pelham, *A System of Notation* [Boston: W. Pelham, 1808]). In 1813 Thomas Embree promoted a corrected orthography closely modeled after Franklin's own, and three years later, Samuel Boyle proposed a twenty-six-character alphabet that, demonstrating a preposterous failure of imagination, invented no new characters, instead using the numbers 2 through 9: "2 aw, 3 ah, 4 hoo, 5 eth, 6 the, 7 esh, 8 ezhay, 9 eng" (Thomas Embree, *Orthography Corrected* [Philadelphia: Dennis Heartt, 1813]; Samuel Boyle, *Orthography Corrected* [Richmond, Va., 1816], 7). A notable exception to the nationalist tenor of the pre-1812 proposals is Jonathan Fisher's "philosophical alphabet." Fisher graduated from Harvard in 1792 and the same year, while studying at Harvard Divinity School, invented his philosophical alphabet in order to save paper. He used it all his life as a pastor in Blue Hill, Maine. See Raoul N. Smith, "The Philosophical Alphabet of Jonathan Fisher," *American Speech* 50 (1975): 36–49; Raoul N. Smith, *The Language of Jonathan Fisher, 1768–1847* (Tuscaloosa: University of Alabama Press, 1985); and Mary Ellen Chase, *Jonathan Fisher: Maine Parson, 1768–1847* (New York: Macmillan, 1948).

47. NW, *Dissertations,* 393–94; NW, *Collection of Essays and Fugitiv Writings* (Boston: I. Thomas & E. T. Andrews, 1795), xi.

48. *American Magazine* (April 1788), 347. NW's "Dissertation concerning the Influence of Language on Opinions and of Opinions on Language" was published in the *American Magazine* in May and reprinted in NW, *Collection of Essays,* 222–28. NW to Hudson & Goodwin, September 4, 1788. *LNW,* 79–80. NW to Mupel and Hafwell, September 7, 1788, NWP, box 1. *ANW,* 252–61. After Webster left, the society re-formed as the Friendly Club, a learned society of more eclectic interests. See Bryan Waterman, "The Friendly Club of New York City: Industries of Knowledge in the Early Republic," Ph.D. dissertation, Boston University, 2000.

49. Mary Stevenson to BF, September 26, 1768, *Writings of Benjamin Franklin,* 5:215. NW, *Dissertations,* 394, 399. NW to Mrs. Mary Coxe, April 14, 1786, *NLNW,* 1:114. On the prominent backing Webster had lined up, see Timothy Pickering to John Gardner, July 4, 1786. As Webster wrote to Washington, "Should I ever attempt it, I have no doubt that I should be patronized by many distinguished characters" (NW to GW, March 31, 1786). BF to NW, June 18, 1786. To Franklin Webster replied that he was "more and more convinced from the present sentiments and spirits of the Americans that a judicious attempt to introduce it needs but the support of a few eminent characters to be carried into effect" (NW to BF, June 23, 1786, *LNW,* 52–53). Ramsay was a particular supporter of Webster's. In his memoirs, Webster called Ramsay "a gentleman who, through life, manifested a particular friendship for N.W." (*ANW,* 146), and when Ramsay published his popular history of the American Revolution, in 1789, he praised Webster: "The principles of their mother tongue were first unfolded to the Americans since the revolution by their countryman Webster. Pursuing an unbeaten track, he has made discoveries in the genius and construction of the English language, which had escaped the researches of preceding philologists" (*The History of the American Revolution* [Philadelphia, 1789], 2:322).

50. *NLNW,* 1:117. NW to Timothy Pickering, December 18, 1791, *NLNW,* 1:309. *BWNW,* 337. In 1786 Pickering encouraged Webster to publish his lectures, on the grounds that "deliberate reading may procure disciples where transient hearing failed" but cautioned him to tone down his attacks against southerners, warning that "multitudes in the States southward of N. England are too proud and conceited to admit or

think that they can receive instructions from that quarter" (Timothy Pickering to NW, July 29, 1786). The financial consequences for Webster were newly serious. On October 26, 1789, he married Rebecca Greenleaf, and pledged to support his family properly. He wrote in his diary on his wedding day, "I begin a profession, at a late period of life," and pledged himself to earn a living as a lawyer (*ANW*, October 26, 1789). NW to GW, September 2, 1790, *LNW*, 85–86. Review of NW, *Collection of Essays and Fugitiv Writings, in Universal Asylum and Columbian Magazine* (November 1790): 333.

51. Ezra Stiles to NW, August 27, 1790, *NLNW*, 1:288. Jeremy Belknap to Ebenezer Hazard, September 14, 1790, *NLNW*, 1:297. NW to TP, *NLNW*, 1:309.

52. [London] *Critical Review* 21 (1797): 175–77. [London] *Monthly Review* 23 (1797): 356. [James Savage], "Webster's Grammar, Dictionary, &c. &c.," *Monthly Anthology* 8 (March 1810): 148.

53. Ellis, *After the Revolution*, 164. Other remarks quoted in Warfel, *Noah Webster*, 73, 322, 269, 42. *Diary of William Dunlap (1766–1839)*, New-York Historical Society Collections (New York: Benjamin Bloom, 1930), 1:21–22. On the problem of not liking NW, see Jill Lepore, "Historians Who Love Too Much: Reflections on Microhistory and Biography," *Journal of American History* 88 (2001):129–44.

54. Ebenezer Hazard to Jeremy Belknap, August 26, 1788, *NLNW*, 1:185.

55. NW, *A Grammatical Institute*, 3. NW, *Dissertations*, 405–6.

2. A UNIVERSAL ALPHABET

1. NW to The Public, March 4, 1797, *LNW*, 145–47. NW, "The Revolution in France, Considered in Respect to its Progress and Effects," in *A Collection of Papers on Political, Literary, and Moral Subjects* (New York, 1843), 41. Thomas Dawes to Noah Webster, February 9, 1795, *NLNW*, 1:397.

2. NW to The Public, July 19, 1796, *LNW*, 138.

3. Le Rapport Barère and Le Rapport Grégoire, in *Une Politique de la langue: La Révolution française et les patois*, by Michel de Certeau, Dominique Julie, and Jacques Revel (Paris: Gallimard, 1975), 295, 297, 302. "Nous avons révolutionné le gouvernement, les lois, les usages, les mœurs, les costumes, le commerce et la pensée même; révolutionnons donc aussi la langue." "Citoyens, la langue d'un peuple libre doit être une et la même pour tous." "Au moins six millions de français . . . ignorent la langue nationale." My translations. See also David A. Bell, "Lingua Populi, Lingua Dei: Language, Religion, and the Origins of French Revolutionary Nationalism," *American Historical Review* 100 (1995): 1403–37, and Paul Cohen, "Courtly French and Peasant Patois: The Making of a National Language in Early Modern France," Ph.D. dissertation, Princeton University, in progress.

4. WT to the Citizen President of France, June 12, 1794, *PWT*, 279–80.

5. WT, *Cadmus: Or, a Treatise on the Elements of Written Language* (Philadelphia, 1793), 27–28; 216–17. On WT's biography, see *PWT*, Editor's Introduction, xxxi–liii.

6. WT to John Coakley Lettsom, January 8, 1795, *PWT*, 295.

7. NW to GW, December 16, 1785, *LNW*, 37–38; *PWT*, xlix. Thornton lived in a boardinghouse at the corner of Market and Fifth streets (with fellow boarder James Madison); Webster lived in a similar establishment on Cherry Street. *PWT*, xliii–xliv; NW boarded with "Mrs. Ford" (*ANW*, 223, 237; a "Mary Ford" is listed in the 1793 Philadelphia Register as living at 46 Cherry Street). Thornton attended Quaker meetings as a

member; Webster attended more or less out of curiosity at the Friends' quiet form of worship ("Not a word said") and also because he was smitten with a young Quaker woman ("I was very attentive, to the silent exhortations of a pretty of sixteen") (*ANW,* 246, 245, 233, 350). Thornton also courted a sixteen-year-old Quaker (*PWT,* xliv).

8. WT, *Cadmus,* 10. Text after Webster's name has also been crossed out and is illegible. "Cadmus," ms. in WTP, reel 5, 2936. Indeed, Thornton was particularly engaged by an English work with which Franklin as a boy had been nearly obsessed, Bishop John Wilkins's *Essay towards a Real Character and a Philosophical Language* (1668). Wilkins's essay differed dramatically from nearly all other English alphabet reform proposals, which essentially aimed to perfect the Roman alphabet the better to fit the English language. Wilkins instead proposed a nonalphabetic universal writing system by establishing, first, a "philosophical language" of categories to describe the world and, second, a notational system to record them. In effect, Wilkins aimed to do for language what musical notation did for music (John Wilkins, *Essay towards a Real Character and a Philosophical Language* [London, 1668]). On Franklin's interest, see editor's note in *PBF,* 15: 300.

9. WT to John Coakley Lettsom, November 26, 1795, *PWT,* 340. See also his notes on the origin of the project in WTP, reel 5, 2876. WT's interest in scripts dates to at least as early as the late 1770s, when he wrote diary entries in a kind of shorthand. He also copied passages about language in a commonplace book he kept in 1786. When he read Wilkins and Webster is unclear. WT recorded extracts from various authors on the subject of language in his notebook of 1786 (WTP, reel 7) and in undated notes (reel 5). In earlier diaries, he wrote in a kind of shorthand; see, for example, the diary entry for October 14, 1779 (reel 7).

10. WT to John Coakley Lettsom, November 18, 1786, *PWT,* 31. WT, "General Outlines of a Settlement on the Tooth or Ivory Coast of Africa" [1786], *PWT,* 38–41. For more, see Gaillard Hunt, "William Thornton and Negro Colonization," *Proceedings of the American Antiquarian Society* 30 (1921): 32–61. See also WT to John Coakley Lettsom, November 18, 1786, *PWT,* 30–35. On such ventures more broadly, see Stephen J. Braidwood, *Black Poor and White Philanthropists: London's Blacks and the Foundation of the Sierra Leone Settlement, 1786–1791* (Liverpool: Liverpool University Press, 1994).

11. Of the northern blacks Thornton met, "They are, and with great propriety, very cautious," he reported to Lettsom, "and desire the most particular information relative to the intended settlement" (WT to John Coakley Lettsom, February 15, 1787, *PWT,* 43). In March, his "Address to the Heart, on the Subject of African Slavery," urging his readers, "AWAKE! ye whose hearts are attuned to sympathy!," was printed in the *Newport, Rhode Island, Herald* (WT, "Address to the Heart, On the Subject of African Slavery," *Newport, Rhode Island, Herald,* March 1, 1787; rep. *PWT,* 49–53). See also exchanges on the subject between Thornton and Sharp and Brissot in PWT.

12. NW, *Effects of Slavery, on Morals and Industry* (Hartford, Conn., 1793).

13. WT to Samuel Hopkins, September 29, 1790, *PWT,* 117–18. WT to Anthony Taylor and the African Union Society, January 13, 1791, and WT to the President and Members of the Council of the Virgin Islands, February 22, 1791, in *PWT,* 123, 129.

14. WT to Thomas Wilkinson, July 31, 1791, *PWT,* 152. WT, *Cadmus,* 27–28, 11, 16–18.

15. Sir William Jones, *Dissertation on the Orthography of Asiatick Words,* in Jones, *Works* (London, 1807), 3:253–318. *Literary Magazine and American Register* 3

(1805): 360. See also Robert A. Ferguson, "The Emulation of Sir William Jones in the Early Republic," *New England Quarterly* 52 (1979): 3–26. On Jones, see Garland Cannon, *The Life and Mind of Oriental Jones: Sir William Jones, the Father of Modern Linguistics* (Cambridge, England: Cambridge University Press, 1990).

16. WT to John Coakley Lettsom, May 5, 1792, *PWT,* 181.

17. CV, *Simplification des langues orientales* (Paris, 1795). On CV's plans to migrate to the United States, see CV, *A View of the Soil and Climate of the United States of America,* trans. Charles Brockden Brown (Philadelphia, 1804), vi. On CV, see Jean Gaulmier, *Un Grand Témoin de la révolution et de l'empire, Volney* (Paris, 1959), and Gilbert Chinard, *Volney et l'Amérique d'après des documents inédits et sa correspondance avec Jefferson* (Baltimore: Johns Hopkins University Press, 1923).

18. Gaulmier, *Volney,* 313. See also WT to Volney, April 1, 1797, *PWT,* 389–90. WT to John Coakley Lettsom, November 26, 1795, *PWT,* 339–40. CV to WT, January 9, 1796, *PWT,* 368. "Nous avons, sans le savoir, travaillé sur le même sujet et presque dans les même vues [my translation]." The interest in alphabets that Volney had in common with Thornton he also shared with fellow republican Thomas Jefferson, who, in 1798, complained that his "busy life" had not permitted him "to indulge in a pursuit to which I felt great attraction": "facilitating the study" of Anglo-Saxon by "reducing the infinite diversities of it's [*sic*] unfixed orthography to single and settled forms" (TJ to Herbert Croft, October 30, 1798, *Writings of Thomas Jefferson,* ed. Andrew A. Lipscomb and Albert E. Bergh [1903–4], 18:361–64).

19. See CV, *L'Alphabet européen appliqué aux langues asiatiques* (Paris, 1819), x–xi. On CV's election to the Asiatic Society on the basis of his *Simplification,* see *L'Alphabet européen,* vi. Peter Duponceau mentioned Volney's *Alphabet europeén* as a continuation of Jones's in a letter to JP, July 7, 1820 (*LJP,* 287). WT to Anthony Fothergill, October 10, 1797, *PWT,* 427.

20. Alexander DeConde, *The Quasi-War: The Politics and Diplomacy of the Undeclared War with France, 1797–1801* (New York: Scribner, 1966), 87.

21. CV, *A New Translation of Volney's Ruins* (Philadelphia, 1804; rep. ed. New York: Garland Publishing, 1979), introduction by Robert D. Richardson, Jr., v–viii. On Jefferson's relationship with Volney, see Chinard, *Volney et l'Amérique.* Cobbett quoted in *Volney en Amérique,* 98. CV, *A View of the Soil and Climate,* vi–viii.

22. NW to GW, April 20, 1794, *LNW,* 117–18; emphasis in original. NW, *Revolution in France,* 31. NW to CV, July 10, 1796, *LNW,* 137. On NW reading Volney's *Travels,* see his diary entry for July 27, 1792, *ANW,* 300. NW to Volney, July 10, 1796, *LNW,* 136–38, and a memo attached to it by NW, as reprinted in *NLNW,* 1: 407.

23. *PWT,* xlv; Warfel, *Noah Webster,* 228–29. NW to the Public, March 4, 1797, *LNW,* 145–47. NW, "Revolution in France," 24. NW, *American Minerva,* January 14, 1795.

24. WT to Jacques Pierre Brissot de Warville, February 13, 1793, *PWT,* 235. WT to the Citizen President of France, June 12, 1794, *PWT,* 279–80.

25. CV, *A View of the Soil and Climate,* xiv–xv. Charles Brockden Brown, who translated Volney's treatise for an American audience, observed wryly in the translator's preface, "Fortunately for Volney, circumstances have prevented him from publishing his observations on the government and manners of the people" (CV, *A View,* translator's preface, xxii).

26. John C. Miller, *Crisis in Freedom: The Alien and Sedition Acts* (Boston: Little, Brown, 1951), esp. 188–89; James Morton Smith, *Freedom's Fetters: The Alien and*

Sedition Laws and American Civil Liberties (Ithaca, N.Y.: Cornell University Press, 1966).

27. TJ to James Madison, May 3, 1798, *Writings of TJ,* ed. Ford, 7:248; see also 257, 262, and TJ to James Madison, April 26, 1798, 7:245, and TJ to James Madison, June 7, 1798, 7:267. WT to Benjamin Stoddert, June 28, 1798, *PWT,* 465.

28. Jedidiah Morse, *A Sermon Exhibiting the Present Dangers, and Consequent Duties of the Citizens of the United States of America* (1799).

29. NW to Theodore Sedgwick, January 2, 1795, *LNW,* 124–25. NW to Timothy Pickering, July 7, 1797, Pickering Papers, Massachusetts Historical Society. NW to Joseph Priestley, January 20, 1800, *LNW,* 214–15.

30. NW, "To the Public," *Connecticut Herald,* August 12, 1806. Scudder, *Noah Webster,* 51. WT to Jacques Brissot de Warville, November 29, 1788, *PWT,* 81.

31. Dunlap, quoted in *PWT,* xxxi–xxxii.

32. Robert Aitken to WT, June 1, 1793, WTP, reel 1. [London] *Monthly Review* 16 (1795): 197. George Turner sent Thornton a copy of this review in 1799 (Turner to WT, June 2, 1799, *PWT,* 497–98. *Quarterly Review* X [1814]: 528–29).

33. Lemuel Lengthy, "To the Editor of the Analectic Magazine," *Analectic Magazine* 3 (1814): 405.

34. *Connecticut Journal,* June 4, 1800.

35. "An Enemy to Innovation" [Joseph Dennie], *Gazette of the United States,* June 10, 1800. Republican attacks on NW quoted in Warfel, *Noah Webster,* 234.

36. Thomas Dawes to NW, August 1, 1809, *NLNW,* 2:71. However, Dawes did find another printer who would oblige. NW to John Jay, June 9, 1813, *NLNW,* 2:120; NW to Thomas Dawes, July 13, 1809, *NLNW,* 2:71. The standard Roman alphabet came to shape American culture. See Patricia Crain, *The Story of A: The Alphabetization of America from "The New England Primer" to "The Scarlet Letter"* (Stanford, Calif.: Stanford University Press, 2000).

37. Quoted in Warfel, *Noah Webster,* 228.

38. *Port Folio* 2 (May 29, 1802), 167a; emphasis in original.

39. WT, *Outlines of a Constitution for a United North and South Columbia* (Washington, D.C., 1815). In the introduction, Thornton noted that he had drafted the plan "about the year 1800."

3. A NATIONAL ALPHABET

1. Samuel Lorenzo Knapp, *Lectures on American Literature* (New York, 1829), 28. John Howard Payne, "The Life of George Gist (1835)," in "Notable Persons in Cherokee History: Sequoyah or George Gist," *Journal of Cherokee Studies* 2 (1977): 389. Charles Francis Adams, ed., *Memoirs of John Quincy Adams, Comprising Portions of his Diary from 1795 to 1848* (New York: AMS Press, 1970), 7: 526.

2. Knapp, *Lectures,* 25. Jeremiah Evarts to Rufus Anderson, March 12, 1828, Papers of the American Board of Commissioners of Foreign Missions, Houghton Library, Harvard University, Letters from Mr. Evarts, 1824–1831, ABC: II, v. 2, item 115. Thanks to John Demos for this reference. On the ABCFM, see Joseph Tracy, *A History of the American Board of Commissioners of Foreign Missions* (Worcester, Mass., 1840).

3. Adams, *Memoirs,* 7:502, 526, 539. On the 1828 delegation and treaty, see William G. McLoughlin, *Cherokee Renascence in the New Republic* (Princeton, N.J.: Princeton

University Press, 1986), 411–17, and Charles C. Royce, *The Cherokee Nation of Indians: A Narrative of their Official Relations with the Colonial and Federal Governments* (Washington, D.C., 1887), 101–21.

4. Sequoyah is supposed to have kept not only a series of voluminous diaries and journals but notes for a history of the Cherokee people and of their language. None of these apparently have survived, although in 1971 a writer named Traveller Bird, allegedly a direct descendant, claimed to have a treasure trove of Sequoyah's writings, including "more than six hundred documents written by George Guess himself on thick ruled ledger books, small leather-bound note books, scraps of paper, edges of early eighteenth and nineteenth century newspapers, white buckskin, corn shuck paper, and mulberry and cedar bark" (Traveller Bird, *Tell Them They Lie: The Sequoyah Myth* [Los Angeles: Westernlore Publications, 1971], 143). Bird's account has been dismissed as spurious (see Raymond Fogelson, "On the Varieties of Indian History: Sequoyah and Traveller Bird," *Journal of Ethnic Studies* 2 [1974]: 105–12; John White, "Elaborate Fabrication," *The Indian Historian* 5 [1972]: 45–46; and Traveller Bird's reply in *The Indian Historian* 6 [1973]: 40), and my attempts to contact him in 1997 failed. There are a host of conflicting contemporary accounts of Sequoyah's life, the most important of which are noted here. Samuel Lorenzo Knapp, a Washington editor, interviewed Sequoyah, with the aid of interpreters, when he visited Washington in 1828 (*Lectures,* 25–29). That same year American Board missionary Samuel Austin Worcester wrote numerous reports on Sequoyah's invention to the American Board. John Howard Payne, an actor and dramatist (best known as the author of "Home Sweet Home") who visited the Cherokees in 1835 in preparation for writing a history of the Cherokee people, recorded an account of Sequoyah's life, given to him by a Cherokee named George Lowery ("The Life of George Gist [1835]," in "Notable Persons in Cherokee History: Sequoyah or George Gist," *Journal of Cherokee Studies* 2 [1977]: 385–92). Philologist and former Secretary of the Treasury Albert Gallatin described Sequoyah's work in "A Synopsis of the Indian Tribes" (*Transactions and Collections of the American Antiquarian Society* 2 [1836]: 92–93). The following year John Stuart, a U.S. Army captain, reported meeting Sequoyah in Arkansas (*A Sketch of the Cherokee and Choctaw Indians* [Little Rock, 1837], 18–22). In a journal and letters written in 1841, Ethan Allen Hitchcock, serving as a U.S. Army officer, noted conversations with Cherokees in Arkansas who had met Sequoyah (Ethan Allen Hitchcock, *A Traveler in Indian Territory,* ed. Grant Foreman [Cedar Rapids, Iowa: Torch Press, 1930], 67–68, 241–42). Also, long after Sequoyah's death George Lowery's granddaughter Wahnenauhi recorded her recollections of him (Jack Frederick Kilpatrick, ed., *The Wahnenauhi Manuscript: Historical Sketches of the Cherokees* [Washington, D.C.: Government Printing Office, 1966], 196–99, 209–11). Biographies written after Sequoyah's death are generally sketchy and in considerable disagreement with one another. The best of these is probably Grant Foreman, *Sequoyah* (Norman: University of Oklahoma Press; rep. 1970). See also George Everett Foster, *Se-quo-yah, The American Cadmus and Modern Moses* (Philadelphia, 1885; rep. AMS, 1979). William A. Phillips, "Sequoyah," *Harper's Magazine* (September 1870), is derivative. A more recent, if brief, biographical study is Jack F. Kilpatrick, *Sequoyah of Earth and Intellect* (Austin, Tex.: Encino Press, 1965). A surprisingly thorough comparison of conflicting biographical information can be found in John B. Davis, "The Life and Work of Sequoyah," *Chronicles of Oklahoma* 8 (1930): 149–80.

5. "Literary and Intellectual Statistics," *New England Magazine* (December 1831): 466. Another example: "Sequoyah, the inventor of the Cherokee Alphabet, is a most interesting personage, but would be still more so, were he a full-blooded Indian. He is the son of a white man and a half-breed woman, and this circumstance essentially detracts from the wonderful character of his discoveries in arts and letters" (Jared Sparks and C. C. Felton, Review of Thomas L. McKenney and James Hall, *History of the Indian Tribes of North America,* volume 1, *North American Review* 47 [1838]: 146).

6. On Cherokee history, see especially William G. McLoughlin, *Cherokee Renascence in the New Republic* (Princeton, N.J.: Princeton University Press, 1986). See also Henry Thompson Malone, *Cherokees of the Old South: A People in Transition* (Athens: University of Georgia Press, 1956), and James Mooney, *Historical Sketch of the Cherokee* (Chicago: Aldine Publishing Co., 1975).

7. Samuel A. Worcester, *Missionary Herald,* February 1826, 47–49. On Webster's spelling book in mission schools: Worcester reported in 1827 the use of "Webster's table of similar words," "Webster's Spelling Book," and "Webster's Table 21"; Elias Boudinot also requested supplies including "I doz. Webster's Spelling Book" (Althea Bass, *Cherokee Messenger* [Norman: University of Oklahoma Press, 1936], 45–46, 66). See also George E. Foster, *Literature of the Cherokees* (Ithaca, N.Y., 1889), 25. Cherokee tradition, quoted in Foster, *Literature of the Cherokees,* 9–10. One Cherokee folktale, recorded by anthropologists in the 1920s, specified that writing was the unique provenance of whites from the moment of creation: "When people first began to live, there were Whites and Indians. Somebody came to the people bringing a printed book. He first offered it to the Indians, but they didn't like it. Then He turned to the Whites and offered them the book. They took it. . . . He also offered a bundle of barks and roots, which was medicine, to the White people, but they did not want it. He then turned around to where the Indians were, offered it to them, and they took it. There were people who did not want either the book or the bundle, and laughed so much at both that their faces turned all black and their eyes white with laughing. Those were the black people" (Jack Frederick Kilpatrick and Anna Gritts Kilpatrick, *Eastern Cherokee Folktales: Reconstructed from the Field Notes of Frans M. Olbrechts* [Washington, D.C., 1966, Bureau of American Ethnology bull. 196, No. 80], 443). That this tradition emphasizes the inferiority of blacks is no surprise; many Cherokees owned African slaves (Theda Perdue, *Slavery and the Evolution of Cherokee Society, 1540–1866* [Knoxville: University of Tennessee Press, 1979]).

8. Knapp reported that when Sequoyah was serving in the Creek War, a letter found on a prisoner caused him and his comrades to debate "whether this mysterious power of the *talking leaf,* was the gift of the Great Spirit to the white man, or a discovery of the white man himself?" Sequoyah "strenuously maintained the latter," and when, after the war, he found himself confined to his cabin on account of his lameness, "his mind was again directed to the mystery of the power of *speaking by letters*" (Knapp, *Lectures,* 465–66). G. C., To the Editor, *Cherokee Phoenix,* August 13, 1828. Writing in 1889, Wahnenauhi recalled that "Sequoyah did not speak the English language, and understood only a few words, of which he could make but little use; though he had seen but few books, he had learned something about them, and how distant friends could communicate with each other by writing. He was convinced that if a written language was beneficial to one people, it would be equally so to another so he determined to make this for his people" (Kilpatrick, *The Wahnenauhi Manuscript,* 198). Such tales of the

origins of Cherokee writing may be fruitfully compared with what Henry Louis Gates calls "the trope of the talking book" in African-American slave narratives (*The Signifying Monkey: A Theory of African-American Literary Criticism* [New York: Oxford University Press, 1988], 127–69).

9. Knapp, *Lectures,* 26. Payne, "Life of George Gist," 387–88. The process Sequoyah followed is typical of nineteenth-century invented writing systems. See Albertine Gaur, *The History of Writing* (London: British Library, 1984), 131–34. For a similar account of Sequoyah's process, see Tracy, *A History of the American Board,* 147–48. See also Willard Walker and James Sarbaugh, "The Early History of the Cherokee Syllabary," *Ethnohistory* 40 (1993): 70–94.

10. *Panoplist* (August 1807), 128.

11. American Board quoted in Bass, *Cherokee Messenger,* 31. John Gambold to Schulz, September 1, 1824, quoted in William G. McLoughlin, *Cherokees and Missionaries, 1789–1839* (New Haven, Conn.: Yale University Press, 1984), 64.

12. John Gambold to Thomas L. McKenney, January 7, 1817, quoted in McLoughlin, *Cherokees and Missionaries,* 64. As John Pickering reminded his readers in his *Essay on a Uniform Orthography for the Indian Languages* in 1820, "Until a few years past . . . these neglected dialects, like the devoted race of men, who have spoken them for so many ages, and who have been stripped of almost every fragment of their paternal inheritance except their language, have incurred only the contempt of the people of Europe and their descendants on this continent; all of whom, with less justice than is commonly supposed, have proudly boasted of the superiority of their own more cultivated languages as well as more civilized manners" (JP, *Essay on a Uniform Orthography,* 2–3). On interest in Indian languages, see Edward G. Gray, *New World Babel: Languages and Nations in Early America* (Princeton, N.J.: Princeton University Press, 1999); H. Christoph Wolfart, "Notes on the Early History of American Indian Linguistics," *Folia Linguistica* 1 (1967): 153–71; Jill Lepore, "Wigwam Words," *American Scholar* 70 (Winter 2001): 97–108; and Anthony F. C. Wallace, *Jefferson and the Indians: The Tragic Fate of the First Americans* (Cambridge, Mass.: Harvard University Press, 1999), 318–25.

13. William G. McLoughlin, *Champions of the Cherokees: Evan and John B. Jones* (Princeton, N.J.: Princeton University Press, 1990), 35–37. See also John Heckewelder to Peter Duponceau, March 4, 1820, Heckewelder, Letters, American Philosophical Society.

14. Peter Duponceau to Daniel Butrick, September 7, 1818, Historical and Literary Committee Letterbook, vol. 2, pp. 19–21, American Philosophical Society. Daniel Butrick to Peter Duponceau, October 29, 1818, Archives, American Philosophical Society. D. S. Butrick and D. Brown, *Tsvlvki Sqclvclv: A Cherokee Spelling Book* (Knoxville, Tenn., 1819). McLoughlin, *Champions,* 35–37. On the Brainerd Mission, see Robert Sparks Walker, *Torchlights to the Cherokees: The Brainerd Mission* (New York: Macmillan, 1931), and Joyce B. Phillips and Paul Gary Phillips, eds., *The Brainerd Journal: A Mission to the Cherokees, 1817–1832* (Lincoln: University of Nebraska Press, 1998). Butrick and Brown's spelling book also caught the attention of Peter Stephen Duponceau, a Philadelphia lawyer, armchair linguist, and corresponding secretary of the American Philosophical Society's Historical and Literary Committee, formed in 1815 and very much dedicated to the study of America's indigenous languages. Duponceau, like Jefferson, was passionate about the study of native American

languages as a crucial literary, scientific, and cultural endeavor of the new nation. Jefferson was eager to document the languages' antiquity; Duponceau hoped to discover an American poetics. In the early nineteenth century Duponceau, along with his close friend JP (whom Duponceau nominated to membership in the American Philosophical Society in 1820), the Moravian missionary John Heckewelder, Jefferson's former secretary of the treasury Albert Gallatin, and, before his death, Jefferson himself, constituted a core group of scholars interested in American Indian languages (see Andresen, *Linguistics in America,* chapter 2). In the summer of 1818 Duponceau had chanced to meet two young Cherokees traveling through Philadelphia on their way to Cornwall, and, through them, learned of Butrick and Brown's Cherokee spelling book (Peter Duponceau, July 27, 1818, Historical and Literary Committee Letterbook, vol. 2, p. 15, American Philosophical Society). See also John Gambold to Peter Duponceau, July 20, 1818, "Vocabularies and Other manuscripts relating to Indian Languages," American Philosophical Society. For more on Duponceau's work, see *Report of the Corresponding Secretary to the Historical and Literary Committee* (Philadelphia, 1819). In many ways, Duponceau modeled his comparative linguistic work and his quest for a native American literary tradition after the work of Sir William Jones. He also closely followed in the tradition of Constantin Volney; in 1835 the French Institute awarded Duponceau the coveted Volney Prize.

15. Timothy Pickering to Mrs. Pickering, October 31, 1783, *NLNW,* 1: 96. On JP, see Mary Orne Pickering, *Life of John Pickering* (Boston, 1887), hereafter *LJP.* JP to Timothy Pickering, June 3, 1799, *LJP,* 142. On JP's philological work, see Andresen, *Linguistics in America,* 104–10. Andresen discusses the overlap in Pickering's interest—and that of other linguists—in both American English and American Indian languages and argues for the need to study them together (75).

16. JP, *A Vocabulary or Collection of Words and Phrases . . . To Which is Prefixed a Memoir on the Present State of the English Language in the United States* (Cambridge, Mass., 1815), 3, 11. JP to Timothy Pickering, February 17, 1817, *LJP,* 260. Simon Colton to Simeon Baldwin, September 8, 1809, excerpted in Warfel, *Noah Webster,* 321–22. "I expect to encounter the displeasure of some of our American reformers, who think we ought to throw off our native language as one of the badges of English servitude, and establish a new tongue for ourselves. But I have the satisfaction to know that the best scholars in our country treat such a scheme with derision; they, on the contrary, are solicitous to retain the peculiar advantages we derive from a language which is common to ourselves and the illustrious writers and orators of our mother country" (JP to Horace Binney, July 15, 1816, *LJP,* 258–59).

17. On Hiram Bingham, see Hiram Bingham, *A Residence of Twenty-one Years in the Sandwich Islands* (1847; Rutland, Vt.: Charles E. Tuttle Co., 1981); and Char Miller, ed., *Selected Writings of Hiram Bingham, 1814–1869* (Lampeter, Wales: Edwin Mellen Press, 1988). On Hopoo's visit, see *LJP,* 291. The Foreign Mission School was founded after the conversion of another Hawaiian, Henry Obookiah (Edwin Welles Dwight, *Memoirs of Henry Obookiah* [Elizabethtown, N.J., 1819]). On the history of the Foreign Mission School, see John Demos, *The Heathen School: A Story of Hope and Betrayal in the Age of the Early Republic* (New York: Knopf, forthcoming).

18. JP to Hiram Bingham, October 19, 1819, *LJP,* 291–92. JP, *An Essay on a Uniform Orthography for the Indian Languages* (Cambridge, Mass., 1820), 1–2, 9. TJ to JP, February 13, 1822, *LJP,* 318.

19. David Brown to the Baron de Champagne, May 1, 1823, in Bass, *Cherokee Messenger*, 42. David Brown to JP, September 4, 1823, *LJP*, 332, and David Brown to JP, undated, *LJP*, 333. David Brown to the Corresponding Secretary of the ABCFM, September 20, 1824, in Rufus Anderson, *Memoir of Catherine Brown, A Christian Indian of the Cherokee Nation* (Boston, 1825), 46–47. On Brown, see also Mary Alves Higginbotham, "The Creek Path Mission," *Journal of Cherokee Studies* 1 (1976): 72–86.

20. JP to TJ, February 10, 1825, *LJP*, 335. In reply, Jefferson expressed admiration for Pickering's *Cherokee Grammar* but regretted that it must be considered more academic than practical: "We generally learn languages for the benefit of reading the books written in them; but here our reward must be the addition made to the philosophy of language" (TJ's reply to JP, February 20, 1825, *LJP*, 335–36). On TJ's views of American Indian languages, see Gray, *New World Babel*, ch. 5; and Wallace, *Jefferson and the Indians*, 310–26.

21. JP to Baron Wilhelm von Humboldt, November 27, 1827, *LJP*, 352–53. A handwritten note, signed by Rufus Anderson and dated 1850, in the Houghton Library copy of Pickering's *Grammar*, explains: "The work was discontinued by Mr. Pickering in consequence, I believe, of some distrust in the knowledge & accuracy of David Brown's knowledge of the language." But Pickering himself cited Sequoyah's invention as the cause of his abandonment of the project. See also Bass (*Cherokee Messenger*, 35): "The Prudential Committee of the American Board had appropriated $500 toward the publication of the Cherokee grammar [by Pickering and Brown] when word reached Boston that the Cherokees had a system of writing of their own that was transforming the whole nation. They had burst into literacy, while the Board was perfecting a scheme to make them literate."

22. [David Brown], September 2, 1825, enclosed in Thomas L. McKenney to Secretary of War, December 13, 1825, in *American State Papers, Indian Affairs* 2 (Washington, D.C., 1834): 653. At least one source claims that "David Brown assisted Sequoyah with the alphabet" (Katherine McKinstry Duncan and Larry Joe Smith, *The History of Marshall County, Alabama* [Albertville, Ala.: Thompson Printing, 1969], 17), and certainly some speculation on that subject seems warranted, but the claim is probably unprovable.

23. *Missionary Herald* 23 (December 1827): 382. Jedidiah Morse did not report on it in 1822; Morse left New Haven with his youngest son, Richard, May 10, 1820, and traveled for two years (David Brown aided Morse; he conveyed a request for information to Charles Hicks); Hicks's letter to Morse, printed in his report, mentions education only in English language; Morse's report includes a report from the Reverend A. Hoyt on the progress of Cherokee mission schools, dated October 1, 1821, but this also makes no mention of Sequoyah. Morse's report is reprinted in large part in E. Raymond Evans, ed., "Jedidiah Morse's Report to the Secretary of War on Cherokee Indian Affairs in 1822," *Journal of Cherokee Studies* 6 (1981): 60–78.

24. Foreman, *Se-quo-yah*, 29. McLoughlin, *Champions*, 39. Kass-ti-ga-tor-skee, or the Feathered Arrow, "Examination of an Article in the 'North American Review,' " *United States Literary Gazette* 4 (August 1826): 264.

25. John Ridge to Albert Gallatin, March 10, 1826, reprinted in William C. Sturtevant, "John Ridge on Cherokee Civilization in 1826," *Journal of Cherokee Studies* 6 (1981): 86–87. Mooney, *Historical Sketch*, 167. William G. McLoughlin and Walter H. Conser, Jr., "The Cherokees in Transition: A Statistical Analysis of the Federal Cherokee Census

of 1835," *Journal of American History* 64 (December 1977): 692–93. On Cherokee literacy, see Carmeleta L. Monteith, "Literacy among the Cherokee in the Early Nineteenth Century," *Journal of Cherokee Studies* 9 (1984): 56–73; Willard Walker, "The Design of Native Literacy Programs and How Literacy Came to the Cherokees," *Anthropological Linguistics* 26 (1984): 161–68; Willard Walker, "Notes on Native Writing Systems and the Design of Native Literacy Programs," *Anthropological Linguistics* 11 (1969): 148–66; and Catherine Corman, "Reading, Writing, and Removal: Native American Literacies, 1824–1835," Ph.D. dissertation, Yale University, 1998.

26. JP to Humboldt, November 27, 1827. *Missionary Herald* (February 1826). On Worcester, see Althea Bass, *Cherokee Messenger: A Life of Samuel Austin Worcester* (Norman: University of Oklahoma Press, 1936). JP, "Indian Languages," *Cyclopaedia Americana* (Philadelphia, 1830–31), 600.

27. Anderson, *Memoir of Catherine Brown*, 18, 44. McLoughlin, *Champions*, 80, 57.

28. Samuel Worcester, *Missionary Herald* (July 1827). Worcester in 1835, quoted in Bass, *Cherokee Messenger*, 189.

29. JP to Humboldt, December 27, 1827.

30. Joseph Priestley, *A Course of Lectures on the Theory of Language and Universal Grammar* (Warrington, England, 1762), 31–36. Realizing that Chinese is really a mixed writing system, most later eighteenth-century writers departed from Priestley and classified it in a category unto itself. This revised ranking of scripts—pictographic, hieroglyphic, syllabic, and alphabetic—placed syllabaries in a similar stage of development as Chinese writing.

31. James Ewing, *The Columbian Alphabet* (Trenton, N.J., 1798), 8.

32. JP to Humboldt, December 27, 1827. Albert Gallatin, "A Synopsis of the Indian Tribes [1836]," *Transactions and Collections of the American Antiquarian Society* 2 (1836): 92–93.

33. Roy Harris, *The Origin of Writing* (London: Duckworth, 1986), 114.

34. Harris, *Origin of Writing*, 41, 87.

35. Intriguingly, Albert Gallatin, unlike John Pickering, wasn't much bothered by Sequoyah's having failed to take the final, civilizing step toward alphabetic literacy. "In practice," Gallatin observed, "and as applied to his own language, the superiority of Guess's alphabet is manifest, and has been fully proven by experience." Perhaps, to Gallatin, there seemed something sublimely suitable about this not-fully-civilized people's using a not-fully-alphabetic kind of writing (Gallatin, "Synopsis," 92–93).

36. On Cherokee as better than English orthography, see the Reverend Ezekiel Rich's report to Congress in 1844 (Reverend Ezekiel Rich, "New Project for Reforming the English Alphabet and Orthography" [U.S. Serials vol. 4, no. 442, House Document 126: February 19, 1844]).

37. Bingham, *Residence*, 155, 153.

38. JP, "Article XI," *North American Review* 28 (1829): 501, and JP, *Remarks on the Indian Languages of North America from the Encyclopedia Americana, Volume VI, Published in 1831* (1836), 597. JP to Humboldt, November 27, 1827.

39. See William G. McLoughlin, "Thomas Jefferson and the Beginning of Cherokee Nationalism, 1806 to 1809," *William and Mary Quarterly* 32 (1975): 547–80.

40. Elias Boudinot, *An Address to the Whites* (Philadelphia, 1826), reprinted in Theda Perdue, ed., *Cherokee Editor: The Writings of Elias Boudinot* (Knoxville: University of Tennessee Press, 1983), 73–74.

41. NW to Eliza Webster Jones, February 15, 1832, NWP. As Pickering wrote in 1830, the prospect of the Cherokees' forced removal from their homelands "is rendered the more embarrassing because we have ourselves for forty years past been encouraging them to abandon hunting, and to become agriculturalists and manufacturers, and thus adopt the condition of civilized people. They consider it peculiarly grievous and unjust in us, under all the circumstances, to oblige them to abandon their country; and I confess I think they have much reason on their side" (JP to William Humboldt, March 29, 1830, *LJP,* 380).

42. McLoughlin and Conser, "A Statistical Analysis." John Howard Payne, "The Cherokee Cause [1835]," *Journal of Cherokee Studies* 1 (1976): 19.

43. Elias Boudinot, "To the Public," *Cherokee Phoenix,* February 21, 1828. Henry T. Malone, "The Cherokee Phoenix: Supreme Expression of Cherokee Nationalism," *Georgia Historical Quarterly* 34 (1950): 163.

44. Quoted in Willard Walker, "The Design of Native Literacy Programs," 162. *Missionary Herald* (December 1827). Willard Walker, "The Roles of Samuel A. Worcester and Elias Boudinot in the Emergence of a Printed Cherokee Syllabic Literature," *International Journal of American Linguistics* 51 (1985): 610–12. For bibliographies of materials printed in the syllabary, see George E. Foster, *Literature of the Cherokees* (Ithaca, N.Y., 1889), bibliography, 1–28; Raymond Yamachika, "Cherokee Literature: Printing in the Sequoyan Syllabary since 1828 with a Bibliography," master's thesis, University of Oklahoma, 1961, 112–211. James Constantine Pilling, *Bibliography of the Iroquoian Languages* (Washington, D.C., 1888).

45. Worcester quoted in Perdue, "The Sequoyah Syllabary," 122. See also *Missionary Herald* (February 1826). JP to Humboldt, November 27, 1827.

46. Elias Boudinot to Herman Vaill from New Echota, January 23, 1829, Herman L. Vaill Collection, Manuscripts and Archives, Yale University. Ann Lackey Landini, "The 'Cherokee Phoenix': The Voice of the Cherokee Nation, 1828–1834," Ph.D. dissertation, University of Tennessee, 1990. See also Theda Perdue, "Rising from the Ashes: The *Cherokee Phoenix* as an Ethnohistorical Source," *Ethnohistory* 24 (1977): 207–18.

47. McLoughlin, *Champions,* 39, 81–83. Monteith, "Literacy among the Cherokee," 69–70. Theda Perdue makes a similar argument about the nativist nature of the invention in "The Sequoyah Syllabary and Cultural Revitalization," in *Perspectives on the Southeast: Linguistics, Archaeology, and Ethnohistory,* ed. Patricia Kwachka (Athens: University of Georgia, 1994), 116–25.

48. Payne, "Life of George Gist," 389.

49. Foreman, *Se-quo-yah,* 31. Hitchcock, *Traveler,* 242.

50. Payne, "Life of George Gist," 390. Stuart, *Sketch,* 20–21. Anna and Jack Kilpatrick, *Chronicles of Wolftown: Social Documents of the North Carolina Cherokees, 1850–1862* (Washington, D.C.: U.S. Government Printing Office, 1966).

51. JP to Humboldt, November 27, 1827.

52. NW to William G. Webster, April 8, 1838, *NLNW,* 2: 354–55.

53. Walker, "Design of Native Literacy Programs," 162. John Ridge to Albert Gallatin, 87. Payne, "Life of George Gist," 390.

54. "On account of Sequoyah's declining health, he was advised to travel. He had thought much of the Legend of the Rocky Mountain Cherokees, and the hope of satisfying his curiosity with regard to this myth made him anxious to take a westward trip; he was also very desirous of seeing and exploring the western outlet belonging to the

Cherokees" (Kilpatrick, *Wahnenauhi Manuscript,* 209–11). Companion quoted in Foreman, *Sequoyah,* 49.

55. Kilpatrick, *Wahnenauhi Manuscript,* 209–11. Foreman, *Sequoyah,* 69–71.

4. NATURAL LANGUAGE

1. Charles Francis Adams, ed., *Memoirs of John Quincy Adams, comprising portions of his Diary from 1795 to 1848* (Philadelphia, 1875), 7:434–37, 458. See also Lewis Weld, *An Address delivered in the Capitol* (Washington, D.C., 1828), and THG to Eli Todd, February 12, 1828, Henry Barnard Papers, Connecticut Historical Society.

2. THG, *A Sermon on the Duty and Advantages of Affording Instruction to the Deaf and Dumb* (Concord, N.Y., 1824); reprinted in Henry Barnard, *Tribute to Gallaudet: A Discourse in Commemoration of the Life, Character, and Services, of the Rev. Thomas H. Gallaudet, L.L.D., delivered before the citizens of Hartford, January 7th, 1852. With an appendix containing history of deaf-mute instruction and institutions, and other documents* (Hartford, Conn.: Brockett & Hutchinson, 1852), 180–81. This was Gallaudet's standard fund-raising sermon, and Adams's references, although they do not identify it by title, suggest that the sermon Gallaudet delivered in Washington was based on, if not identical to, this text.

3. Adams, *Memoirs,* 437–38. THG quoted in Henry Winter Style, *A Biographical Sketch of the Reverend Thomas Hopkins Gallaudet, L.L.D.* (Philadelphia, 1887), 7, 9, and in Heman Humphrey, *The Life and Labors of the Reverend T. H. Gallaudet, LL.D.* (New York, 1857), 20–21.

4. Hiram Bingham to Samuel Worcester, May 11, 1819, *Selected Writings of Hiram Bingham, 1814–1869* (Lampeter, Wales: Edwin Mellen Press, 1988), 92–93. Biographical treatments of Gallaudet are few. See Style, *A Biographical Sketch;* Barnard, *Tribute to Gallaudet;* Humphrey, *Life and Labors;* Edward Miner Gallaudet, *Life of Thomas H. Gallaudet, founder of deaf-mute instruction in America, by his son, Edward Miner Gallaudet* (New York: H. Holt & Co., 1888). The only recent full-length study of Gallaudet is confined to his work with the deaf: James John Fernandes, "The Gate to Heaven: T. H. Gallaudet and the Rhetoric of the Deaf Education Movement," Ph.D. dissertation, University of Michigan, 1980.

5. Quoted in Barnard, *Tribute,* 14.

6. Histories of deaf education include J. A. P. Barnard, "The Education of the Deaf and Dumb," *North American Review* 38 (1834): 307–57; Harlan Lane, *When the Mind Hears: A History of the Deaf* (New York: Random House, 1984); and Douglas Baynton, *Forbidden Signs: American Culture and the Campaign against Sign Language* (Chicago: University of Chicago Press, 1996). See also Oliver Sacks, *Seeing Voices: A Journey into the World of the Deaf* (Berkeley: University of California Press, 1989).

7. THG, "A Journal of some occurrences in my life which have a relation to the Instruction of the Deaf and Dumb," GP, box 1. All details pertaining to Gallaudet's trip to Europe are taken from this journal, unless otherwise indicated.

8. WT, "On teaching the Surd, or Deaf and consequently Dumb, to Speak," in *Cadmus,* 94–110. JP, "Article XI: Elementary Instruction," *North American Review* (Boston: Frederick T. Gray, 1829), 28 (new ser. 19): 499. [London] *Monthly Review* 16 (1795): 197.

9. Juan Pablo Bonet, *Reducción de las Letras y Arte para Enseñar a Hablar los Mudos* (Madrid, 1620), trans. H. N. Dixon, *Simplification of the Letters of the Alphabet and*

Method of Teaching Deaf-Mutes to Speak (Harrogate, England, 1890). Melchor Yebra, *Libro Llamado Refugium Infimorum* (Madrid, 1593). Pereire quoted in Lane, *When the Mind Hears,* 82.

10. Noam Chomsky, *Aspects of the Theory of Syntax* (Cambridge, Mass.: MIT Press, 1965), *Reflections on Language* (New York: Pantheon, 1975), and *Language and Mind* (New York: Harcourt, 1968). Steven Pinker, *The Language Instinct* (New York: William Morrow, 1994).

11. Charles-Michel de l'Épée, *Institution des sourds et muets par la voie des signes méthodiques* (Paris, 1776).

12. Dugald Stewart, "Some Account of a Boy Born Blind and Deaf," *Transactions of the Royal Society of Edinburgh* 7 (1815): 39, 46. See also THG to Mason Fitch Cogswell, July 11, 1815, GP, box 2.

13. THG to Mason Fitch Cogswell, April 11, 1816, GP, box 2; emphasis in original.

14. Style, *Biographical Sketch,* 22. On Gallaudet and Fowler's marriage, see E. M. Gallaudet, *Life of Gallaudet,* 141–56.

15. Reverend J. M. Wainwright, April 9, 1818, in "Institution at Hartford for instructing the deaf and dumb," *North American Review* 7 (1818): 127.

16. THG, "On Teaching the Deaf and Dumb," *Christian Observer* 18 (1819): 786. J. A. P. Barnard, "The Education of the Deaf and Dumb, *North American Review* 38 (1834): 337, 316–17.

17. "Methods of Teaching Written Language to the Deaf and Dumb, in the American Asylum at Hartford, in the state of Connecticut," *Academician* 1 (July 10, 1819): 336.

18. THG, "On the Natural Language of Signs," *AADD* 1 (1848): 56–57.

19. Laurent Clerc, "Address to the Connecticut Legislature," in Christopher Krentz, ed., *A Mighty Change: An Anthology of Deaf American Writing, 1816–1864* (Washington, D.C.: Gallaudet University Press, 2000), 13–14. THG, "On Oral Language and the Language of Signs," *Christian Observer,* 26 (1826): 465–68. De l'Épée quoted in Harlan Lane, ed., *The Deaf Experience: Classics in Language and Education,* trans. Franklin Philip (Cambridge, Mass.: Harvard University Press, 1984), 181.

20. THG, "On Teaching the Deaf and Dumb," *Christian Observer* 18 (1819): 648. Gallaudet asked Hiram Bingham to try sign language on the native Owhhyheeans (Hawaiians) and received a favorable report. Moreover, "another of our missionaries, in India," Gallaudet announced in 1826, "has expressed to me the same opinion" (THG, "On Oral Language and the Language of Signs," *Christian Observer,* 26 [1826]: 464). In 1848, two years before his death, Gallaudet published his comparison, suggesting, for instance, that the Indians' sign for *sun* was identical to that used by deaf white Americans: "The forefinger and thumb are brought together at tip, so as to form a circle, and held upwards towards the sun's track" (THG, "On the Natural Language of Signs," *AADD* 1 [1848]: 59). Sign language was indeed common as a lingua franca among Pawnee, Shoshone, Arapahoe, Cheyenne, Crow, and Sioux Indians, as reported in W. P. Clark, *The Indian Sign Language* (Philadelphia, 1885; rep. Lincoln: University of Nebraska Press, 1982). Lane, *When the Mind Hears,* 282.

21. Hiram Bingham to Samuel Worcester, May 11, 1819, 88. *LJP,* 291. JP to Hiram Bingham, October 19, 1819, *LJP,* 291–92. Hiram Bingham to Samuel Worcester, May 11, 1819, *Selected Writings of Hiram Bingham,* 86–87.

22. THG, "The Language of Signs as Auxiliary to the Christian Missionary," *Christian Observer* 26 (1826): 592–93. "The Deaf and Dumb Asylum," *Religious Intelligencer* 7 (1822–23): 406–7.

23. THG, "Language of Signs as Auxiliary to the Christian Missionary," 592–93. "Deaf and Dumb Asylum," 407. Hiram Bingham to Samuel Worcester, May 11, 1819. Hiram Bingham was indeed pressed for time. Leaving Cornwall, he began preparing for his journey: in six short months he needed to complete his studies at Andover, meet with John Pickering, learn a new language, visit his parents in Bennington, Vermont, and introduce them to Thomas Hopoo. Perhaps most difficult of all, he also needed to find a wife. In order that its foreign missionaries avoid the temptations of native women, the American Board insisted that all be married and bring their wives along. Bingham unfortunately had no prospects in sight. Luckily, just weeks before his scheduled departure he met and courted Sybil Moseley, a young woman as passionate about missionary work as he was, a woman "rejoicing in prospect of suffering" (Sybil Moseley to the Calvin Binghams, October 3, 1819, *Selected Writings of Hiram Bingham,* 110).

24. "Deaf and Dumb Asylum," 407; emphasis in original. Bingham apparently became close to Gallaudet, who delivered the sermon at Hiram and Sybil's wedding, just days before they set sail for the Pacific (Thomas H. Gallaudet, "An Address, delivered at a Meeting for Prayers, with reference to the Sandwich Mission, in the Brick Church in Hartford," October 11, 1819, *Selected Writings of Hiram Bingham,* 111–21).

25. James Woodward, "Historical Bases of American Sign Language," *Understanding Language through Sign Language Research,* ed. Patricia Siple (New York: Academic Press, 1978), 333–48.

26. THG, "On the Natural Language of Signs," *AADD* 1 (1848): 58. THG, "On Teaching the Deaf and Dumb," *Christian Observer* 18 (1819): 784; emphasis in original. Laurent Clerc to Reverend J. M. Wainwright, in "Institution at Hartford for instructing the deaf and dumb," *North American Review* 7 (1818): 135–36.

27. Horace Mann, "Seventh Annual Report of the secretary of the [Massachusetts] Board of Education," *Common School Journal* 6 (1844): 75, 79, 81; emphasis mine.

28. THG to Horace Mann, May 13, 1844, GP, box 2.

29. J. J. Flournoy, "Reply to Objections," *AADD* 10 (1858): 140–51. See also John Vickrey Van Cleve and Barry A. Crouch, "A Deaf State," in *A Place of Their Own: Creating the Deaf Community in America* (Washington, D.C.: Gallaudet University Press, 1989), 60–70; Margret A. Winzer, "Deaf-Mutia: Responses to Alienation by the Deaf in the Mid-Nineteenth Century," *AAD* 131 (1986): 29–32, and Barry A. Crouch, "Alienation and the Mid-Nineteenth Century American Deaf Community: A Response," *AAD* 131 (1986): 322–24. The debate over the deaf state is reprinted in Krentz, ed., *Mighty Change,* 161–211.

30. "The Plans for a Community of Deaf-Mutes: Editorial Remarks," *AADD* 10 (1858): 138, 137.

31. William W. Turner to J. J. Flournoy, December 6, 1855, *AADD* 8 (1856): 118–19. Edmund Booth, "Mr. Flournoy's Project," *AADD* 10 (1858): 76.

32. "Mr. Flournoy to Mr. Turner," December 21, 1855, *AADD* 8 (1856): 123.

33. "Mr. Flournoy to Mr. Turner," October 3, 1857, *AADD* 8 (1856): 43–44. "Proceedings of the Third Convention of the New England Gallaudet Association of Deaf-Mutes," *AADD* 10 (1858): 213, 215.

34. Crouch, "Alienation," 322. William W. Turner to J. J. Flournoy, December 6, 1855, 119; "Mr. Flournoy to Mr. Turner," December 21, 1855, 123. Booth, "Mr. Flournoy's Project," 75.

35. "We wish to have, if possible, as sequestrated people, nothing to do with what is an ever threatening and pregnant bane to mar the harmony of our country, and to peri-

odically menace the Union" (Flournoy, "Reply to Objections," 151). Flournoy actively participated in the African colonization movement (as did Thomas Hopkins Gallaudet, himself an ardent advocate of colonization). Indeed, Flournoy claimed to be so essential to the movement that he would never himself be able to migrate to Gallaudet: "I have long been attempting to play a sort of moral reformer in Georgia, to induce the deportation of the slaves to Liberia, and I fear, if I should go west now, I should be abandoning a sacred duty I owed to my God and my countrymen, to, feeble as I am, endeavor to save the republic by the expulsion of the national 'bone of contention'" (quoted in "Mr. Chamberlain and others on Mr. Flournoy's Project," *AADD* 10 [1858]: 89).

5. STRANGE CHARACTERS

1. [Washington] Daily National Intelligencer, May 20, 1828. *Boston Evening Gazette,* August 16, 1828. On Abd al-Rahman's dress, see Terry Alford, *Prince among Slaves* (New York: Harcourt Brace Jovanovich, 1977), 110–11. Contemporaries referred to Abd al-Rahman Ibrahima in many ways ("Prince" among them) and rarely spelled his name the same way twice. A modern transcription of his own Arabic signature reads "Abd al-Rahman Ibrahim." But, especially as spoken, Arabic names in West Africa typically end in vowels; hence "Ibrahima" also appears commonly in the primary sources. Alford refers to Abd al-Rahman as Abd al-Rahman Ibrahima, a standard that I follow here. "Ibrahim" is the correct standard Arabic orthography, but "Ibrahima" reflects Abd al-Rahman's African roots. Documentary evidence pertaining to Abd al-Rahman's life, as well as a biographical introduction, has been assembled by Allan D. Austin in his collection *African Muslims in Antebellum America: A Sourcebook* (New York: Garland, 1984), 121–63; hereafter *AMAA*. Much quoted material in this chapter comes from *AMAA;* in all cases, both the original and the pages in Austin will be cited.
2. Adams, *Memoirs,* 7: 541. This latter entry, dated May 22, was expurgated from Adams's published diary; it is cited in Alford, *Prince among Slaves,* 128–29.
3. Adams, *Memoirs,* 7: 541. On Adams's Harvard professorship, see Paul C. Nagel, *John Quincy Adams: A Public Life, a Private Life* (New York: Knopf, 1997), 159–88.
4. P. K. Wagner, "To the Freemen of Louisiana," [New Orleans] *Louisiana Advertiser,* October 25, 1828; in *AMAA,* 214.
5. "Abduhl Rahahman," *African Repository* 4 (October 1828): 246; in *AMAA,* 175. For a fascinating discussion of other dubious tales in antebellum America, see Ann Fabian, *Unvarnished Truths: Personal Narratives in Nineteenth-Century America* (Berkeley: University of California Press, 2000).
6. "The Unfortunate Moor," *African Repository* 3 (February 1828): 365; in *AMAA,* 135. "Abduhl Rahahman's History," *African Repository* 4 (May 1828): 81; in *AMAA,* 148.
7. "Abduhl Rahahman's History," 81; in *AMAA,* 147–48.
8. "The Moorish Prince," *Providence Manufacturer's & Farmer's Journal,* August 21, 1828; in *AMAA,* 151–45.
9. See especially Henry Clay to Andrew Marschalk, January 12, 1828; in *AMAA,* 196–97.
10. [Washington] *Daily National Intelligencer,* May 8, 1828.
11. "Abduhl Rahahman, The Unfortunate Moorish Prince," *African Repository* 4 (May 1828): 80; in *AMAA,* 147.

12. Circular of the Colonization Society, May 1, 1828; in *AMAA*, 193.

13. "Abduhl Rahahman," *African Repository* 3 (May 1828): 78; in *AMAA*, 145–46. "Abduhl Rahahman," *African Repository* 4 (October 1828): 245; in *AMAA*, 174.

14. "The Unfortunate Moor," 367; in *AMAA*, 136.

15. "The Unfortunate Moor," 366; in *AMAA*, 135–36. THG to AR, May 15, 1828; in *AMAA*, 154–56.

16. AR to THG, June 7, 1828; in *AMAA*, 157.

17. See Alford, *Prince among Slaves*, 163.

18. Excerpts from THG's sermon were reprinted in the *African Repository* 4 (October 1828): 243–50; in *AMAA*, 173, 175.

19. On Muslim literacy, and on Muslims in the Atlantic slave trade more generally, see Sylviane A. Diouf's invaluable *Servants of Allah: African Muslims Enslaved in the Americas* (New York: New York University Press, 1998), esp. ch. 4.

20. On Omar Ibn Said, see *AAMA*, 445–523.

21. Diouf, *Servants of Allah*, 117.

22. Ibid., 136–37, 134.

23. Edward Everett, *Abdul Rahahman, Orations and Speeches on Various Occasions* (Boston, 1859), 3:188. Everett continued: "He was said to be still master of several African languages. . . . He spoke the English language without accent. . . . Besides his knowledge of literal Arabic, he was acquainted with several of the living dialects of West Africa" (188–89). THG in "Abduhl Rahahman," *African Repository* 4 (October 1828): 245; in *AMAA*, 175.

24. *New England Palladium*, August 12, 1828.

25. Henry Louis Gates, "The Trope of the Talking Book," in *Signifying Monkey: A Theory of African-American Literary Criticism* (New York: Oxford University Press, 1988), 127–69.

26. Olaudah Equiano, *Equiano's Travels: his autobiography; the interesting narrative of the life of Olaudah Equiano or Gustavus Vassa the African*, abr. ed. Paul Edwards (London: Heinemann, 1967), 132–33, 151–52. Equiano's story has recently been questioned; see Vincent Carretta, "Olaudah Equiano or Gustavus Vassa? New Light on an Eighteenth-Century Question of Identity," *Slavery and Abolition*, 20 (December 1999): 96–105.

27. Blight, "Introduction: 'A Psalm of Freedom,' " in Frederick Douglass, *Narrative of the Life of Frederick Douglass, an American Slave, Written by Himself*, ed. David W. Blight (Boston: Bedford Books, 1993), 4. See also Janet Duitsman Cornelius, *"When I Can Read My Title Clear": Literacy, Slavery, and Religion in the Antebellum South* (Columbia: University of South Carolina Press, 1991).

28. Douglass, *Narrative*, 57–58.

29. Ibid., 61–63.

30. Quoted in E. Jennifer Monaghan, "Reading for the Enslaved, Writing for the Free: Reflections on Liberty and Literacy," *Proceedings of the American Antiquarian Society* 108 (2000): 317.

31. Ibid., 326–37, 339. David Walker, *David Walker's Appeal, in Four Articles, Together with a Preamble, to the Coloured Citizens of the World, But in Particular, and Very Expressly, to those of the United States of America*, ed. with an introduction by Charles M. Wiltse (New York: Hill & Wang, 1965), 29, 53.

32. [John Russwurm?], *Freedom's Journal*, August 29, 1828, 79; in *AMAA*, 159.

33. "Languages of Africa," *United States Literary Gazette* 3 (February 15, 1826): 396.

34. Joseph E. Worcester, Article IV, *North American Review* 45 (1837): 89.

35. "The Unfortunate Moor," 366; in *AMAA*, 135.

36. Cyrus Griffin, in *Natchez Southern Galaxy*, June 12, 1828; in *AMAA*, 139–40.

37. "The Unfortunate Moor," 366; in *AMAA*, 135.

38. *Freedman's Journal*, September 6, 1828, 186; fuller accounts in *AMAA*, 163–66.

39. Andrew Marschalk, October 16, 1828, handbill; in *AMAA*, 198, 202.

40. *Natchez Statesman and Gazette*, October 23, 1828; in *AMAA*, 197 (original contract), 211 (breach of contract).

41. P. K. Wagner, "To the Freemen of Louisiana," [New Orleans] *Louisiana Advertiser*, October 25, 1828; in *AMAA*, 214–15. Emphasis in original.

42. Ibid.; in *AMAA*, 216.

43. [P. K. Wagner], [New Orleans] *Louisiana Advertiser*, November 4, 1828; in *AMAA*, 226.

44. Three years after Abd al-Rahman's death, Momolu Duwalu Bukele, an African Vai native of Liberia, had a vision, altogether different from Gallaudet's. "I had a dream, in which a tall, venerable looking white man appeared to me," he told the visiting German linguist S. W. Koelle. In Bukele's dream, the white man showed him a script in which he could write in his own language. But when Bukele awoke, "he could not remember the signs which had been told him by night." Undaunted, he set about studying his language, convinced that "his people might write letters as they did in Monrovia." After some time Bukele and a small group of friends devised a syllabic script of forty to sixty characters. This he shared with his people, whose rapid acquisition of literacy astounded visiting missionaries. Bukele's syllabary was first reported in 1834, when American Board missionaries John Leighton Wilson and Stephen Wynkoop reported it in journals and letters sent to the American Board's headquarters in Boston. "The Vey people," Wilson reported, have "recently invented a system of writing in which although it has not been more than one year since it was commenced, they have already written volumes. . . . Some of their characters are evidently Arabic, some resemble Hebrew characters—most of them resemble no written characters that we have ever seen." How had Bukele, an uneducated trader, invented such a script? Although he was illiterate, he was familiar with both Arabic and European writing. Writing in 1849, Koelle assumed that Bukele had come up with the idea for the script after visiting mission schools in Monrovia. Recently several scholars have questioned this assumption. After all, Bukele devised a syllabary, not an alphabet, and he borrowed no characters from either the Arabic or Roman alphabet. Yet because he devised his script in a very short time, no more than two years, it seems unlikely that he invented it from whole cloth. Perhaps, these scholars have suggested, he borrowed the idea of syllabic writing from Sequoyah's script, brought to Liberia by American Board missionaries, who, like Hiram Bingham, envied its success. Some American Board missionaries in Liberia were themselves Cherokees; at least one of them was known to use the Vai script. In any event, missionaries among the Vais, like missionaries to the Cherokees, soon attempted to put the script to their own use, building types and printing religious tracts (though they achieved much less success than had Cherokee missionaries). S. W. Koelle, *Narrative of an Expedition into the Vy Country* (London, 1849), 21–24. On the Vai script, see Peter T. Daniels and William Bright, *The World's Writing Systems* (New York: Oxford University Press, 1996), 593–98. On its origins, see O. Bates, ed.,

"The Origin of the Vai syllabary," *Harvard African Studies* 1 (1917): 290–92; P. E. H. Hair, "Notes on the Discovery of the Vai Script, with a Bibliography," *Sierra Leone Language Review* 2 (1963): 36–47. On the Cherokee connection, see Svend E. Holsoe, "A Case of Stimulus Diffusion: A Note on Possible Connections between the Vai and Cherokee Scripts," *Indian Historian* 4 (1971): 56–57. My thanks to Konrad Tuchsherer for sharing his research on this connection with me (Konrad Tuchsherer to the author, personal communication, May 6, 1999).

45. On AR's journey and last days, see the documents in *AMAA,* 233–38.

46. "Abduhl Rahahman, the Unfortunate Moorish Prince," 77–81; in *AMAA,* 144–48.

47. The original is in the John Trumbull Papers, Yale University. Translations are provided in *AMAA,* 243, n8, although I relied on new translations by Jeremy Berndt (e-mail to author, July 19, 2001).

48. Diouf, *Servants of Allah,* 123.

49. "Abduhl Rahahman, The Unfortunate Moorish Prince," 80; in *AMAA,* 146.

50. P. K. Wagner, "The Prince of Timboo," [New Orleans] *Louisiana Advertiser,* October 30, 1828; in *AMAA,* 218.

6. UNIVERSAL COMMUNICATION

1. All descriptions of the festivities are taken from C. T. McClenachan, *Detailed Report of the Proceedings had in Commemoration of the Successful Laying of the Atlantic Telegraph Cable* (New York, 1863).

2. SM to Norvin Green, July 1855, *SMLJ,* 2: 345.

3. Charles F. Briggs and Augustus Maverick, *The Story of the Telegraph and a History of the Great Atlantic Cable* (New York, 1858), 21–22.

4. See Samuel Prime, *The Life of Samuel F. B. Morse* (New York, 1875), 665.

5. Quoted in *SMLJ,* 2: 483.

6. Jedidiah Morse to SM, February 21, 1801, SMP, box 1. SM to Jedidiah and Elizabeth Morse, September 20, 1812, SMP, box 3. For biographies of Morse, see Prime, *Life; SMLJ;* and, most usefully, Carleton Mabee, *The American Leonardo: A Life of Samuel F. B. Morse* (New York: Knopf, 1944).

7. SM to Jedidiah and Elizabeth Morse, August 17, 1811, SMP, box 2; emphasis mine.

8. *SMLJ,* 2: 26.

9. SM to Richard and Sidney Morse, July 18, 1832, SMP, box 11.

10. Richard Cary Morse to SM, November 28, 1833, SMP. William Dunlap, *A History of the Rise and Progress of the Arts of Design in the United States,* new edition, illustrated, edited, with additions by Frank W. Bayley and Charles E. Goodspeed (Boston: C. E. Goodspeed & Co., 1918), 3: 98.

11. *SMLJ,* 2: 27–28. SM to James Fenimore Cooper, February 21, 1833, SMP, box 11. See also SM to Sidney and Richard Morse, July 18, 1832, SMP, box 11.

12. My brief history of the telegraph is principally derived from James Reid, *The Telegraph in America* (New York, 1879), and Tom Standage, *The Victorian Internet: The Remarkable Story of the Telegraph and the Nineteenth Century's Online Pioneers* (London: Weidenfeld & Nicolson, 1998).

13. "Quelle brilliante destinée . . . , les sciences et les arts ne réservent-ils pas à une République qui, par son immense population et par le génie de ses habitants, est appelée à devenir la nation enseignante de l'Europe!" "L'établissement du télégraphe

est, en effet, la meilleure réponse aux publicistes qui pensent que la France est trop étendue pour former une république. Le télégraphe abrège les distances et réunit en quelque sorte une immense population en un seul point" (Alexis Belloc, *La Télégraphie historique* [Paris, 1889], 80–84); my translation.

14. WT, *Outlines of a Constitution for a United North and South Columbia* (Washington, D.C., 1815), 14.

15. *SMLJ*, 2:6. SM to George Clarke, June 30, 1834, *SMLJ*, 2:27. *SMLJ*, 2:28–33. On this transition, see also Brooke Hindle, "From Art to Technology and Science," *Proceedings of the American Antiquarian Society* 96 (1986): esp. 30–32.

16. SM, *Foreign Conspiracy against the Liberties of the United States* (New York, 1835). SM to A. S. Willington, May 20, 1835, SMP, box 11. SM, *Imminent Dangers to the Free Institutions of the United States through Foreign Immigration* (New York, 1835), 28.

17. SM to A. S. Willington, May 20, 1835, SMP, box 11.

18. *SMLJ*, 2: 61–62, 65. Draft of "The Petition of Samuel F. B. Morse of New York in the country and State of New York" to the Commissioner of Patents, September 28, 1837, SMP, box 12.

19. *Journal of Commerce*, January 29, 1838, in *SMLJ*, 2:75.

20. *SMLJ*, 2:266–67. Quoted in Oliver W. Larkin, *Samuel F. B. Morse and American Democratic Art* (Boston: Little, Brown, 1954), 177.

21. As Allan Nevins has written, Morse "of course did not originate the idea of the use of electromagnetism in telegraphy, and simply made himself ridiculous when he so asserted. But it seems clear that the Morse code was truly Morse's" (Allan Nevins, "Introduction," in Mabee, *American Leonardo,* xi).

22. "Electric Telegraph," *Richmond* [Virginia] *Inquirer,* January 26, 1847, in Morse's scrapbook, SMP, box 61. *SMLJ*, 2:61–68. "The Telegraph," from the *Chicago Daily Tribune,* December 22, 1847; pasted in Morse's scrapbook, SMP, box 61.

23. For this episode, see Prime, *Life,* 492–97.

24. "Electro and Animal Magnetism," *Congressional Globe,* February 21, 1843. Prime, *Life,* 496.

25. SM to the Congress of the United States, June 3, 1844, in Prime, *Life,* 507. J. Cutler Andrews, "The Southern Telegraph Company, 1861–65: A Chapter in the History of Wartime Communication," *Journal of Southern History* 30 (1964): 319.

26. "The Telegraph," *New York Sun,* November 6, 1847, in Morse's scrapbook, SMP, box 61. "Election Yesterday," *Poughkeepsie* (New York) *Telegraph,* November 8, 1848, in Morse's scrapbook, SMP, box 61.

27. Quoted in Daniel J. Czitrom, *Media and the American Mind: From Morse to McLuhan* (Chapel Hill: University of North Carolina Press, 1982), 11–12, and in Annteresa Lubrano, *The Telegraph: How Technology Innovation Caused Social Change* (New York: Garland, 1997), 152.

28. Quoted in Carl F. Kaestle, *Pillars of the Republic: Common Schools and American Society, 1780–1860* (New York: Hill & Wang, 1983), 214.

29. Richard B. Kielbowicz, "The Telegraph, Censorship, and Politics at the Outset of the Civil War," *Civil War History* 40 (1994): 97. Paul J. Scheips, "Union Signal Communications: Innovation and Conflict," *Civil War History* 9 (1963): 402.

30. *The Constitution, An Argument on the Ethical Proposition of Slavery, The Letter of a Republican . . . and Prof. Morse's Reply* (New York, 1863), 6. David Bates, *Lincoln in the Telegraph Office* (New York, 1907).

31. SM to Sidney Morse, December 29, 1857, *SMLJ*, 2:389–90. *SMLJ*, 2:331.

32. SM to James Wynne, May 2, 1860, SMP, box 52.

33. B. [Samuel F. B. Morse], *The Present Attempt to Dissolve the American Union, a British Aristocratic Plot* (New York, 1862), 38, 11.

34. SM to George L. Douglas, April 2, 1862, *SMLJ*, 2:418–19. SM to Amos Kendall, July 23, 1862, *SMLJ*, 2:420.

35. *SMLJ*, 2:289–90. SM to Sidney Morse, August 7, 1848, SMP, box 52. SM to Richard Morse, July 29, 1848; in Mabee, *American Leonardo*, 304–5.

36. SM to L. J. Anderson, January 24, 1853, SMP. Thanks to Kenneth Silverman for this reference.

37. In 1837, Henry Griswold, also from Utica, enrolled in the school. He was recorded as having become deaf at an unknown age from scarlet fever. It seems likely that Henry was either Sarah's brother or her cousin and that the two cases of deafness in the same family were related. Henry's deafness was probably profound, for he stayed at the school for seven years, two years more than the usual course of instruction. Perhaps both children's conditions were congenital but, in Sarah's case, not recognized until she was one. Or perhaps Henry and Sarah, especially if they lived in the same house, were sickened by the same bout of scarlet fever, the nation's leading cause of deafness and a sickness that might have caused Sarah's fall. The two causes, "fall" and "scarlet fever," often appear together in the records, as in "A fall followed by scarlet fever" or "A fall or scarlet fever" (H. P. Peet, "List of Pupils of the New York Institution," *AADD* 6 [1854]: 206).

38. *Nineteenth Annual Report of the Directors of the New-York Institution for the Instruction of the Deaf and Dumb . . . for the Year 1837* (New York, 1838), 8, 10.

39. *Fifteenth Annual Report of the Directors of the New-York Institution for the Instruction of the Deaf and Dumb . . . for the Year 1833* (New York, 1834), 68.

40. Laurent Clerc to John C. Spencer, February 18, 1827, Laurent Clerc Papers, Yale University. Mabee, *American Leonardo*, 363.

41. *Fifteenth Annual Report*, 68.

42. SM to Sarah Morse, 1857, *SMLJ*, 2:373–74.

7. VISIBLE SPEECH

1. AMB, *Visible Speech: A New Fact Demonstrated* (London, 1865), 8–14.

2. Alexander J. Ellis, "The Reader," [London] *Morning Star*, September 3; reprinted in Bell, *Visible Speech*, 24–29.

3. AGB to AMB, January 7, 1871, AGBP, Family Correspondence. (This collection is also available through the Library of Congress's Web site at memory.loc.gov/ammem/bellhtml/bellhome.html.) For a comprehensive and penetrating biography of the younger Bell, see Robert V. Bruce, *Bell: Alexander Graham Bell and the Conquest of Solitude* (Boston: Little, Brown, 1973).

4. *Deaf-Mute Voice*, February 2, 1889; AGBP, The Deaf, Correspondence. For Bell's fuller scientific explanation of his invention, see AGB, "Researches in Telephony," *Proceedings of the American Academy of Arts and Sciences* 12 (1876–77): 1–10.

5. Richard Lepsius, *Standard Alphabet for Reducing Unwritten Languages and Foreign Graphic Systems to a Uniform Orthography in European Letters* (London, 1855). See especially Lepsius's history of efforts to standardize the alphabet, 8–24. Henry's diary quoted in Bruce, *Bell*, 40.

6. Bruce, *Bell*, 20, 29–30. AMB's father, Alexander Bell, a failed actor, had also taught elocution and had authored *The Practical Elocutionist* (1834), as well as *Stammering, and Other Impediments of Speech* (1836). Bernard Shaw, *Pygmalion* (London: Penguin, 1986), 6. Stanley Weintrub, ed., *Bernard Shaw: The Diaries, 1885–1897* (University Park: Pennsylvania State University Press, 1986), 1: 30.

7. AMB, *Visible Speech*, 42–46; 13, 19, 21–22, 26, 27, 34–37. Bell's Visible Speech is an example of what the linguist Roy Harris calls phonetic iconicity, the idea that how we write illustrates the movement of our lips and tongues. In 1772 the Englishman Charles Davy had proposed that the letters of the Greek alphabet had originally represented the position of the tongue and lips when making particular sounds (for example, the shape of the letter O mirrors the rounding of the lips when that sound is produced). Charles Davy, *Conjectural Observations on the Origin and Progress of Alphabetic Writing* (London, 1772). Many linguists before and after Davy made similar kinds of claims about early alphabets, but they are now widely discredited, not least because no early alphabets had vowels and because as some linguistic historians now believe, writing was invented as writing, not as a representation of speech. In other words, writing was first more like drawing or counting than an attempt to document speech. Harris, *Origins of Writing*, ch. 4.

8. AMB, *Visible Speech: The Science of Universal Alphabetics* (London, 1867); AMB, *English Visible Speech for the Million* (London, 1868). See also, for example, AMB, *Universal Line-Writing and Steno-Phonography; On the Basis of "Visible Speech"* (London, 1869).

9. Bruce, *Bell*, 54–55.

10. [William Dwight Whitney], "Bell's Visible Speech," *North American Review* (1868): 356–57, 351, 355–56, 347, 354, 358.

11. Bruce, *Bell*, 35–37. See also "Making a Talking Machine," undated, AGBP, Article and Speech Files; The Notebook of Alexander Graham Bell, AGBP, Article and Speech Files, Folder: "Autobiographical Writings," 1904–10, undated.

12. Bruce, *Bell*, 14, 20–21; Richard Winefield, *Never the Twain Shall Meet: Bell, Gallaudet, and the Communications Debate* (Washington, D.C.: Gallaudet University Press, 1987), 12. Eliza Symonds Bell to AGB, December 12, 1875, AGBP, Family Correspondence. AGB also, later in life, sent his mother an improved ear trumpet (Eliza Symonds Bell to AGB, 1876, AGBP, Family Correspondence).

13. After a lecture, the elder Bell mentioned using Visible Speech to teach the deaf and "said that teaching the deaf to speak was not his idea but his son's who had devoted much time to working out a method and was very hopeful of results" (article by Alexander Graham Bell, August 15, 1904, AGBP, Article and Speech Files, Folder: "Autobiographical Writings," 1904–10, undated).

14. On Bell's methods, see AGB to AMB, Eliza Symonds Bell, and Carrie Bell, April 16, 1871, AGBP, Family Correspondence. AGB to AMB, Eliza Symonds Bell, and Carrie Bell, December 1, 1871, AGBP, Family Correspondence; emphasis in original.

15. Mabel Hubbard to AGB, July 26, 1876, AGBP, Family Correspondence. AGB to AMB, Eliza Symonds Bell, and Carrie Bell, October 20, 1874, AGBP, Family Correspondence. AGB to AMB, February 3, 1877, AGBP, Family Correspondence; emphasis in original. AMB to AGB, February 8, 1877, AGBP, Family Correspondence.

16. AGB to AMB and Eliza Symonds Bell, May 24, 1875, AGBP, Family Correspondence.

17. See Bruce, *Bell*, 121. AGB to AMB, Eliza Symonds Bell, Carrie Bell, Charles J. Bell, May 6, 1874, AGBP, Family Correspondence.

18. *Deaf-Mute Voice,* February 2, 1889; AGBP, The Deaf, Correspondence. For Bell's fuller scientific explanation of his invention, see AGB, "Researches in Telephony," *Proceedings of the American Academy of Arts and Sciences* 12 (1876–77): 1–10.

19. AGB to AMB, March 10, 1876, AGBP, Family Correspondence.

20. Although his engagement to a deaf woman initially occasioned some hostility between Bell and his parents, they were soon reconciled, and Bell's mother wrote him, "I assure you I feel quite complimented by your selecting a deaf lady for your wife, as it proves you have not been deterred by your Father's experience with me." She did, however, request that Mabel "learn the double handed finger alphabet for me" since she should, "for her own safety, know either one or the other"—that is, the one-handed American finger alphabet or the two-handed British (Eliza Symonds Bell to AGB, December 12, 1875, AGBP, Family Correspondence). See also AGB to Eliza Symonds Bell, August 18, 1875, AGBP, Family Correspondence; and Eliza Symonds Bell to AGB, August 23, 1875, AGBP, Family Correspondence.

21. AGB to Mabel Hubbard Bell, undated, AGBP, Family Correspondence. Mabel Hubbard to Alexander Graham Bell, 1876, AGBP, Family Correspondence.

22. AGB to Gardiner Greene Hubbard, November 23, 1875, AGBP, Family Correspondence. AGB to AMB, Eliza Symonds Bell, and Carrie Bell, October 20, 1874, AGBP, Family Correspondence.

23. United States Centennial Commission, *Reports and Awards, Group XXV* (Philadelphia, 1877), 21. AGB to Mabel Hubbard, December 6, 1876, AGBP, Family Correspondence; emphasis in original.

24. AGB to Mabel Hubbard, June 21, 1876, AGBP, Family Correspondence. Mabel Hubbard to AGB, July 26, 1876, AGBP, Family Correspondence.

25. AGB to AMB and Eliza Symonds Bell, July 7, 1876, AGBP, Family Correspondence.

26. AGB to Mabel Hubbard, November 22, 1876, AGBP, Family Correspondence, Mabel Hubbard Bell, AGBP, Family Correspondence. AGB to Mabel Bell, September 9, 1878, AGBP, Family Correspondence.

27. AGB to Mabel Bell, September 9, 1878, AGBP, Family Correspondence.

28. Bell and his father also collaborated on a manual alphabet using the symbols of Visible Speech (AMB to AGB, March 10, 1873; and AMB to AGB, February 23, 1873, AGBP, Family Correspondence).

29. AGB to AMB, Eliza Symonds Bell, and Carrie Bell, April 17, 1872, AGBP, Family Correspondence.

30. Winefield, *Never the Twain Shall Meet,* 15–16. See also AGB to AMB, Eliza Symonds Bell, and Carrie Bell, April 17, 1872, AGBP, Family Correspondence. AGB to AMB, Eliza Symonds Bell, and Carrie Bell, May 15, 1872, June 17, 1872, AGBP, Family Correspondence.

31. AGB, *Upon a Method of Teaching Language to a Very Young Congenitally Deaf Child* (Washington, D.C.: Gibson Brothers Printers, 1883). See AGB to AMB, Eliza Symonds Bell, Carrie Bell, July 1, 1873, AGBP, Family Correspondence.

32. AGB, "Visible Speech as a Means of Communicating Articulation to Deaf-Mutes," *AADD* 17 (January 1872). See also the manuscript in Article and Speech Files, AGBP.

33. Alexander Graham Bell, *Facts and Opinions Relating to the Deaf* (London, 1888), 1–9. AGB, "The Education of the Deaf" (unpublished ms., October 28, 1889), AGBP.

34. AGB, "Upon the Formation of a Deaf Variety of the Human Race," *Memoirs of the National Academy of Sciences* 2 (1883): 194, 179, 180; all emphases in original. In this contention, Bell found much support in the scientific community. Most of the scientists

he consulted said they had "no doubt whatever" about Bell's conclusions, although many expressed the belief that the process would be very slow and would take many, many generations (AGB, *Facts and Opinions,* 89–106). But many of the deaf educators who responded to Bell's survey were furious at his suggestion that marriage between deaf men and women ought to be discouraged. Albert Hardy, superintendent of a Wisconsin school, wrote, "So far as I can judge, this matter is simply a 'bugbear.' I do not think there is even a possibility of a 'race of deaf-mutes' resulting from intermarriage of deaf-mutes" (AGB, *Facts and Opinions,* 80).

35. AGB, "Upon the Formation of a Deaf Variety of the Human Race," 217–18. AGB to Thomas B. Berry, May 14, 1884, AGBP, The Deaf, Correspondence.

36. AGB to AMB, Eliza Symonds Bell, and Carrie Bell, January 27, 1873, AGBP, Family Correspondence. Mabel Hubbard Bell to Eliza Symonds Bell, May 22, 1878, quoted in Beverly W. Brannan, "Alexander Graham Bell: A Photographic Album," *Quarterly Journal of the Library of Congress* 34 (1977): 81.

37. AGB, "Education of the Deaf."

38. AGB, "Upon the Formation of a Deaf Variety of the Human Race," 218–19. The only event that would make such circumstances worse would be "to reduce the sign-language to writing, so that the deaf-mutes would have a common literature distinct from the rest of the world," a "form of ideography like the Egyptian hieroglyphics."

39. AGB to Mary E. Bennett, August 30, 1913, AGBP, The Deaf, Correspondence.

40. AGB, "Upon the Formation of a Deaf Variety of the Human Race," 220–21.

41. [Samuel Silas Curry], *Alexander Melville Bell: Some Memories with Fragments from a Pupil's Note-Book* (Boston: School of Expression, 1906), 17–18.

42. AGB, "Is Race Suicide Possible?," *Journal of Heredity* 11 (1920): 341. See also Bruce, *Bell,* 417–20.

EPILOGUE: MEN OF PROGRESS

1. Michael Kammen, *Mystic Chords of Memory: The Transformation of Tradition in American Culture* (New York: Knopf, 1991), 47.

2. Of the nineteen "men of progress" in Schussele's painting, only three devised something other than industrial machinery: William Morton (anesthesia), Isaiah Jennings (friction matches), and Morse (whose invention very much supported industrialization).

3. See Arthur A. Ekirch, Jr., *The Idea of Progress in America, 1815–1860* (New York: AMS Press 1944).

4. "People of Progress," *American Heritage* (November 1999): www.americanheritage.com/99/nov/083.htm.

5. For a recent report on these debates, see Suzanne Daley, "Use of English as World Tongue Is Booming, and So Is Concern: In Europe, Some Fear National Languages Are Endangered," *New York Times,* April 16, 2001.

6. For a discussion of this subject, see Naomi S. Baron, *Alphabet to Email: How Written English Evolved and Where It's Heading* (London: Routledge, 2000).

7. Graffiti is a registered trademark of Palm, Inc.

8. Conrad H. Blickenstorfer, "From the Editor," and Shawn Barnett, "Jeff Hawkins: The Man Who Almost Single-Handedly Revived the Handheld Computer Industry," *Pen Computing* 33, www.pencomputing.com/palm/Pen33/hawkins2.html.

9. With five minutes of practice, first-time users of Graffiti are able to achieve 97 percent accuracy in getting their computers to recognize their letters (I. Scott MacKenzie and S. Zhang, "The Immediate Usability of Graffiti," *Proceedings of Graphics Interface,* www.yorku.ca/mack/GI97a.html).

10. Blickenstorfer, "From the Editor." MacKenzie and Zhang, "Immediate Usability," 4. On "National Graffiti," see www.sergem.net/interpilot/index.html.

11. Oliver Wolcott to NW, May 3, 1794, *NLNW,* 1:383.

12. *Handbook for the Palm III ™ Handheld* (Santa Clara, Calif.: Palm, Inc., 1998). Bill Gates, *Business @ the Speed of Thought: Succeeding in the Digital Economy* (New York: Warner Books, 1999); all quotations are from chapter excerpts at www.speed-of-thought.com.

Acknowledgments

"Hi, Mommy."
"Hi, Gideon."
"Who dat?"
"A man."
"What name?"
"Finley."
"He pretty."
"Mmm-hmm."
"Nother one?"
"Okay."
"What name?"
"Noah."
"Big head."
"Mmm-hmm."
"Nother one?"

I was sitting at my miserable, crashy computer this morning, trying to write these acknowledgments, when my two-year-old son Gideon managed to open the door that separates my study from the rest of the house. Hoorah, a reprieve! I pulled him up onto my lap and searched my desk for something that would interest a toddler, something not chewable. All I could find was my little red hand-held mini–slide previewer and my pile of 35-mm color slides of portraits of the men in this book, a pile I always keep at hand for the mixed purposes of inspiration and procrastination. Gideon is more or less obsessed with names these days, so the slide show pleased him immensely. And me, too.

I've dragged out those slides a bit more publicly on more than a few occasions before this. Portions of this book have been delivered at lectures and conferences, where I've always received helpful comments and opinions eloquently expressed (though none as wonderful as "He pretty"). I've presented parts of this work at the Bunting Institute at Radcliffe; the Charles Warren Center at Harvard; Harvard's Center for International Affairs; the Omohundro Institute for Early American History and Culture's Microhistory Conference; the Edinburgh meeting of the Society for the History of Authors,

Readers, and Printers; the Massachusetts Historical Society; Brandeis University; and the History Department and Humanities Center at Boston University.

Gideon learned the alphabet while I was revising this manuscript (with the help of a set of rubber letters that stick to the walls of the bathtub), making me think about literacy in wholly new ways. But I've been blessed with the assistance of infinitely more proficient readers than he. Bruce Schulman heroically read the whole manuscript, much of it more than once, as did my fine editor, Jane Garrett, while the floating membership of a writing group to which I belong read the lion's share: Elizabeth Abrams, Mia Bay, Steve Biel, Catherine Corman, James Cullen, Hildegard Hoeller, Kristin Hoganson, Christina Klein, Jane Levey, Sarah Luria, Alec Marsh, Julie Reuben, and Laura Saltz. Michael Kammen and John Demos generously offered comments on an early draft. My parents, too, gave it a read, for which I am immensely grateful. And Ann Fabian, Amy Kittelstrom, and Bryan Waterman read all of it, at the very end, for which I can never thank them enough. Douglas Baynton, James McCann, and Robert Bruce each offered advice about specific chapters, while Clifford Backman, Jeremy Berndt, Barbara Diefendorf, and Robert Hoffmeister helped with tricky translations from Latin, Arabic, French, and American Sign Language. I've also talked through the project many times with Jane Kamensky, whose collaboration on our Web magazine, *Common-place* (www.common-place.org), has made me excited about being a historian all over again.

Gideon was born soon after I began this book, and he's newly a big brother as I complete it. Miraculously, two maternity leaves have helped make this book possible, though both have been characterized by moments like the day at a writing group meeting not too long ago when we critiqued a chapter draft while I nursed, burped, diapered, and rocked baby Simon. More generous still has been the support of fellowships at the Boston University Humanities Center and Radcliffe Institute, as well as a research grant provided by the American Philosophical Society and funds from BU's American Studies and University Research Opportunities Program, which have allowed me to employ the invaluable assistance of Danielle Lightburn, Amy Kittelstrom, and Katherine Stebbins-McCaffrey.

I've also benefited immensely from the generous staff at the libraries of Boston University, Harvard, and Yale, as well as at the archives where I conducted the bulk of the research for this project: the American Antiquarian Society, the American Philosophical Society, the Amherst College Library, the Boston Athenaeum, the Connecticut Historical Society, the Historical Society of Pennsylvania, the Library Company of Philadelphia, the Jones Library in Amherst, the Library of Congress, and the Massachusetts Historical Society. And, although I never did research there, I've found daily moral and intellectual support at the tiny O'Neill neighborhood branch of the Cambridge Public Library, in the company of the best librarians I know.

This book is more or less the first thing I've written without first rehearsing it with my best friend, Jane Levey, who died the day after Gideon was born. I worry the work is weaker for the loss, but I know too that I have since been taken care of by good friends, new and old, among them Adrianna Alty, Kathleen Dalton, Deb Favreau, Benjamin Filene, Lisa Lovett, Dan Penrice, Julie Reuben, Bruce Schulman, Rachel Seidman, Denise Webb, and Wendy Weitzner. And most of all, by Gideon and Simon's dad, Timothy Leek, who likes to leave the study door unlocked.

Cambridge
April 2001

Index

Abd al-Rahman Ibrahima, 11, 111–35, *illus. 114*, 150, 189, 190, 191, 220*n1*, 222*n44*; and American Colonization Society, 118–20, 127, 128; Arabic "Lord's Prayer" of, *illus. 134*; "autobiographies" of, 132–4, *illus. 133*; and black abolitionists, 128–30; literacy of, 116, 122, 126, 128; as slave, 114–16; in Washington, 111–13, 117–18

abolitionism, 125, 128–30, 134, 155, 156

Académie Française, 23

acculturation, resistance to, 87, 89

Adams, John, 54–5

Adams, John Quincy, 63, 86, 91–3, 112, 113, 116, 117, 129–30, 135, 217*n1*

African colonization schemes, 47, 48, 56, 57, 109, 117–19, 126, 128

African languages, 48, 49, 51, 56, 68, 127, 221*n23*; *see also specific languages*

African Repository, 118, 127, 132

Alford, Terry, 114

Alien and Sedition Acts (1798), 54–5, 59

Allston, Washington, 7

alphabetic code, 149–50, *illus. 152*

alphabets, 4, 45, 56, 76; computer-friendly, 193–4; distinction between syllabaries and, 77–8; dot-and-dash, *see* Morse code; manual, 97, 98, *illus. 101*, 105, 171, 180, 182; perfect, 49, 67, 70–3, 75, 96; reformed, 31–5, *illus. 32*, 38; universal, 43, 44, 46, *illus. 47*, 48–52, 56–7, 60, 68, 163–70, 189; *see also specific alphabets*

American Academy of Arts and Sciences, 71

American Annals of the Deaf and Dumb, 108

American Asylum for the Deaf and Dumb, 91, 99–100, 103–5, 107, 108, 119, 158, 176, 180

American Board of Commissioners of Foreign Missions, 64, 69, 72–5, 78, 83, 104, 119, 165, 210*n4*, 214*n21*, 219*n23*, 222*n44*

American Breeders Association, 185

American Colonization Society, 117–18, 120, 127, 128, 131

American Heritage, 191

American language, 4–7, 16–18, 29–30, 49, 56, 58–60, 142; national character and, 21, 22, 58; opposition to development of, 70–2; pronunciation of, 22–3, *illus. 24*, 35; spelling and, 21–4, 30–9; unity and, 27, 40–1

A NOTE ABOUT THE AUTHOR

Jill Lepore was born in Worcester, Massachusetts, in 1966. She received a B.A. degree from Tufts University, an M.A. from the University of Michigan, and a Ph.D. from Yale University. She was an assistant professor of history at the University of California, San Diego, 1995–96; a fellow at the Charles Warren Center, Harvard University, 1996–97; and a fellow at Radcliffe's Bunting Institute, 1999–2000. Since 1996 she has been on the faculty of Boston University, where she is currently an associate professor of history. She is the author of *The Name of War: King Philip's War and the Origins of American Identity,* which won the Bancroft Prize, Phi Beta Kappa's Ralph Waldo Emerson Award, the Berkshire Conference of Women Historians' Book Prize, and the New England Historical Association's Book Award. With Jane Kamensky she founded *Common-place,* an online history magazine (www.common-place.org).

A NOTE ON THE TYPE

This book was set in a typeface called Primer, designed by Rudolph Ruzicka
(1883–1978). Mr. Ruzicka was earlier responsible for the design of Fairfield and
Fairfield Medium, Linotype faces whose virtues have for some
time been accorded wide recognition.

The complete range of sizes of Primer was first made available in 1954,
although the pilot size of 12-point was ready as early as 1951. The design of the
face makes general reference to Linotype Century—long a serviceable type,
totally lacking in manner and frills of any kind—but brilliantly
corrects its characterless quality.

Composed by North Market Street Graphics,
Lancaster, Pennsylvania

Printed and bound by Quebecor Printing,
Martinsburg, West Virginia

Designed by Iris Weinstein